'An impressive display of comparative history, coherent and well written, and convincingly argued. It is very likely to be considered a milestone development in the time to come.'

John Thornton, Professor of History, Boston University

War was a central theme in the world history of the late fifteenth and sixteenth centuries, with military capability and activity central to its states, societies, economies and cultures. *War in the World: A Comparative History 1450–1600* provides an account of warfare in the period, placing it in global context. It offers a corrective to a narrative that has emphasised European developments and obscured the history of non-European military systems and cultures of war.

Highlighting conflict between non-Western powers, which constituted most of the conflict around the world, as well as giving due attention to warfare between Western and non-Western powers, Black emphasises the breadth and variety of military trajectories and connections. This comparative context also provides a framework for considering the idea of a European-based Military Revolution. A wide-ranging account of world military history in a period of substantial development, the book will be essential reading for those interested in global history and conflict.

War in the World: A Comparative History 1450–1600 is designed as a companion volume to Jeremy Black's *Beyond the Military Revolution: Warfare in the Seventeenth Century World.*

Jeremy Black is Professor of History at the University of Exeter, UK. He is a leading authority on early-modern British and continental European history, with special interest in international relations, military history, the press, and historical atlases. His recent publications include *The English Seaborne Empire, The Age of Total War, Using History, Naval Power* and *Beyond the Military Revolution.*

Also by Jeremy Black: *Beyond the Military Revolution: War in the Seventeenth Century World*

War in the World

A Comparative History
1450–1600

Jeremy Black

First published 2011 by
PALGRAVE MACMILLAN

Palgrave Macmillan in the UK is an imprint of Macmillan Publishers Limited, registered in England, company number 785998, of Houndmills, Basingstoke, Hampshire RG21 6XS.

Palgrave Macmillan in the US is a division of St Martin's Press LLC, 175 Fifth Avenue, New York, NY 10010.

Palgrave Macmillan is the global academic imprint of the above companies and has companies and representatives throughout the world.

Palgrave® and Macmillan® are registered trademarks in the United States, the United Kingdom, Europe and other countries.

ISBN   978–0–230–29858–3   hardback
ISBN   978–0–230–29859–0   paperback

This book is printed on paper suitable for recycling and made from fully managed and sustained forest sources. Logging, pulping and manufacturing processes are expected to conform to the environmental regulations of the country of origin.

A catalogue record for this book is available from the British Library.

A catalog record for this book is available from the Library of Congress.

10   9   8   7   6   5   4   3   2   1
20   19   18   17   16   15   14   13   12   11

Printed and bound in Great Britain by
CPI Antony Rowe, Chippenham and Eastbourne

For Fran Noble and Alex Aylward

Contents

Preface

War as military history, and war cause, moulder, and consequence of change, are the key themes of this book. War was a central theme in the world history of this period and military capability and activity were central to its states, societies, economies and cultures. This book presents an account of late fifteenth- and sixteenth-century warfare in a global context, and, as such, is a corrective to a general body of work that has emphasised Western developments to an extent that the history of non-Western military systems and cultures of war are frequently obscured. In order to offer this corrective, there is a stress on conflict between non-Western powers, which constituted most of the fighting around the world, as well as due attention to warfare between Western and non-Western powers. Moreover, the stress on conflict between non-Western powers has the additional value of providing a comparative context for conflict in the West, while discussion of warfare between Western and non-Western powers offers an opportunity to provide an approach to Western warfare that looks at an important dimension of activity.

In this book, because Europe serves as much to describe the Ottoman empire, which throughout the period, but even more from the 1520s, covered most of south-east Europe, as it does to indicate Christian states within Europe, so the latter are described as the West. Christendom would not be a useful term, as one of the more active Christian states was African, that of Ethiopia (Abyssinia).

The emphasis on non-Western powers provides an instructive context within which to consider the influential concept of a Western-based Military Revolution and this book is designed to complement my *Beyond the Military Revolution: War in the Seventeenth Century World* (2011). In the place of the Military Revolution, the stress here will be one on a variety of military trajectories, and it will be suggested that there is no reason to privilege the Western one. This approach provides an opportunity moreover to put Western expansion in context and, in doing so, to show that imperial conquest generally involved, in both the short and the long term, a complex co-operative and incorporating process in which local aid and acceptance were important to the expanding power.

Within the non-West, the emphasis is on Asia, more particularly East, South and South-West Asia. In part, this is because of the variety of effective Asian military systems, which together constitute an Asian counter-example to challenge the idea of a Western-based Military Revolution. However, the distribution of world population is also significant. Figures are approximate and were affected by the devastating impact of the bubonic plague, which hit the population of China, the Middle East and Europe particularly hard in the fourteenth century. Nevertheless, in the mid-fifteenth century, East and South Asia comprised about half the world's population, with another maybe 13 per cent in South-East and South-West Asia together. Europe had about 14 per cent, as did the Americas, with Africa having about 10 per cent. In contrast, Australasia and Oceania had probably less than 0.01 per cent. Western expansion to the Americas led to the devastating spread of measles and smallpox, greatly reducing their populations.

This study builds on my *European Warfare, 1494–1660* (2002), but greatly expands its scope. As I cannot expect everyone to have read the earlier work, I have reprised some of its argument, but fuller detail on European developments can be found in that study.

I see this book not as a solo work, but as an important contribution to a debate in which others have made and will continue to make valuable contributions. If my work is seen to rest alongside and to provoke fresh discussion, that will be success enough. I benefited from the opportunity to give the first annual Alan Villiers Memorial Lecture at Oxford in 2010, to speak at Brigham Young and Pennsylvania State universities the same year, and, in particular, from participating in 'The Limits of Empire in the Early Modern World', a 2009 conference in honour of Geoffrey Parker, a much valued mentor and friend. In honouring his contribution, I also want to draw attention to the inspiration of scholars now, alas, dead. The Preface to my volume in the *Cambridge Illustrated Atlas of Warfare* (1994) thanks three such, David Aldridge, Matthew Anderson and Jan Glete. Looking to the past, I also recall my visit in 1976 to Iran, Afghanistan and Pakistan in which I had the opportunity to walk terrain and visit sites that are difficult to grasp from photographs and books. More recently, I have benefited from the opportunity to visit sites in the Mediterranean and the Far East. Maps are useful for locating places mentioned in the text. These days, maps can readily be found online, while for atlases it is useful to consult the *DK Atlas of World History* (1999), and the works referred to in its bibliography, notably Joseph Schwartzberg's *Historical Atlas of South Asia* (2nd edn, 1992), the *New Cambridge Modern History Atlas* (1970), and J.D. Fage's *Atlas of African History* (1958).

Preface

I am most grateful to Harald Kleinschmidt, Rudi Matthee, Gervase Phillips, Mark Stevens, David Trim, and two anonymous readers for their comments on all of an earlier draft and to Pradeep Barua, Giancarlo Casale, Karl Friday, Albrecht Fuess, Simon Pepper, Louis Sicking and Kenneth Swope for their comments on sections of an earlier draft. I have benefited from advice from Peter Lorge. Kate Haines has proved a very supportive editor, whether based at Basingstoke or in Kigali, and Juanita Bullough helped considerably as copy-editor. None is responsible for any errors that remain. It is a great pleasure to dedicate this book to good friends with many thanks for time together, not least Devon walks and evening meals.

Jeremy Black

1 *Introduction*

Fundamentals

If change, but variety in change, is a key theme of this book, then it is important to consider the earlier background to the period, both because that provides a context within which change can be assessed and because it helps explain this variety. Two significant socio-political themes emerge from this background, first the warfare of large states or empires and their opponents, and, secondly, warfare on a different scale involving both smaller states and societies that were not organised for deploying significant forces. This distinction is different to the standard one between settled societies and nomadic or semi-nomadic peoples, but, in practice, the two distinctions capture features of an overall matrix of military activity in which scale, political development, social characteristics, and environmental constraints were linked and mutually interacting.

Nomadic and semi-nomadic peoples generally relied on pastoral agriculture or slash-and-burn shifting cultivation, were less populous, and their governmental structures were less developed. These people did not therefore tend to develop comparable military specialisation, especially in fortification and siegecraft. A good example is provided by the peoples of highland South-East Asia,[1] or those of New Guinea and most of Borneo. While the agricultural surplus and taxation base of settled agrarian societies permitted the development of logistical mechanisms to support permanent specialised military units, nomadic peoples generally lacked such units, and had far less organised logistical systems. In war, these peoples and others lacking a defined state system often relied on raiding their opponents, and generally sought to avoid battle; although there was also frequently endemic violence between villages, clans and tribes. As a result, many, if not most, settlements were fortified.

Partly, however, because of a neglect of such people, but also as a result of the standard emphases, both in the history of war and, more specifically, in the study of the warfare of states, much of the discussion of the nature of conflict focuses on battle, more particularly battle between specialised military units. As a result, much of the discussion fails to give sufficient weight to the alternative 'little war' of raids, skirmishes, and small-scale clashes that were far more frequent aspects of war, both for nomadic or semi-nomadic peoples and for settled societies with specialised units. Moreover, this 'little war' was an important feature of 'big war' that could undermine or undo the consequences of victory in battle. This level of conflict was one in which the mobility of cavalry and light infantry proved particularly valuable, while battlefield formations and tactics were largely irrelevant.

As yet, there has been no systematic study of 'little war', although it was one in which distinctions between the regular forces of the state engaged in such fighting and irregulars were often far from clear. Moreover, irregular forces could be very substantial and several represented bodies with some of the attributes of independent statehood, for example the Cossacks. The range of such forces and conflict requires emphasis and they should not be seen as necessarily less effective than the 'high end' of warfare, represented by large-scale battles on land and sea, and the regular sieges of well-prepared fortresses.

Linked to these tensions over the relative significance of different types of conflict comes those over the description of warfare. For example, in the scholarship on Central Asian and pre-colonial sub-Saharan African conflict, there is a contrast between the argument that much, probably most, conflict was, as raiding war, qualitatively different from Western warfare, and, on the other hand, the claim that 'real' warfare, similar to that practised in the West, can be seen, and not simply what is dismissed as raids. Looked at differently, and challenging the use of Western terminology that downgraded warfare in other parts of the world, raiding can also be seen as real warfare. This issue is further confused by the extent to which military cultures have been constructed and greatly simplified, not least by misleading external categorisation in terms of militarism or passivity.[2]

The issue of subsequent academic construction is indeed pertinent when discussing the inherent military cultures of particular societies, although, at the same time, war-making was in fact culturally specific in particular societies.[3] Moreover, the culture of war could change in its characteristics and/or manifestations, as when Japan in the early seventeenth century essentially gave up war while maintaining many of the social and cultural attributes of bellicosity.

These factors all played a role in the pull-and-push dynamics of military activity; the dynamics arising from the demands placed upon the military and, on the other hand, the possibilities that it could offer. Military capability and action were framed in accordance both with the tasks or goals that political and military contexts gave rise to, and with the possibilities they created. These pull-and-push dynamics could be seen in terms of strategies, operations and tactics, each of which reflected tasks and possibilities. The dynamics could also be seen in force structures, notably the varied emphases on numbers of troops as opposed to experience, infantry as opposed to cavalry, and firepower as opposed to mobility.

At the same time, alongside differences between particular types of conflict, there were fundamentals to warfare in the early fifteenth century, fundamentals that remained pertinent throughout the period covered by this book. Most obviously, but so taken for granted by contemporaries that it was scarcely subject for mention, the conduct of warfare in all societies was very much the duty of men. Women were closely involved, notably because their agricultural labour was crucial to the economic survival of societies at war, and also as victims, whether directly or indirectly, and whether physical, mental, social or economic.[4] In particular, the rape and enslavement of women were habitual in raiding warfare. Nevertheless, the direct involvement of women as fighters was exceptional.

Secondly, the relatively low level of applied technology, and in even the most developed societies, ensured that all warfare remained subject to environmental and physical constraints which were common worldwide. The absence of any real understanding of infectious diseases, for humans and animals, combined with low agricultural productivity and the limited nature of industrial activity to ensure that population figures were low everywhere, by modern standards, and that the potential pool of warriors was restricted, although the armies deployed in the field were often larger than those deployed today. Moreover, the predominance of agriculture produced fighting men who, in areas of cultivation, were most available outside the harvesting season. A need for troops encouraged enslavement and slave raiding not only to provide labour but also to increase the pool of warriors, particularly in Islamic societies, or, at least, the auxiliaries necessary for conflict, such as porters carrying supplies and rowers propelling galleys.

Moreover, most labour was probably exerted by generally malnourished human or animal muscle, while other power sources were natural and fixed: water and wind power and the burning of wood, a bulky and immobile product. These power sources could not be moved with armies or fleets, which limited the mobility of the latter and made their operations dependent on resources obtained en route, most obviously with wind-powered ships. The nature of technology was such that there were no rapid communications on land or sea, which affected the movement of soldiers, supplies, and messages everywhere in the world. Nevertheless, there were notable examples of highly developed communications systems, for example the pony express of the Mongols, the runners of the Incas, the use of galleys in the Mediterranean, and the widespread employment of beacons.

Scale as well as speed was at issue. By 1450, no state had dispatched and sustained major naval and amphibious forces across the Atlantic or Pacific, let alone to the other side of the world, although such forces had been used at closer range, as with the unsuccessful Mongol invasions of Japan and Vietnam.

Returning to differences, the tasks and possibilities confronting military forces on land and sea were subject to perception, contingency and testing, and there was no fixed nature of warfare that could be affected by technological change, most obviously gunpowder. Indeed, given that the rise of gunpowder weaponry and its impact is an important theme in this study, it is necessary, at the outset, to stress that it is mistaken to see this rise as the sole theme. Moreover, such weaponry impacted on a very varied and dynamic global military environment, and these variations helped influence, if not determine, the response to this weaponry, and thus affected its influence.

In 1450–1600, especially 1450–1540, many established states were to be brought down by conquerors, including the Aztec empire of Mesoamerica (Mexico), the Inca empire of the Andes, both at the hands of Spanish conquerors; Byzantium (the Eastern Roman empire), the Mamluk empire of Egypt, Syria and Palestine, and the Jagiello kingdom of Hungary, all at the hands of the Ottoman Turks; the Aqquyunlu confederacy, which ruled Iran and Iraq, at the hands of Safavid invaders; and the Lodi Sultanate of Delhi, at those of Mughal invaders. Each of these successes indicated the effectiveness of force as a medium of change, as well as the frequency of war; and several of the conflicts highlighted military differences between particular cultures, in some cases major differences.

The Mongols

The situation of the Mongols was a direct continuation of centuries of conflict, conflict that has attracted particular attention in the case of Eurasia, as the sources are better there. Conflict frequently reflected the tension between settled societies and attackers, but this tension was also more complex than this explanation suggests because, alongside conflict and tension, there was frequent military co-operation across this border. Such co-operation rested on a careful politics of mutual advantage. For example, Chinese relations with nomadic and semi-nomadic peoples of the extensive steppe lands to the north-west and north, notably the

Mongols, rested on a combination of force with a variety of diplomatic procedures, including *jimi* or 'loose rein', which permitted the incorporation of 'barbarian' groups into the Chinese realm. Their chiefs were given Chinese administrative titles, but continued to rule over their own people in the traditional fashion, which assisted the policies of divide and rule that were important to the Chinese influence in the steppe.

Such management spectacularly broke down in the thirteenth century, and this failure contributed directly to the starting point, for part of the world, of a process of change that offers an alternative to the Western European focus, in discussing and explaining change, on Western European trans-oceanic activity from the 1490s. The latter emphasis reflects a more general Western assumption that modernity as a distinctive condition began in the period 1450–1550 and that an early modern period beginning then is a helpful tool for historical analysis.[5] This approach, however, has limited value as far as most of the world is concerned. Indeed, the Chinggisid (descendants of Temüjin, Chinggis Khan) Mongol empire of the thirteenth century has been claimed as the starting point for continuous global history since it led to the beginning of interlinking exchange-circuits of technologies, ideas, and even diseases. Moreover, it has been suggested that the Mongol rulers deliberately helped such circuits in order to strengthen their system, which took further already-existing links along the silk roads west from the Orient, and was particularly important to relations between China and Iran.[6] Both were overrun by the Mongols who, also conquering southern Russia, Turkestan (Central Asia), and Iraq, advanced as far as (although not conquering) Poland, Hungary, Serbia, Syria, Java and Japan, thus creating the largest contiguous empire in the world.

Weaponry and tactics were both important to Mongol success, but organisation more so. Defining the challenge for many other military systems, the Mongols used cavalry, specifically mounted archers, to provide both mobility and firepower, and such archers remained a key military force across much of the world into the seventeenth century and, in some cases, beyond. Storing compressive and tensile energy by virtue of its construction and shape, allowing it to be smaller than the longbow, their compound bow was a sophisticated piece of engineering. Mongol skill in employing bows and arrows was tactically crucial, with horsemanship being particularly important. The Mongols used short stirrups, which had a major advantage over long stirrups for accurate fire, as the rider's torso was free of the horse's jostlings, while his legs acted as shock absorbers. The use of short stirrups required greater ability as a rider as it was easier to be unhorsed, but their use helped provide a steady firing platform, although skill was also necessary to shoot arrows in any direction and also when riding fast. Standing in the stirrups provided more accuracy than bareback riding or the use of cavalry saddles. A Song general noted of the Mongols, 'It is their custom when they gallop to stand semi-erect in the stirrup rather than sit down.'

Aside from skill in riding, the Mongols also benefited from the hardiness of the horses. As in the savannah lands of West Africa, the emphasis was on small breeds of horses, employed more for mobility than for shock.[7] In turn, control over the major breeding and rearing areas of effective horses of this type provided a major advantage, notably for the Mongols. Such control remained very important to the geopolitics of military power. The Mongols, moreover, were adept at cavalry tactics, such as feigned retreats, and at seizing and using the tempo of battle. Cavalry was crucial to the envelopments that characterised many of their battles. The Europeans had nothing to match them. The Mongols also had heavier cavalry lancers as part of their well-balanced mobile forces. As another instance of variety, the cavalryman of the West African savannah was armed with lance, sword and javelins, as well as bows.

Fighting skill alone did not suffice. Temüjin, known as Chinggis Khan, or fierce, firm, resolute leader, who was named khan, or overlord, of the Mongols in 1206 after a period of sustained tribal warfare, restructured their army, uniting the nomadic tribes into a single force, as well as appointing commanders on the basis of talent, and not of blood-right. He displayed exceptional leadership. In addition, the Mongol culture and way of life provided a ready-made manpower pool of trained warriors used to extensive travel over large areas. Mongol logistical support was highly effective because it reflected and mirrored their normal nomadic state. The Mongols were effectively logistically self-contained in their early conquests, and used local knowledge and resources effectively when they needed to bring up heavier siege equipment.

Moreover, the Mongol tsunami method of conquest was especially effective: they invaded and devastated a large region, but then withdrew and held only a small section of territory. The Mongols thus created a buffer zone that made it impossible to attack them and also weakened the enemy's resources. Also, by only occupying small chunks of territory, they did not tie down troops in garrison duty. Instead, a relatively small force could control the region while the civil administration moved in and integrated territories into the empire. Then, the border troops moved forward and added new territory. This tidal-wave process – the large invasions, then pulling troops back, then surging forward again like a wave – allowed the Mongols to fight on multiple fronts without overextending themselves.[8] This process lasted until the reign of Möngke Khan (1250–9), a grandson of Chinggis

Khan, under whom administrative reforms permitted a maximising of their resources, enabling the Mongols to send huge armies, such as that under Hülegü which captured Baghdad, a centre of Muslin civilisation, in 1258, an attack referred to by Saddam Hussein in 2003 when seeking to mobilise Iraqi public support against invasion by an American-led international coalition.

As with that of other successful steppe peoples, the military skill of the Mongols depended in part on making a transition to city-taking conflict. To move from raiding and victory in battle to seizing territory required an ability to capture fortified positions, and, largely by using Chinese expertise, the Mongols acquired skill in siege warfare during the numerous campaigns required to conquer the Jurchen Jin empire of northern China and the Song empire of southern China, campaigns that represented the most impressive use of force in the thirteenth century. The lengthy nature of the sieges was possible only because of Mongol organisation and persistence, while their ability to elicit and coerce support was also important. Similarly, the Mongols developed a navy from captured Chinese maritime resources, acquiring the relevant expertise from the Chinese and the Koreans. The latter provided the better ships, and for his unsuccessful invasions in 1274 and 1281, Khubilai drew on resources from his entire East Asian empire not just China.

The Mongol ethos was also important, as, if opponents refused to accept terms, the Mongols employed terror, slaughtering many, in order to intimidate others. This policy may have increased resistance, but also encouraged surrender. Success also helped the Mongols, at least initially, to maintain cohesion as well as to win support from other steppe peoples. No other state matched their military strength nor, on land, was any to do so in the period 1450–1600. Indeed, the idea of development in military history has to address this contrast, as it is all too easy to assume that the passage of time automatically brought greater strength and lethality, which is a view far more correct for the nineteenth and twentieth centuries than for earlier periods.

After the death of Möngke, a civil war over the throne ensued, and then rivalry between other Chingissid princes tore the inheritance into four empires: the Empire of the Great Khan, the Khanate of the Golden Horde, the Chagatai Khanate, and the Il-Khanate. Defining the political context across much of Eurasia, these were still far-flung empires, especially the first, which united China, included the Mongol homeland, and held sway over Korea, Tibet, and much of South-East Asia. Khubilai, the Great Khan, a grandson of Chinggis, moved the capital from the steppe to Beijing in 1264.

The fourteenth century was an age of Mongol decline, in part because of conflict within the ruling élite, but other factors also played a role. In China, corruption in the bureaucracy angered many, as did animosity between the rulers and ruled, natural disasters, and less competent rulers. The Mongols were driven from China by rebellions in 1356–68: the establishment of the Ming dynasty of Zhu Yuanzhang in 1368 followed the flight of the Mongol emperor from Beijing back to the steppe ahead of the approaching Chinese army.

Having effectively controlled or threatened much of Eurasia, the withdrawal and decay of the Mongols offers an appropriate starting point for the subsequent military history of much of Eurasia. A range of weapons played a role in this history. Thus, in India, the impact of improved cavalry, not least more effective mounted archers, was increased in the thirteenth and fourteenth centuries by developments in siege technology, notably the introduction of trebuchets, counterweight ballistic machines, from the Middle East, as well as of gunpowder, fired in bombs by ballistic machines or used for sapping under the walls, from China via the Mongols.[9]

Timur

A new power emerged in Central Asia in the person of Timur the Lame (1336–1405; later called Tamerlane), who modelled himself on the Mongols and claimed descent from Chinggis, a significant source of legitimacy, although, in fact, he was not a Chinggisid. Timur married Chinggisid princesses so that he could have the title of Güregen or son-in-law. Timur provided a clear instance of the potential of steppe forces. He filled the vacuum left by the Mongols and employed the same methods. Having gained control of the Chagatai Khanate, Transoxiana, where his capital was at Samarqand, Timur conquered the city of Herat in Afghanistan in 1381, before successfully turning on Persia (Iran), and then he attacked the Golden Horde. Prestige and legitimacy were important as Timur wished to demonstrate his superiority over Toqtamysh, the Golden Horde khan, who had earlier gained his position as a protégé of Timur. Victory was followed by the sacking of the capital, New Sarai, and Timur rerouted the Central Asian trade routes to converge on Samarqand. Timur pressed on to sack Delhi (1398), a traumatic event for the Islamic sultanate of Delhi that left it greatly weakened, followed by turning west to capture Baghdad and Damascus in 1401.

Next year, with rumours circulating of his plans for global conquest, Timur turned against the Ottoman Turks, defeating them at Ankara on 20 July: after a long struggle, Timur's army, which was mostly cavalry, was victorious, not least because much of the Ottoman cavalry defected or abandoned the field. Subsequently, in a pattern that was frequent, the Ottoman infantry was finally broken: the cavalry struggle tended to decide the fate of any battles which increased the significance of cavalry. At the time of his death in 1405, Timur was planning to invade China.[10]

The two great nomadic empires of Chinggis and Timur, and, in particular, alongside their cavalry lancers, their light cavalry armed with compound bows, had been exceptionally successful in extending their sway, not least because China, Europe, and the states of South and South-West Asia, really had no answer to the sort of power they deployed. This situation remained partly true for centuries, although the sixteenth century indicated that, alongside reliance on using mounted archers against mounted archers, as in the frequent conflicts between the Safavids and the Uzbeks, fortifications and firearms could act as important force-multipliers in successfully resisting their attack.

However, although the nomadic empires had more organisation than is often appreciated and were more than simply raiding empires, they lacked the density of resources that the Europeans and Chinese were to command. Moreover, the political decay of these nomadic empires, which was brought about through lack of legitimating principles, frequent succession struggles, and absence of a common ethnic base, rather than military limitations, provided opportunities for other powers. Timur, in particular, failed to plan for the future. Yet, these problems were scarcely unique to nomadic empires, and the territorial changes in Christian Europe between 1400 and 1600 often reflected similar factors. Timur's son and successor, Shāhrukh (r. 1405–47), lacked his father's dynamism and aggression, and under his rule, based in Herat, Timurid government became increasingly sedentary.

The Americas

Extensive steppe grasslands were an important basis for light cavalry, but this was not the natural or military environment of war across much of the world. The horse was not native to the Americas nor to Australasia and Oceania, and was not found across much of Africa south of the savannah belt, in part due to disease. However, far-flung empires were not created by cavalry only. The successive empires of the Andean chain in South America, including the Chimú empire (c. 700–1475) and, far more, the Inca empire (1438–1532), showed what could be achieved by infantry-based armies. The Incas conquered the Chimú and spread their power into modern Ecuador and central Chile, although their technology was relatively unsophisticated. Subject peoples were used to provide the porters that ensured the logistics of their far-flung campaigns.

The Incas' counterpart in central Mexico, although scarcely on the same grand scale, was the Aztec empire, which gained control of much of the region in a series of campaigns in the fifteenth century, while also making adroit use of alliances. Like the Incas, the Aztecs were highly militaristic. Huitzilipochtli, the God of War, was a major force in their religion.

There were no empires, however, across most of the Americas, let alone Australia, Siberia and Oceania, where native peoples fought with wood, bone or stone weapons. Instead, population densities in these regions were low, and both settlement and authority were dispersed. That, however, did not mean that there were no wars or conquests. Indeed, accounts of aboriginal peoples as essentially pacific are seriously misleading and fail to appreciate the consequences of a lack of state authority to limit conflict. For example, in northern Canada, the Dorset culture of the Palaeo-Eskimos of the eastern Arctic was overwhelmed from about 1000 by the Thule people of northern Alaska, whose kayaks, float harpoons and sinew-backed bows made them more effective hunters of whales. On land, the Thule gained mobility from dogsleds. The Dorset people were killed or assimilated.

Further south, in southern Ontario, where, because it was warmer, it was possible to cultivate crops, the spread of settlement led by 800 to the construction of villages protected by palisades, and, eventually, by double palisades, which created a series of defendable cul-de-sacs. These agricultural societies fought: in about 1300, the Pickering people conquered and partly assimilated the Glen Meyer, while, in the fifteenth century, the Huron conquered the St Lawrence Iroquois. In North America, there was 'public' warfare, in the form of conflict between tribes, but also 'private warfare': raids with no particular sanction, often designed to prove manhood.

Africa

There was a similar pattern in Africa to that in the Americas. Alongside wide-ranging polities, such as the Malinke empire of Mali in the thirteenth century, there were many areas in which there were no such polities, for example South-West Africa. Moreover, as in Asia, nomadic herders pressed when they could on settled peoples. Thus, in the thirteenth century, the Banu Marin advanced from the fringes of the Sahara to overrun Morocco. Subsequently, Abu'l-Hasan, the 'Black Sultan' (r. 1331–51) of the Marinid dynasty in Morocco, overran the Maghrib (North-West Africa), capturing the city of Tunis in 1347, but found it impossible to defeat the Christians in Spain when he invaded in 1340.

Alongside Islam, there was a spread from North Africa to inland west Africa, from at least the fourteenth century, of larger breeds of horses, new equestrian techniques, and new tactics of cavalry warfare. As with Eurasia, changes in cavalry capability proved significant, which focused attention on the supply of horses. Cavalry was particularly important in the *sahel*, the savannah belt to the south of the Sahara, which was suitable cavalry terrain; but, in turn, this reliance on cavalry increased the dependence of operations on the availability of water and fodder, especially grass.

Europe

Compared to the range and sway of the great Asian conquerors, their (Christian) European counterparts were insignificant. On the global scale, European (Western) impact was limited. The Russian principalities were unable to prevail against the powers to their east, had to pay tribute, notably to the Golden Horde, and found themselves the victims of high rates of slave raiding, much of which fed the slave trade via the Black Sea to the Near East and the Mediterranean. As another instance of limited impact, the Vikings established settlements in Greenland and (far more briefly) North America, but could not maintain them. At a far larger scale, the Crusades to the Near East, first proclaimed in 1095 and pursued with great energy over the following two centuries, failed.

Moreover, although the Muslims were driven from most of Spain, while, thereafter, there was Spanish and Portuguese expansion into the Atlantic islands and Morocco;[11] there was also a significant shift of success away from Christian Europe in the fourteenth and fifteenth centuries on its south-eastern boundaries. This shift was particularly apparent after the defeat of the allied Balkan army at Kosovo in 1389, following which the Ottoman Turks reduced Serbia and Wallachia (southern Romania) to tributary status. The Ottomans combined the classic mobility and fluidity of Asian light cavalry tactics with an effective use of infantry. They were helped by a further victory at Nicopolis in 1396 in which Western cavalry, many from France, advanced impetuously through the Ottoman infantry, only to be broken on the Ottoman gun lines and then driven back and routed by the Ottoman cavalry reserve.[12]

The Ottoman advance was greatly delayed by the impact of Timur, whose victory at Ankara in 1402, which led to the capture and imprisonment of sultan Bayezid I, the victor of Nicopolis, was followed by the reversal of Ottoman dominance over much of Anatolia. Indeed, Timur's victory was celebrated in Constantinople (Istanbul), the capital of the embattled and truncated remnant of the Byzantine (Eastern Roman) empire. Subsequently, the Ottomans' advance was adversely affected by civil warfare, but, in the 1430s, they resumed their pressure, driving the Venetians from the city of Thessalonica in 1430 and overrunning much of Serbia in 1439.

Another large crusade was launched in 1443 in response to the Ottoman successes, and it was initially successful. The Hungarians captured the cities of Nis and Sofia, and supported rebellion against Ottoman rule in the Balkans; but, in 1444, the predominantly Hungarian army was heavily defeated by the Ottomans under sultan Murad II (r. 1421–44, 1446–51) at Varna on the Black Sea. The Crusader army totalled about 16,000 men, the Ottomans close to 60,000. King Wladislas I of Hungary (Wladyslaw III of Poland) was killed on the battlefield.[13] Four years later, the Hungarians were defeated again at Kosovo; Ottoman successes underlining the weaknesses of Western warmaking and military organisation.

Western warmaking was varied, with the French emphasis on heavy cavalry and castles not matched in Spain where, instead, there was a far greater stress on light cavalry. This cavalry proved more effective against the Moors, less expensive, and better attuned to the arid environment in Spain, although heavy shock cavalry still had a value in battle which indeed led to the hiring of Christian knights for conflicts between Islamic rulers in Spain and North Africa.

Infantry was of particular significance in northern Italy, the Swiss cantons, Flanders and Scotland. Combining infantry with firepower, the English developed archery. Their longbowmen, however, lacked the tactical and operational flexibility of Central Asian archers. The longbowmen were sometimes mounted for movement on campaign, and indeed Philip II of Spain, when he visited England in 1554, was to have a bodyguard of 100 mounted English archers. However, longbowmen could not fire from the saddle and, even if they rode to the battle, tended to fight on the defensive. This situation meant that their men at arms were also required to fight on foot, sacrificing their mobility and shock effect in the process. This practice ensured that armies with longbowmen as their core component depended on being attacked; a general problem with infantry forces in the period.

The relative limitations of longbowmen is instructive as there is a tendency to treat archers as progenitors for the subsequent introduction of hand-held gunpowder weaponry and, more generally, to present the development of infantry, especially when armed with bows or handguns, as the route to military proficiency. This teleological approach has led to a slighting of the variety of medieval warfare, not least the value of cavalry, and to a misleading account of the changes in this warfare, including those through the use of pole arms, pikes, field fortifications, wagon forts, and the continued development of heavy and light cavalry.

A more significant problem than the failing of particular arms was posed by the difficulty of turning victory in battle into a permanent settlement, as the English discovered in Scotland and France in the fourteenth century. This problem recurred in the early fifteenth century in the latter stages of the Hundred Years War between the kings of England and France (1337–1453). In support of dismounted men-at-arms, Henry V of England's archers helped defeat the successive advances of the French at the battle of Agincourt in 1415, and Henry subsequently conquered the Duchy of Normandy and the valley of the Seine. He was helped by his use of siege artillery but these did not prove to be decisive, and mining and starvation tended to be the methods used to bring a successful conclusion to a siege. Henry owed his overall success to the continuing divisions between the Burgundian and Orleanist branches of the French royal family. Although, by the Treaty of Troyes of 1420, Henry was recognised as the heir to Charles VI of France, his area of control did not extend south of the Loire Valley, and did not include the Burgundian domains of eastern France.

The struggle continued with Charles VI's son, Charles VII (r. 1422–61), rejecting the claims of Henry V's infant son, Henry VI (r. 1422–61, 1470–1). The French suffered further defeats, notably at Verneuil (1424), where they were assisted by a large Scottish expeditionary force. This battle was on a similar scale to Agincourt, and illustrated the effectiveness of the English archers. In the battle, fully-armoured Italian *condottiere* (mercenary) cavalry, riding barded (armoured) horses, and with arrow-proof armour, rode down the English archers and broke the English front line. However, the English reformed and successfully used the lightly-clad archers in support of the men-at-arms in the close-quarter fighting that followed.

Nevertheless, the English forces became over-extended, and home support began to wane. This led to a major English reversal at Orleans, where their siege works were incomplete due to a lack of manpower, which allowed a French army, whose morale was restored by a charismatic peasant girl, Joan of Arc, to break the siege in 1429 and to inflict a series of defeats on the retreating English forces. The political context, however, was the crucial factor for continued English success, and when, in the mid-1430s, they lost the support of Philip 'the Good' (r. 1419–67), the powerful Duke of Burgundy, their defeat became inevitable. The surprising thing is that the English occupation of Normandy, Anjou, Maine and Gascony lasted as long as it did, but the collapse in 1450 was spectacularly swift, and was aided by an effective use of siege cannon by the French.

Gunpowder

The genesis of gunpowder weaponry was a long one. It had first developed in China, where the correct formula for manufacturing gunpowder was discovered in the ninth century. An established arsenal to produce gunpowder existed by the mid-eleventh, effective metal-barrelled weapons were produced in the twelfth, and guns were differentiated into cannon and handguns by the fourteenth.

Each of these processes in fact involved many stages. Although the ability to harness chemical energy was a valuable advance – and cannon have been referred to as the first workable internal combustion engines – gunpowder posed serious problems if its potential as a source of energy was to be utilised effectively. It was necessary to find a rapidly burning mixture with a high propellant force, while an increased portion of saltpetre had to be included in order to transform what had initially been essentially an incendiary into a stronger explosive device. Saltpetre was not easy to obtain.

The effectiveness of cannons was limited by their inherent design limitations throughout the fifteenth century. Large siege bombards were extremely heavy and cumbersome to move and position, and confronted all armies that used them with a major logistical problem. The use of a separate breech chamber to hold the powder and the shot made them slow to load, and the requirement to cool down after firing limited their rate of fire. Great skill was required by the gunsmiths to hammer lengths of wrought iron together to ensure that the seams were able to withstand the pressures generated within the barrels. In 1460, James II of Scotland died while laying siege to Norham Castle when one of his Flemish bombards exploded beside him, as the wedge holding the breech chamber in place was blown out.

However, the employment of improved metal casting techniques, that owed a great deal to the casting of church bells, and the use of copper-based alloys, bronze and brass, as well as cast iron, made cannons lighter and more reliable, as they were able to cope with the increased explosive power generated by 'corned' gunpowder. Improved metal casting also allowed the introductions of trunnions that were cast as an integral part of the barrel, with the improved mobility that this gave, along with higher rates of fire. The introduction of more powerful and stable 'corned' gunpowder and iron cannonballs, supplemented by canister, or grape shot, and mortars combined with the advances in casting and metallurgy alluded to above, made cannons more flexible and effective. Around 1420, 'corned' powder was developed in Western Europe, the gunpowder being produced in granules which kept its components together and led to it being a more effective propellant, providing the necessary energy, but without dangerously high peak pressures. Furthermore, the use of potassium sulphate, rather than lime saltpetre possibly from about 1400, helped limit the propensity of gunpowder to absorb moisture and deteriorate.[14] As a result of these changes, the military possibilities offered by gunpowder were to become increasingly apparent in Europe in the mid-fifteenth century.

Maritime Power

However, it was far from clear at that stage that gunpowder was to help lead to greater relative power on the world stage for the West. The same was true of maritime power. A Portuguese amphibious expedition had seized the city of Ceuta in Morocco in 1415 beginning what was to be a major commitment to conquest there, Portuguese settlement of the Atlantic island of Madeira began in 1424 and of the Azores in the 1430s, and in the 1440s the Portuguese explored the coast of West Africa as far as modern Guinea.

At the same time, however, the Chinese were far more wide-ranging and powerful. In 1161, gunpowder bombs fired by catapults helped the navy of the Song to defeat that of the Jurchen Jin. Such bombs were also used by the Mongol rulers of China in naval operations, including their unsuccessful invasions of Japan in 1274 and 1281, while the Ming fleet possibly carried cannon from the 1350s. In contrast, although shipboard cannon were used earlier, the first naval battle in which European guns were used by both sides occurred at Chioggia in 1380 between the two leading European naval powers: the Venetians defeated the Genoese. Each was able to support its naval strength on the profits of maritime commercial empires, while this strength helped sustain the trade and bases that were central to these empires.

Under the Ming, a series of seven expeditions was sent into the Indian Ocean between 1405 and 1433 under Admiral Zheng He (1371–1433), and, at considerable expense, Chinese power was made manifest along much of its shores. The largest ships carried seven or eight masts, although claims that they were nearly 400 feet in length have been questioned, not least as the dimensions do not correspond to the figures for carrying capacity, tonnage and displacement. Nevertheless, these were probably the largest wooden ships built up to then and, thanks to watertight bulkheads and several layers of external planking, they were very seaworthy. A stele erected by Zheng He explained his mission as one of spreading a Chinese world order of peace that held barbarianism at bay: 'Upon arriving at foreign countries, capture those barbarian kings who resist civilization and are disrespectful, and exterminate those bandit soldiers that indulge in violence and plunder. The ocean route will be safe thanks to this.'[15] Indeed, Chinese patronage was important to the commercial strength of the leading South-East Asian entrepôt of Malacca (Melaka) and the Indian entrepôt of Cochin.

Conclusion

At the same time that, on land, they were pressing south-west into the uplands of South-East Asia and also attempting, albeit unsuccessfully

in the face of guerrilla warfare, to control Dai Viet (North Vietnam), the
Chinese under Zheng He, in a major show of force designed to extend the
Ming tributary system, reached Zabid, the capital of the Tahirid sultan of
Yemen, and Mogadishu in Somalia. On the third expedition, the Chinese
successfully invaded Sri Lanka in about 1411. In addition, they intervened
in Sumatra in 1407 and 1415.[16] South Asian trading patterns were affected
by the expeditions. Just as on land there was no reason to assume that
the Western armies were superior in weaponry, tactics and organisation,
so it was by no means clear that the West would dominate the oceans and
eventually, therefore, the world.

2 Conflict, 1450–1500

War very much brought dramatic outcomes in the mid-fifteenth century. It led to a major check for the world's leading military power, Ming China, saw the end of a millennium-long power, Byzantium (the Eastern Roman empire), and brought to a near-complete close the possession of French territories by the ruler of England. These varied outcomes, however, also showed the difficulty of establishing any clear pattern in military success. In particular, whereas some of these victories owed at least something to the use of gunpowder, this was not the case with others.

At the same time, it is not always easy to recreate what happened in battles, and, therefore, to understand the reasons for success.[1] Tactical formations certainly appear to have meant less in terms of fighting quality than the experience and morale of troops. The size of forces was also important, as was the ability of commanders to influence the tempo of the battle, in particular by retaining reserves or by rallying and redirecting cavalry. Command skills were also involved in the choice of position, and, specifically, in an understanding and assessment of detailed topography. This assessment affected a host of actors, including the advantage of height and slope for all arms, of sight lines for archers, musketeers and cannon, and the softness of the ground, which made cavalry advances particularly difficult. Command skills and unit experience were also bound up in the achievement of co-operation between the varied arms, which was a key force-multiplier and was more significant than in modern warfare, as most modern troops have similar weaponry.

In the case of fortifications, it is also important not to focus on what is seen as the cutting-edge of change, such as the Western *trace italienne* system of anti-cannon fortifications, as most positions were not fortified at the scale and expense of the best-defended locations, and, as a result, most sieges did not match the lengthy efforts mounted against the latter. Indeed, many positions were carried by assault. Nevertheless, the role of fortified positions, and most towns were walled, was such that many campaigns revolved around attempts to take them and, in response, to relieve threatened or besieged positions. As a result of the latter, sieges led to battles, as at

War in the World

Ghajdewān in 1514 and Pavia in 1525. Fortifications were most of value when combined with field forces able to relieve them from siege.

China

One of the most significant battles of mid-century saw victory for an army that did not employ firearms. On 1 September 1449, the Yingzong emperor was captured and his army destroyed at Tumu after a foolish advance into the steppe against the Mongols had been followed by a disastrous retreat in which the rearguard had been destroyed, next by the mistaken establishment of a waterless camp that had been swiftly surrounded by the well-led Mongols, and then by the destruction of the Chinese army when it tried to break out. Access to fresh water was a key tactical and operational issue in some parts of the world, but not in others.

The defeat greatly influenced Ming policy and brought to an end a period in which the Ming had launched numerous offensives beyond the Great Wall and taken the war to the Mongols.[2] Instead, the Ming thereafter largely relied on a defensive strategy based on walls. In the immediate aftermath of the battle, the Mongol leader, Esen (r. 1439–55) an Oirat or western Mongol, not a Chinggisid, did not attack the capital, Beijing, but, instead, returned home with his loot. This move gave the Ming the opportunity to decide to remain in Beijing, to make defensive preparations, and to entrust rule to the emperor's half-brother, Jingdi. When Esen subsequently advanced, he failed to capture cities including Beijing, and this failure encouraged a new Ming emphasis on fortifications, first to protect strategic passes. Later, especially in the 1470s, the Great Wall of the first Qin emperor was reconstructed and there were also new fortifications.

Similarly, Korea, a Chinese tributary state, which had lost part of its north-east in the early fifteenth century to conquest by the Jurchens (who were based in what is now Manchuria and the Russian Far East), launched attempts at reconquest from 1434 and established a chain of defensive positions to consolidate the frontier, using resettlement as part of the process. Resettlement was more generally part of the process by which states sought to consolidate control, notably in the face of nomadic attacks. Such resettlement was frequently linked to fortifications, walls, and military colonies.

The Chinese defensive strategy, which also reflected the widespread agrarian rebellions of the 1440s that allegedly left over a million dead, was part of a wider process of Chinese caution seen most clearly in the abandonment of the voyages to the Indian Ocean and also in the acceptance of a loss of control over Dai Viet (North Vietnam). New-found Chinese caution from mid-century did not mean an end of interest in the steppe. Instead, as part of a process in which they did not rely solely on the walls, the Ming devoted considerable attention to maintaining influence through a tributary system designed to protect their vulnerable northern frontier, the vulnerability of which was enhanced from 1421 when the capital was moved from Nanjing to Beijing. Whereas, prior to 1450, the Chinese had launched numerous campaigns against the Mongols as far as the Orkhon, Onon and Kerulen Rivers, thereafter the Mongols initiated more of the conflicts and forced the Ming onto the defence[3], although the Ming also still used offensive operations to seize resources and keep nomadic foes off-balance. Moreover, dealing with outsiders, from the Jurchens to the north-east to the Tanguts in Qinghai, the Chinese sought to maintain influence when they could not wield control. Indeed, the Tangut lands, occupied from 1403 to 1513, were thereafter influenced by linkage through tributary status.

To the Chinese, the tribute system was designed to ensure stability in a peaceful system of nominal dependence on the Emperor, with this dependence in theory defining the real presence and ranking of foreigners. Confirming the succession of foreign rulers ensured, in Chinese eyes, their legitimation as well as their vassalage, and this was an aspect of the Chinese attempt to exploit divisions among their neighbours. These divisions were important to China's relative security. Disunity among the Mongols was particularly significant, notably that between the eastern and western Mongols, the Khalkhas and the Oirats. Thus, Batu Möngke, the leader of the eastern Mongols, crushed the western Mongols in the early 1410s, but disunity continued. Moreover, Esen, the Oirat leader, was killed in a rebellion in 1455. His death was followed by renewed warfare within the Mongol world, not least between the Khalkhas and the Oirats, with Mandaghol (r. 1473–9) finally unifying the Khalkhas, and his son Dayan (r. 1479–1517) defeating the Oirats and then attacking China.

Alongside receiving tribute and waging war, Chinese rulers were capable of dealing with other powers in practical terms as in effect equals, and in some periods even approached formal parity in diplomatic practice. Trade and tribute were also related in the complex relations between China and neighbours or near-neighbours, such as the Timurid lands of Central Asia. Trade certainly served military purposes by enabling the Chinese to exchange tea for the militarily-capable horses that were not obtainable in China, horses needed for the cavalry and as draught animals. This trade was badly hit by the failure of 1449.[4] The offer of goods by envoys and the receipt, in return, of Chinese goods provided a way to ensure mutual profit, but this relationship was also unstable, not least as it relied on each side finding the same value in the goods exchanged. In 1466, the Ming imprisoned and subsequently executed the Jurchen leader, Dongshan, who had led an embassy to complain about the gifts given by the Chinese in return for tribute. The killing of Jurchen leaders was important to a major campaign in 1466–7 in which 50,000 Chinese and 10,000 Korean troops advanced north. In response to this pressure, the Jurchen re-established tributary relations with China, although, as a reminder of the partial nature of most such successes, Jurchen raids continued.

Dai Viet (North Vietnam) recognised the nominal suzerainty of Mongol China in 1288 and was conquered by the Ming in 1407; but the need, for the Chinese as for other powers, to win acquiescence in conquest was shown with the serious resistance that began in 1418 and that led to the Ming expulsion in 1428. The ability of Dai Viet to acquire firearms capability to match that of the Ming was valuable in this resistance; but, equally, the Chinese allegedly had captured Vietnamese experts, who then helped in the manufacture of firearms in the Chinese department established to do so in 1407. In practice, the political situation was more important in explaining the Chinese failure.

If tributary ritual did not ensure compliance, notably later from Dai Viet, nevertheless the Chinese tributary system served as a way to mediate international relations, and thus to avoid war. The latter process was crucial to Ming military history, as war-avoidance became its central policy from the mid-fifteenth century. Indeed, the ritual of the tributary system could serve to disguise and confirm changes of power that were unwelcome to China, such as the Dai Viet increase in power by means of conquering the state of Champa in what is now the southern part of Vietnam from 1471: the Champa capital, Vijaya, fell five years later. In theory, China maintained its moral and practical superiority, but, in practice, the tribute system alleviated tension.

Firearms were not a key element. The use of cannon and other firearms had spread from China to Burma, Cambodia, Siam, Vietnam and elsewhere in the fourteenth century; while the Japanese received crude guns in the fifteenth. However, China lost the lead in handheld firearms. Its cannon were not particularly good in the fifteenth and sixteenth centuries, the manufacture of muskets was primitive, and there was a lack of experimentation in new methods of using handguns on the battlefield. Instead, the Chinese emphasis in countering opponents was on improvements in logistics, for example the Grand Canal from the Yangtze River to Beijing so as better to mobilise and support large forces.[5] The ability to move large quantities of supplies from the prime agricultural regions to the frontier areas, where large armies had to be supported in order to fulfil strategic and operational goals, was a central theme in Chinese geopolitics. It was to be important to the Manchu conquest of Xinjiang in the eighteenth century.[6]

Alongside the decision whether to use troops against foreign powers, there was a frequent need, for China as for other powers, to employ them against rebels. For example, in the 1450s, there were frequent operations against non-Han peoples, especially the Yao and Miao. These were followed in the 1460s and 1470s by operations in southern Sichuan, as well as by the Yongyang rebellion in Hubei. Non-Han peoples were also affected by the expansion of Ming power to the south-west in the large forested upland region that formed a backbone for South-East Asia. This expansion led both to conquest and to large-scale colonisation by Han Chinese.[7]

Japan

War was very much part of Japanese history in this period and, indeed, in the sixteenth century as well; but this warfare was civil conflict until the 1590s when Korea was invaded. Japan's ability to remain in this state, of civil turmoil but without external conflict, reflected the limited extent to which naval power projection necessarily led to such conflict. The Mongol rulers of China had the capability to intervene in Japan, but, having tried unsuccessfully in the late thirteenth century, did not do so, and no other power was capable of considering such action in the late fifteenth century.

In Japan, power from the mid-fourteenth to the mid-fifteenth century was largely wielded by the *shogun*, the head of the warrior [*samurai*] government, as the emperor, whose court was in the city of Kyoto, had no real power and was really a sacred figure. Indeed, the Japanese emperor had far less power than the Emperor in the Holy Roman Empire (Germany, Austria, the Czech Republic, and the Low Countries), even though the power of the latter, in turn, was far less than that of the rulers of empire-states, such as the Ottoman empire and China.

The Ashikaga *shogunate* had begun in 1336, but the *shogun*'s effective power over much of Japan, including the Kantō region, the crucial section of the main Japanese island, Honshu, was limited. The *shugo* (military governors) of the provinces comprising Japan were among the last remaining forces defending centralisation, largely because their principal asset distinguishing them from other powerful warriors in their provinces was their title as *shugo* which was meaningful only in the context of continued imperial control.[8] Nevertheless, the *shugo* were increasingly autonomous as well as affected by opposition by local warriors. Moreover, the leading *shugo* families were hit by succession disputes that had reached the stage of open warfare. In a situation that in some respects paralleled France in the late sixteenth century or England during the Wars of the Roses, the Ōnin War of 1467-77 arose from a succession dispute within the Ashikaga house which was exacerbated by the role of rival *shugo*, both in that dispute and in those within the leading *shugo* houses. Fighting between the contenders in one of the leading *shugo* houses in 1467 was the spur for what became a highly destructive war. Kyoto was the principal site of much of the fighting, but it spread elsewhere and, even though the armies left the city in 1477, the Ōnin War led into the local and regional conflict that characterised much of the age of *Sengoku* (The Country at War) from 1467 to 1568. The Ashikaga *shogunate* had lost its power and the *shugo* network had collapsed in a context of general disorder with ties of vassalage increasingly broken in a society that was very much in flux.

Instead, warrior chieftains emerged, these *daimyō* (literally 'big names') coming largely from the former vassals of *shugo*. The *daimyō* were far more independent of *shoguns* than the constables had been. The authority of *daimyō* rested on successful conflict, and this proved the way to retain the support of vassals. The idea that the latter should be loyal to *daimyō* who inherited their position meant little if the *daimyō* could not win victory and the lands and prestige that came with it.[9] The need for such success helped ensure that betrayal was central to the politics of *daimyō* conflict; and, as a result, treachery played an important role in both battles and the seizure of fortresses. Operations were partly designed so as to display strength, and thus induce surrender and deter treachery.

Central Eurasia

The Mongols, especially the Khalkas and Oirats, who ruled a vast tranche of territory from near Beijing to the southern shores of Lake Baikal, were far from alone in not using firearms. Major Central Asian states to the west were similarly heavily reliant on mounted archers, notably the Chagatai khanate, part of the inheritance of Chinggis Khan, which ruled from Xinjiang to Lake Balkhash; and the Shaybanids, who ruled most of modern Kazakhstan, Uzbekistan and Turkmenistan. The military history of these lands is both obscure and understudied, which helps ensure that the role of mounted archers is undervalued, both there and on the world scale. This under-valuation is ironic, as this form of warfare displayed considerable vitality. Thus, the Ming Chinese used Mongol mounted archers, while in Iraq and much of what is now Iran, the Türkmen cavalry of the Aqquyunlu Confederacy eventually took over in the chaos that followed the death of Timur. Their army was a classic Central Asian one, armed with bows, swords and shields and largely deployed on the battlefield in a two-wing cavalry formation.

Known as the White Sheep Türkmens, the Aqquyunlu from eastern Anatolia established themselves across the Iranian Plateau in 1467–9 at the expense of similar forces, notably the rival Black Sheep Türkmens. In 1468, Uzun Hasan, the head of the Aqquyunlu (r. 1457–78), defeated and killed Jahān Shāh, the chief of the Black Sheep, after which the lands of the latter were incorporated into the Aqquyunlu lands. Kirmán in eastern Iran was conquered in 1469. As a reminder of the danger, of seeing this period principally in terms of the rise of the Ottomans, who, in 1473, defeated, although without overthrowing Uzun Hasan, in 1469 his envoy arrived in Cairo carrying the severed head of Abū Sa'id, the Timurid ruler of Bukhara and Samarqand. This was an impressive display of power, although the envoy was refused permission to have the head, impaled on a spear, paraded through the streets.

Further north, mounted archers were recognised as of value by the Christian principalities of European Russia. In 1456, at Staraia Rusa, Vassily II of Muscovy was able to defeat an army from the powerful city-state of Novgorod that was strong in lancers, by making good use of mounted archers, in part provided by Tatar auxiliaries. As a result, Novgorod was forced to accept Muscovite dominance, an important step in the consolidation of Christian Russia. The city was to be eventually captured in 1477, partly because Ivan III was able to take advantage of social and political divisions in it. Other Rus' principalities were subjugated and otherwise brought under control in the 1450s and 1460s. Staraia Rusa also marked a transition in force structures. Hitherto, Russian principalities had deployed armoured lancers, in part as a consequence of the Byzantine preference for heavy cavalry. In their place, came a shift in cavalry armament and tactics towards archers wearing padded hemp coats, an adaptation to the Central Asian form of warfare that made it cheaper to deploy cavalry.

India

Mounted archers also played a major role in northern India where the (Muslim) Afghan Lodis ruled the sultanate of Delhi from 1451 to 1526. Northern India was disunited and territorially unstable, and its political and military history in the fifteenth century is generally passed over, with scant attention between Timur's conquest in 1398 and the establishment of the Mughal dynasty following Babur's defeat of the Lodis at Panipat outside Delhi in 1526. This lack of attention reflects the general absence of interest in pre-Mughal military history, combined with a sense that it was of limited consequence. While well-founded in terms of the long-term development of warfare and military systems, this sense of limited long-term consequence does not really rise to the challenge of discussing warfare for a given period at a global scale, and notably for important areas with a large population, such as northern India. Moreover, the success of those powers that were to have longer-term significance, such as the Mughals and the Ottomans, is best discussed in the context provided by a consideration of those that did not match them, not least because they were defeated by the first group of powers. Repeatedly in explaining success, it is the ability to ensure and sustain a degree of political cohesion, and to translate this into military capability, that is of note, rather than an unique warfighting style, and this point is relevant for the West as well as for India, China and the Islamic world.

India also witnessed significant military developments in the period, developments that were to help ensure that the Mughal conquest in the sixteenth century proved far more difficult than is suggested by simply referring to victory at Panipat in 1526. In part, these developments were a matter of the spread of gunpowder technology such that its use by the Mughals only gave a limited technology advantage, although far more was at stake. Having benefited from the diffusion of crops such as bananas, sugar cane and sorghum, the highly-populated character of much of northern India was significant, as was the absence of any disease impact comparable to that which the Europeans brought to the New World.

Although beginning earlier in India, the use of cannon spread much more in the fifteenth century, especially in the Muslim sultanates of the Deccan in central-south India, but also from there further north. The use of hand-held firearms fired by means of a matchlock-trigger mechanism also spread. Yet, the effectiveness of firearms remained limited. For example, Indian forts did not tend to fall to cannon, in part probably because of the major improvements in fortifications that had taken place over the previous two centuries, with walls made thicker, the building of round (as opposed to square) towers and of strong projecting bastions to minimise the threat from mining, and adaptations to the walls to enable the installation of defensive artillery. Moreover, forts were increasingly built on steep, rocky hills and in the midst of forests, both of which hindered attack.[10]

Such positions were difficult to attack by storm or siege, which led to an emphasis on blockade, a lengthy process in which the exhaustion of the forts' supplies was countered by the strains on the larger besieging army. As a consequence, there was a stress on obtaining surrender by bribery, which was an aspect of the use of conciliation in order to incorporate new territories and to sustain control over existing ones. This established pattern of Indian campaigning was to be adopted by invaders from poorer areas, such as the Mughals. The difficulty of taking forts contributed to this situation, as it ensured that the martial élite had to be wooed in order to win them over. Once wooed, this élite was employed in campaigning in order to derive benefits from conquest that would ensure their support.

The availability of this martial élite helped provide Indian rulers with the cavalry that made it unnecessary to develop infantry forces, while the latter, whether or not using matchlocks, were vulnerable to cavalry attack, both to the mounted archers, who fired more rapidly, and to heavy cavalry. In contrast, in Western Europe, there was no force of mounted archers capable of challenging the firepower of the infantry; and the lack of this challenge helped the Western Europeans to develop their own form of infantry with its emphasis, by the mid-sixteenth century, on musketeers.

The founder of the Lodi sultanate, Buhlūl, controlled much of the Upper Ganges valley by his death in 1489. This inheritance was expanded by his successors, Sikandar and Ibrahim. Victory in battle played a role, notably in 1495 when the rival Sharqis, who then ruled the area of Bihar, were defeated near the city of Benares; but so also did a politics of primacy and vassalage in which the impression of power helped to ensure a degree of control, albeit an unstable degree.[11] This situation was more generally true of political systems in the period, and it frequently makes it difficult to fix on key occasions of success and failure. Victory was significant, but conflict could also reflect a failure, on one or both parts, to manage the impression of power adequately.

Instability in India reflected in part the weakness of the major states, with the sultanate of Delhi in particular gravely damaged by Timur's sack of Delhi in 1398, while, in south-central India, the Bahmaní kingdom divided from the 1480s into five separate sultanates – Berar, Ahmadnagar, Bidar, Bijapur and Golkonda – as a result of succession disputes and a failure of leadership after the death of a powerful shah. The weakness and disintegration of these and other Indian states arose from the fissiparous character of the Turko-Afghan military society that dominated Islamic India, as well as a more general absence of cohesion in territories that essentially rested on the military prowess of the ruler and his ability to win over support through continued success. In turn, the large number of states that resulted made any conquest lengthy, and a process rather than an event, as the Mughals were to discover.

The Americas

The expansion of imperial systems without the use of firearms was also seen in the New World, most dramatically with the expansion of the Inca empire. Under Tupac Yupanqui (r. 1471–93), there was an expansion not only to the north, defeating the smaller empire of the Chimú in 1476, but, to a greater extent, to the south, into modern central Chile and northern Argentina, in part helped by utilising a more sophisticated governmental system. The chiefdoms to the south of the Inca dominions could not field comparable forces while, conversely, they could be assimilated into the Inca system by becoming subject peoples; although, south of the Maule River in Chile, the Mapuche blocked Inca expansion, just as, from the mid-sixteenth century, Spanish expansion was to be blocked.

The Incas also benefited from the extent to which the farming villagers in the tropical forests to the east of the Andes did not pose a military challenge, no more than the nomadic hunter-gatherers to the south-east. Equally, the Incas did not try to extend their power far into these areas, especially the former, and this limitation represented a sensible response to their environment. In an instance of the wider pattern of environmental adaptation, the forest people used bows and archers, while the Incas, coming from treeless uplands, did not, and this contrast gave the former a marked advantage in conflict. Equally, these forest people did not seek to conquer the uplands.

The Incas held their own territories together by developing an extensive road system which reached from the Equator to just below 35° South, an infrastructure unmatched outside China. Certainly, the Aztecs in Mexico did not match them in scale. Aztec control over otherwise autonomous city states was expressed through tribute payment, and the latter was sustained by a high level of military activity. As with the Incas, this was a matter of infantry who did not have firearms: neither the horse nor gunpowder was yet present in the Americas. Having expanded to the Gulf of Mexico coast, the Aztecs also advanced to the Pacific. The Aztec army had an élite corps that was available year-round, but the bulk of the manpower was of a lower status. In their conflicts, the Aztecs used a variety of techniques. Thus, in the defeat of the Huaxtecs in about 1450, a feigned retreat drew the pursuing enemy into an ambush, a tactic used around the world.

Africa

In Africa, as in the Americas, there was a continuum from states to hunter gatherers via complex farming societies with significant populations and developed settlements, and more simple farming societies. There is a strong tendency to write military history in terms of the states, both because they appear more significant and because the limited sources are far more sparse for any other type of society. That approach, however, risks leaving the military history of much of Africa neglected. It is likely that most of this history was conducted on a far more restricted geographical scale than was the case across much of Asia, in large part because of the difficulty of the terrain and vegetation across much of Africa, combined with the absence of horses. Most sub-Saharan African military history was also on a more restricted scale than that in the Andean chain in South America, although in the latter case there were no horses. The emphasis on the local, added to the limited population of much of Africa and logistical problems, presumably meant relatively small-scale forces.

Yet, there were also factors encouraging the opposite tendencies, those of greater distance and scale. In particular, trade led to a commitment over distance, with trans-Saharan trade routes and those focused on the Indian Ocean proving particularly important. Moreover, specific environments, notably the *sahel* belt of grassland between the Sahara Desert and the forests to the south, and also the uplands of Ethiopia and Zimbabwe, encouraged longer-range military activity. The general result in these areas was the development of larger polities, although the extent to which these should be described as states is controversial. The polities were often linked to trade-routes, notably those across the Sahara, and those focused on the Swahili port cities on the Indian Ocean such as Malindi and Kilwa.

Warfare affected, even altered, the relations both between these polities and between them and their surrounding areas. In particular, in the *sahel* belt of West Africa, an area conducive to cavalry, the dominant state of the early fifteenth century, the Malinke empire of Mali, which had risen to prominence in the early thirteenth century, was surpassed by Songhai, a polity in the Niger valley, with Gao as its major city, that, in the 1460s, began serious raids on Mali. Moreover, Songhai increased its power by overcoming the polities further up the Niger, including those that controlled the towns of Timbuktu and Jenne, both of which, like Gao had been under the control of Mali in the mid-fourteenth century.

Sonni Ali (r. 1464–92), the maker of Songhai expansion, fought every year of his reign. Some of his campaigns, most obviously against the Tuaregs of the Sahara who used raiding to benefit from the wealth of settled societies, can be characterised as defensive; but war was central to the Songhai state, as Sonni expanded his power at the expense of Jenne, captured in 1471, as well as the Fulani of the region of Dendi to the east, and the Mossi states to the south-west. As with the Aztecs, expeditions served to maintain his control over his tributaries. These wars of expansion were continued by Askia Muhammad (r. 1493–1528). Songhai also pressed hard on the Hausa in what is now northern Nigeria, exacting tribute from the city-state of Kano.[12]

More generally, the region was affected by a spread of Muslim influence which led to the establishment of a series of states in the *sahel*, including Kanem and Bornu near Lake Chad, and Tunjur to the east in modern eastern Chad on the pilgrim road to the port of Suakin on the Red Sea en route to Mecca. In contrast to the situation in Central Asia, there was no far-flung empires, certainly none crossing the Sahara and linking the *sahel* states to the North African littoral as there was to be from 1591, when Morocco conquered Timbuktu, and again in the nineteenth century when Egypt conquered Sudan. Instead, the independent states of Makuria and Funj were to the south of Mamluk Egypt.

After a dramatic rise in 1250–60, creating an empire including Syria, Palestine and the Hejaz (western Arabia), Mamluk expansion was limited, while their military culture was conservative, although the Mamluks were able to see off successive Mongol attacks and their empire survived a quarter-millennium, which was a considerable achievement. The Mamluk élite put a premium on cavalry who did not associate the use of firearms with acceptable warrior conduct. They also stressed individual skill in archery and their archery training was top notch.

Mamluk views on firearms have been a topic subject to revision in recent years. It was argued that firearms were regarded as socially subversive, as was also to be the case with *samurai* aversion to firearms in seventeenth to nineteenth century Japan, although, as Japan then was a group of islands that was at peace, the comparison should not be pushed too hard: it relates mostly to the emphasis on élite warriors. Hostility to the use of musketeers obliged successive Mamluk sultans in 1498 and 1514 to disband musketeer units they had raised. Sultan al-Nāsir Muhammad (r. 1496–8), who sought to form a unit of black slaves armed with firearms, was overthrown. Like the Aztecs in Mexico, the Mamluks stressed individual prowess and hand-to-hand, one-to-one, combat with a matched opponent. These values sapped discipline and made them vulnerable to forces that put an emphasis on more concerted manoeuvres and on anonymous combat, particularly employing firepower.

However, recent work has suggested a need for the re-evaluation of these views, and as part of a more positive approach to the Mamluk willingness to reform.[13] It is clear that Mamluk élite soldiers were passionate horse riders while the infantry was reserved for other strata of society. Horse riders could not use firearms at the beginning of the sixteenth century, and there seemed scant reason why the highly-trained Mamluk cavalry élite should dismount when the training required for firearms was not so intensive. Yet, at the same time, the Mamluks turned to firearms, using cannon from the 1360s. Moreover, in their conflict of 1465–71 with shah Suwār, who had deposed his brother as emir of Dhu'l-Kadr and renounced the emirate's ties of vassalage to Egypt, and who the Ottomans secretly backed, the Mamluks employed cannon in their successful captures of the positions of 'Ayntāb (1471), Adana (1471), and Zamanti (1472). In their war with the Ottomans in 1485–91, the Mamluks cast cannon at their camp at Ayas, and used them, alongside ballistas and mangonels, at the siege of Adana. The Ottomans were also able to cast cannon in the field. In this war, the Mamluks encountered firearms in large numbers for the first time, and they immediately started their military reforms. In 1490, the Mamluks used handgunners successfully against the Ottomans, advancing to Kayseri. Under capable leaders, the Mamluks could still check, if not defeat, the Ottomans, but it proved very difficult to finance the war which led to the levying of emergency taxation.[14]

Mamluk reforms faced strong disadvantages from the outset compared to the Ottomans, notably lack of resources, such as iron, and of skilled manpower. The Mamluks tried, but could not cope, while the Ottomans were stronger. Moreover, as a reminder that firearms were not the sole issue, the sultan's overthrow in 1498 was linked to the fact that he was a son of a reigning sultan, that generally in the fifteenth century the dynastic principle had been abolished, and that the old companions of his father resented his staying on the throne as usually the new ruler had to be chosen from among them. In addition, the opposition to the black slaves armed with handguns may have been more of a problem of ethnicity than arms. Cavalry, moreover, remained effective. The key victory over Suwār, that at the Jayhūn river in November 1471, was preponderantly a cavalry struggle. However, rather than discussing such factors, Egyptian literary sources from the seventeenth century had to explain the downfall of the Mamluks and chose to do so with the topic of firearms and the luxury life that had allegedly estranged the élite from their people, an approach that cast a more positive light on the Ottoman rulers of the period.

Further west, the Islamic presence in the Mediterranean was weak. The *Reconquista*, the longstanding reconquest of Spain from the Moors by the Christians, culminated in the capture of Granada in 1492, and was matched by Portuguese and Spanish expansion in Morocco and along the coast of what is now Algeria. The Christian advance in Spain also had a major impact on the maritime situation in the Western Mediterranean as it reduced the coastline and number of ports in Muslim hands. Gibraltar was finally gained by Spain in 1462, while the emirate of Granada brought with it the ports of Malaga and Almeria.

The Ottoman empire

The Ottomans were to overcome the Mamluk empire in 1516–17, but, in the meantime, they had been more famously successful in destroying the Byzantine empire. The fall of Constantinople in May 1453 after 54 days of bombardment and attacks was richly symbolic. A centre of power that had resisted non-Christian attack for nearly a millennium had finally fallen, and to what had in 1300 been a small frontier principality. In 1453, Ottoman numerical superiority (about 80,000 to 10,000 troops) was crucial, but so also was the effective use of gunpowder weaponry thanks to the skilful direction of sultan Mehmed II. The artillery, including about sixty new cannon cast at the effective foundry of Adrianople (Edirne), drove off the Byzantine navy and battered the walls of Constantinople, creating breaches through which the city was stormed.[15] This artillery, which relied to a considerable extent on specialists from Central Europe, served notice on military attitudes and practices that had seemed to protect Christian society. Relying on fortifications to thwart 'barbarians' by offsetting their numbers, dynamism, mobility and aggression, no longer seemed a credible policy.

Although the rest of Christian Europe had sent little support, the fall of Constantinople inflicted a bitter psychological blow on Christendom and signalled the extent to which war could dramatically alter the political order. With emperor Constantine XI dying in the defence of the city, the Eastern Roman empire was reduced to fragments that would soon fall. As well as making their empire contiguous, and gaining a major commercial and logistical base, the Ottomans won great prestige in both the Muslim and Christian worlds, and took over a potent imperial tradition. Their capital moved to Constantinople, while Mehmed took the sobriquet 'the Conqueror' and the Byzantine title of 'Caesar'. He had grown up amidst imperial ideas and sought to realise the longstanding Islamic dream of the conquest of Byzantium, and thus to defy and overcome Christendom. Having done so, Mehmed strengthened the defences of the city by rebuilding its walls.[16]

The period from the fall of Constantinople in 1453 to that of Belgrade to Süleyman I, the Magnificent, in 1521 is not usually seen as one of Ottoman inroads in Europe. Indeed, in 1456, despite deploying at least twenty-seven large bombards and seven mortars besieging the position[17], Mehmed was defeated by the Hungarians under János Hunyadi outside Belgrade, which had already successfully resisted siege in 1440. Belgrade was the key defensive position on the river Danube and, by controlling the river route, protected Hungary from attack from the south. Supply routes relied on rivers, not least in order to move siege artillery. Hungarian success, which included victories at Jaysca (1463), Savacz (1475), and Kenyémezö (1479), helped lessen Christian anxiety about the Ottomans,[18] although, in turn, it made subsequent Ottoman advances against Hungary in the 1520s more frightening. In 1480, moreover, despite deploying a substantial force, Mehmed failed to capture Rhodes. By adopting a scorched-earth policy, the Knights of St John exacerbated the logistical problems facing the besiegers.

Nevertheless, there were important and extensive Ottoman gains which again raise the question of how to assess significance. There were conquests in Albania, Serbia, Bosnia-Herzegovina, Attica, the Morea (Peloponnese), and the Aegean. These conquests involved different kinds of operation. The fall of Corinth, a key position protecting the Morea, in 1458 followed a four-month siege that reflected the Ottoman ability to supply a large army in the field whereas the defenders were starved into surrender. In contrast, the rapidly-concluded and ably-organised conquest of Bosnia-Herzegovina faced guerrilla-type resistance, notably ambushes, leading to a robust Ottoman response including cutting the water supply and/or smoking out resisters, as well as sudden attacks.[19] In the Aegean, the island of Lesbos fell in 1461-2, the fortress of Mitylene surrendering after Ottoman cannon had wrecked much of the walls; while the successful capture of key bases and islands in the war with Venice of 1463–79, for example Negroponte (1470) on the island of Euboea, won the Ottomans the dominant position in the Aegean.

Rather, however, than simply seeing these conquests in terms of some inexorable process, Ottoman steps owed much to a sense of anxiety about the moves of other powers. Thus, the successful invasion of Serbia in 1458 by the Grand Vezir, Mahmud Pasha Angevolić, arose in part due to the success of the Hungarian protégés in the dispute among the Serbian regents. Moreover, the concerted attacks of Hungary and Venice on the Ottomans in 1463, which included the Venetian conquest of most of the Morea in 1463 and an attack on Lesbos in 1464, led to rapid Ottoman responses.

Ottoman capability was shown at Negroponte in 1470 when a fleet was coordinated with an army under Mehmed II that crossed to the island by a bridge of boats. The arrival of an indecisively-led Venetian relief fleet led to Mehmed launching a successful final assault through breaches made by his cannon. In contrast, the Ottomans had relied on both cannon and catapults in their siege of Thessalonica in 1430. Their focus on cannon was aided by the efficiency with which they operated their field foundries.[20]

It was apparent that Christendom faced a new series of invasions and it was unclear whether it might survive. Indeed, in 1480, a 12,000-strong Ottoman amphibious force, convoyed by a fleet of 28 galleys and 104 light galleys and transport vessels, landed at Otranto in south-eastern Italy, within campaigning distance of Rome. The town of Otranto fell, providing the Ottomans with a base. The Western Roman Empire had been extinguished in 476, just over a millennium earlier, and a new conquest of Western Europe appeared imminent. The nearby port of Bari had been an Arab base from 841 to 871, but, since then, the coast of Apulia had been free of Muslim bases. It was easy to understand why war, one of the four horsemen of the Apocalypse, was frequently presented as a Turk. An eyewitness account of the siege of Rhodes was printed in the West and made an impact.[21]

The Ottomans were able to take Otranto and hold it against a Neapolitan force at the same time that they were besieging Rhodes. In both cases, the cannon used by the attacking forces, Ottomans and Neapolitans, were inadequate to guarantee success. This was probably due to their inflexibility and size, and their slow rate of fire and use of stone cannonballs. In both cases, the fortifications were 'pre-bastion' in design.

The Mediterranean was not the sole area of Ottoman expansion. There was also a major drive in the Black Sea region, an area that was far more important strategically and commercially than tends to be appreciated today. Having successfully resisted Ottoman-Tatar attack in 1454, the Genoese port of Kaffa (modern Feodosiya in the south-eastern Crimea) fell in 1475 to an Ottoman expedition of 380 galleys and other ships, establishing the Ottomans in the Crimea and giving them control of a key entrepôt in the slave trade. The port-bases of Kaffa, Kinburn, Kerch, Ochakov and Azov, and the southern shore of the Crimea came under direct Ottoman control, and, from their bases, the Ottomans projected their power into the interior. River valleys were a prime means for this projection. Thus, from Akkerman, captured in 1484, the Dniester valley became a route for Ottoman power, leading Stephen the Great, the ruler of the now exposed principality of Moldavia, to become an Ottoman tributary two years later.

Further east, the khanate of the Crimea, which emerged in 1441 under the Giray dynasty, became an ally from 1475, and a major source of slaves for the Ottomans. The complex relationship indicated the need for caution when thinking about imperial power and expansion: the khan was an Ottoman subject, but received gifts from the Ottomans that were seen as tribute by the khans who had, thanks to their Chinggisid descent, more exalted antecedents. This alliance, which owed much to Ottoman intervention in the divided internal politics of the dynasty, encouraged the Tatars to raid Muscovy to the north, with whom relations became hostile from the 1470s. The Russians were made to pay an annual tribute, but that did not prevent Tatar raiding for slaves. Further east, from their base of Anapa, the Ottomans dominated the region of the Kuban and influenced the Caucasus.

The Ottomans also took control of the southern shore of the Black Sea. First, the Genoese base of Amasra fell to a land and sea offensive in 1460, the city surrendering as there seemed no hope of successful resistance. Then, the Greek kingdom of Trebizond was conquered in 1461, with the fall of the cities of Sinope and Trezibond, ending the leading Byzantine survivor. These successes were achieved by amphibious forces operating in concert with the land army which was under the personal command of Mehmed. A fleet of 100 galleys was sent against Sinope. Moreover, the Muslim Isfandiyari principality to its west was also overrun, with the fortresses of Koyulhisar and Karahisar falling that year after bombardment by Mehmed's cannon.

The Black Sea was now dominated by the Ottomans, giving them control or influence over the lands around the sea, although this position was subject to attack from the north.[22] The Ottoman success was a major geopolitical development, both regionally and in Eurasia as a whole, and it was a change that affected the power politics of Europe by influencing the nature of Russian power.

In contrast, the Golden Horde, the successor state to the Mongol empire in its western conquests, had been divided into Tatar khanates as a result of struggles for leadership in the first half of the fifteenth century, leaving no dominant Islamic force north of the Black Sea. The ability of the khanates of the Crimea, Kazan, the Golden Horde and Astrakhan to block the expansion of Poland-Lithuania and Muscovy/Russia was uncertain. Lithuanian power reached close to the Black Sea, although, under Ivan III 'the Great' (r. 1462–1505), Russian expansion was directed to the north-west and north-east, and not southwards. In 1467–9, Ivan began to take the initiative against Kazan to the east, launching a series of campaigns. He subsequently took advantage of dynastic strife within the khanate, and, in 1487, his troops helped install a sympathetic claimant. Russian firepower was not primarily in the form of firearms. On the Ugra river in 1480, khan Akhmet of the Golden Horde was defeated not so much by the arquebusiers of Ivan III as by his archers. Ivan successfully rejected Tatar overlordship.

The absence of a strong Islamic state to the north of the Black Sea also benefited the Ottomans, for there was no equivalent there to Aqquyunlu Iraq and Mamluk Egypt to restrict their expansion or, indeed, to challenge them in the Black Sea. Instead, it was the Ottomans who came to dominate to the north of the Black Sea, and were thus best placed to recruit local protégés. As a result, the Russian advance south was delayed.

More generally, the Ottomans benefited, both in Europe and Asia, from the absence of any sustained and powerful opposing alliance, a lack that reflected the difficulty of co-operation both across cultural divides and because of the distance and communications issues involved. In 1458, Uzun Hasan (r. 1457–78), the head of the Aqquyunlu or White Sheep confederation of Türkmen tribes, joined a coalition with David Komnenos, ruler of Trebizond, and a number of Caucasian rulers, an alliance that spanned religious divides, and, in 1460–1, this precarious alliance sought the support of European Christendom. However, no powerful anti-Ottoman league able to concert operations was created. The failure of the Ottomans' Islamic opponents to unite was as serious as the comparable failure of the Europeans, and, despite the shared enmity of Uzun Hasan, Hungary and Venice towards Mehmed II, notably in 1464–5 and 1472–3, it proved impossible to create a viable league spanning the two spheres of operations. Thus, the Ottomans profited from their central place location.

At the same time, an awareness of this shared enmity encouraged Ottoman action, not least when there was intervention in areas where the Ottomans already considered themselves the dominant outside force. Uzan Hasan's support for Ishak Bey, a contender for the Karamanid throne, the ruler of Karaman (south-central Anatolia), led in 1464 to the expulsion of Ishak Bey's half-brother, Pir Ahmed, the son of an Ottoman princess who had been installed there with Ottoman approval in 1464. The Ottomans, in turn, drove out Ishak Bey in 1465, although, in 1468, Mehmed displaced Pir Ahmed because he had refused to provide support against the Mamluks. The Karaman issue helped increase Ottoman hostility towards the Aqquyunlu. Similarly, the Knights of St John in Rhodes had sought to co-operate with Karaman against the Ottomans.

The Ottomans also benefited from their military development. Initially relying on mounted archers, *akincis* (raiders) who were essentially freelance, they established, in the second half of the fourteenth century, an infantry that became a centrally-paid standing army eventually armed with field cannon and handguns. The increase in central direction stemmed largely from changes under Murad II and reflected increased control over resources that rested in part on a stronger bureaucracy. As a result, reliance on the *akinci* commandos in frontier zones declined to be replaced by a focus on the officials of the state. A growing stress on handguns was encouraged when the Ottomans encountered Christian European forces using guns in battle. This weaponry served the Ottomans to good effect when they fought the Aqquyunlu in 1473, although much of the Ottoman infantry was not yet armed with handguns. Thus, when Mehmed II had earlier crossed the Taurus mountains in the face of opposition by the Aqquyunlu, he did so with archers and spearmen in his vanguard.[23]

In the 1510s, most of the janissaries still carried bows,[24] and many of those who invaded Egypt in 1517 were armed with spears.[25] Archers continued to be used by the Ottomans in the late sixteenth century, being employed, for example, against the rebellion in Yemen in the 1560s, as well as in the invasion of Cyprus in 1570 and at the (naval) battle of Lepanto in 1571.

On 11 August 1473, at Başkent, the effect of Ottoman cannon and handguns on Türkmen cavalry helped lead to victory over Uzun Hasan, who had unsuccessfully sought firearms from the Venetians because of Ottoman opposition. The victory at Başkent, however, was not simply a matter of technology. The Ottomans under Mehmed II also benefited from having a fortified wagon-position from which to resist cavalry attack, and from both numerical superiority and better discipline.[26] The use of *tábúr cengi*, fortified wagon-positions or camps, was a common technique in resisting cavalry attacks, one seen across the Islamic world as well as in Eastern Europe, for example by the Hussites in Bohemia. In 1476, the Moldavians unsuccessfully used such positions against Ottoman attack.

The initial clashes on 1 and 4 August 1473 had resulted in Aqquyunlu successes, especially on the 1st when a feint retreat led to a rash Ottoman advance that was ambushed, resulting in the death of its commander. Contention over failure to support this advance resulted in the later dismissal of the Grand Vezir and contributed to his execution in 1474. However, on 11 August 1473, the Ottomans were victorious not only in defence but on the attack, and not only on the flanks but also in the centre where Mehmed attacked and defeated the Aqquyunlu centre.[27] The number of factors that can be cited to help explain the outcome serves as a reminder of the need for caution in establishing a general model of military capability based on one factor such as gunpowder weapons. It is also necessary to put battles in their context. Başkent did not lead to an Ottoman conquest of the Aqquyunlu territories, nor, indeed, to any significant territorial advances. By 1478, moreover, when they were used at the battle of Khuy in the conflict over Uzun Hasan's successor, the Aqquyunlu had both field artillery and handguns. They soon both employed and manufactured firearms. At Khuy, the side with the firearms lost.

Despite its many successes in the late fifteenth century, the Ottoman empire then was not to achieve the gains seen in the first half of the sixteenth century. Nevertheless, the expansion of 1450–1500 was far greater than that of any Western state, with the nearest equivalent (although not in population gained) being that of Russia under Ivan III.

Christian Europe

The Western powers also developed the use of gunpowder weaponry, and it had a notable effect in the closing stages of the Hundred Years' War. In 1449–51, English-held Normandy and Gascony fell rapidly to the stronger army of Charles VII of France, not least his impressive train of artillery. The replacement of stone by iron cannon balls, the use of more effective gunpowder, improvements in the transport of cannon, and the development of the trunnion, which made it easier to change the angle of fire, all increased the effectiveness of artillery; although the latter also helped drive up the cost of war as well as posing the formidable logistical challenge of transporting not only the cannon but also the cannon balls and powder. The importance of sieges in conflicts, for example the Polish victory over the Teutonic Order in the Thirteen Years' War of 1454–66, was such that any method that led to a rapid success was valuable. Charles VII's cannon brought the speedy fall of fortified positions, in marked contrast with the time taken in earlier sieges, and also helped lead to victory in battle over English archers at Formigny in 1450. In turn, an English counter-offensive was crushed at Castillon in Gascony in 1453 with siege cannon playing a role in the French victory.[28]

Cannon proved useful against domestic and foreign rulers. Thus, Louis XI of France employed cannon against rebellious barons in the War of the Public Weal (1465–9), as well as against the Dukes of Burgundy between 1465 and 1477, and in repelling an English invasion in 1475. The war with Burgundy involved a conflict between strong artillery powers that included formidable exchanges as, notably, when Duke Philip 'the Good' unsuccess-fully besieged Paris in 1465. In 1444, Burgundian galleys using stern chasers had been employed off Rhodes. Philip's son, Charles 'the Bold' (r. 1467–77), in turn faced a range of powers using artillery.[29]

These successes suggested a new age of warfare, not least when combined with episodes such as the use of cannon to capture the fortresses of Granada, the last Muslim principality in Spain, culminating with the surren-der of the capital, Granada, on 1 January 1492; as well as with the success-ful sieges when Charles VIII of France invaded Italy in 1494, launching the Italian Wars that lasted until 1559. In response, there was a major change in fortification, a change that transformed the value of earlier fortifications and put a considerable burden on budgets. Cannon were most effective against the stationary target of high stone walls, so fortifications were redesigned to provide lower, denser and more complex targets. There were developments and adaptations to resist cannon prior to the better-known *trace italienne* system, but fortifications designed to cope with artillery were first constructed in large numbers in Italy, and were then spread across Europe by Italian architects. In the new system, known as the *trace italianne*, bastions, generally quadrilateral, angled, and at regular intervals along all walls, were introduced to provide gun platforms able to launch effective flanking fire against attackers, while defences were lowered and strengthened with earth. There were similar designs in Japanese castles.

As a prime instance of the challenge-and-response character of military development, these improvement in fortifications lessened the decisive-ness of artillery in siegecraft. The ability to organise and implement such a response, notably if costly as was the *trace italienne*, required resources and a degree of administrative ability, such that, for gunpowder, it has been argued that 'administrative improvements preceded military change, and that military change preceded the introduction of any new military technology… The [earlier European] age of cavalry was really the age of bad infantry, and was a political, not a technological, phenomenon.'[30]

The analysis of a new age of gunpowder-based warfare, however, can be questioned and qualified for a number of reasons. First, the process of change was more complex than implied by referring to the potential of gunpowder, not least as the development and application of an enhanced capability was far less clear-cut than may be suggested.[31] Secondly, detailed scrutiny of the episodes usually cited as evidence of a new capability frequently reveal a number of factors responsible for success. For example, English positions in Normandy fell as a result of treachery as well as cannon, the former proving a relatively inexpensive way to capture positions.

The need to address multiple factors in causation was scarcely new. For example, the heretical Hussite movement in Bohemia (much of the modern Czech Republic) used handgunners in its successful defeat of a series of crusades from 1420 to 1431. Yet, the Hussites also benefited in their series of victories that included Sudomer (1420), Kitkov (1420), and Malešov (1424), from the use of crossbowmen, from the field fortifications that protected both them and their handgunners, from a mastery of terrain, and from the contrast between good Hussite command, especially by Jan Žižka, and the extent to which their attackers were poorly-commanded.

Similarly, Granada's fall owed much to largely German-manned Spanish artillery and offensive artillery tactics, but took a decade of campaigning and was also a product of serious divisions among the defenders, in particular a succession dispute in the ruling house that reflected a major issue with Islamic ruling houses, namely the extent to which both polygamy/concubinage and an absence of primogeniture [inheritance by the eldest male] helped lead to more than one claimant in a situation that was settled with violence. The absence of support for Granada from North Africa was also significant. Moreover, Spanish military capability was not simply a matter of firepower.[32] The size of the invading army was significant as was the use of economic warfare in the shape of the destruction of crops. Furthermore, Moorish cities could resist bombardment only to fall as a result of hunger, which was the case of Malaga in 1487 and in many respects of Granada itself.

Thirdly, and, most pertinently, for understanding the late fifteenth century, there were a number of weapons systems that were effective[33] and, as yet, even in Europe, there was nothing inevitable about the triumph of gunpowder weaponry. This can be seen for example with the major role of cavalry in the French and Burgundian armies. Moreover, the rise of the Swiss to prominence in Western Europe, notably as a consequence of their crucial role in defeating Charles 'the Bold', Duke of Burgundy, in 1476-7, came through their use of the pike.

The employment of pikes had a lengthy genesis in the later medieval period. There were continuities with the spears and halberds (a combined spear and battleaxe) used by the Flemings, as at Courtrai (1302), and the Scots, as at Bannockburn (1314), and also with the halberds employed by the Swiss in the fourteenth century. The halberd was shorter than the pike, but the tactics developed were similar. Pikes were originally utilised as a defensive weapon, but the particular value of pikemen related not only to their ability to sustain a defence, but also to their potential for effective attack. Useless as an individual weapon, because it was heavy and inflexible and could not provide all-round protection, the pike was devastating *en masse* in disciplined formations, its mass providing momentum in attack, while pike squares were not vulnerable to flank attacks. In defence, pikemen could give protection against cavalry, as the pike outreached the lance. Furthermore, while benefiting from their protective firepower, pikemen provided musketeers and halberdiers with the defensive strength otherwise offered by walls or field entrenchments. Other infantry weapons were less able to do so. Yet, the operation of units focused on pikemen required concerted actions that rested on drill and, as with musketry, methodical training, which led to a need for trained, professional infantry, far superior to most medieval levies. This requirement rewarded unit cohesion, and thus the professionalism linked to continuity.

The Swiss gained great prestige as pikemen by their defeat, at both Grandson (2 March 1476) and Murten (22 June 1476), of the combined armed forces of Charles 'the Bold' which had especially strong heavy cavalry units. These victories, both of which were linked to sieges, were not, however, only due to the Swiss pikemen, and their technique of advancing in echelon. Other factors included Charles's poor battlefield leadership (although he was an effective organiser) and the cavalry which the Swiss were provided by their allies, as they had none of their own. The cavalry ensured the harrying of the retreating Burgundians which helped to make Murten a sweeping victory. Charles was finally defeated and killed at Nancy in 1477; but there were few Swiss there and the battle was largely fought by Lorrainers and Germans.[34]

These victories led other powers to hire (France) or emulate (several German rulers) the Swiss in establishing mobile infantry forces largely, especially from the 1490s, composed of pikemen, with the German rulers developing *landsknechte* units. At Guinegate (1479), Maximilian, Archduke of Austria, later Emperor Maximilian I, the son-in-law of Charles 'the Bold', used Flemish pikemen, their pikes copying those of the Swiss, supported by cannon, to beat a French army strong in firepower. Similarly, at Murten, Burgundian artillery had failed to halt the advancing Swiss pikemen. Maximilian's *landsknechte*, raised in Germany, had a higher proportion of pikemen than the Swiss and also favoured handgunners over crossbow-men. The *landsknechte* defeated far larger Frisian forces in 1496 and 1498.

Mercenary bands were particularly important in Italy, the wealthiest part of Europe, and their professionalism and concern to make effective and safe use of their relatively expensive forces ensured that they generally embraced new weapons and formations, as with Bartolemeo Colleoni, a mercenary leader who became Captain General of Venice from 1455 to 1475, and who was a keen advocate of firearms.[35] The Swiss had territorial interests in northern Italy, where they gained territory for their confedera-tion, notably the Ticino in 1512; but in the Italian Wars (1494–1559) they principally acted as mercenaries as rulers were willing to pay for the use of their experienced troops. Mercenaries were also important elsewhere. For example, the failure of the general Polish levy to win over the Teutonic Order in the mid-century Thirteen Years' War led to a reliance on merce-naries who proved particularly effective in the sieges of castles.

Gunpowder led eventually to the supplanting of earlier missile weapons, the crossbow and the longbow, but not that of other weapons, notably the pike which continued to play a major role on the European battlefield until the close of the seventeenth century. Handguns had greater penetrative power than either longbows or crossbows which was particularly impor-tant as, thanks to quenching rather than air-cooling, improved armour was produced in sixteenth-century Europe. However, detailed tests have suggested that handguns were less effective than is sometimes claimed.[36] Handguns were cheaper than bows, but handguns had a limited range and a low rate of fire, were affected by bad weather as rain doused burning matches, and therefore affected ignition, and also damped powder, were harder to make than bows, needed a supply of powder and shot, and were not easy to use from horseback. At Fornovo on 6 July 1495, the artillery duel at the start of the battle between French and Italian forces was inef-fective as rain had dampened the powder. Aside from problems rooted in the mechanical properties of handguns and in the chemical nature of the gunpowder reaction, for example the lack of consistency in purity of the chemical reagents, there were also characteristics of the weaponry that interacted with poor use. Maladroit shooting, notably a lack of steadiness in igniting the match to fire the powder, was one of these. Gunpowder-driven projectiles have markedly higher velocity than earlier weapons, and arrows are much closer to hand-thrown spears in terms of velocity than projectiles fired from handguns. Thus, guns are much deadlier than earlier weapons, but they were also less accurate, shorter range, and slower than the composite recurved bow, and could not be fired from horseback.[37]

The use of the arquebus, the first effective handheld firearm in Europe, spread from the 1460s. This spread appears to have been due not to an instant acceptance of overwhelming capability, but to the use of the arquebus in a particular niche and by a specific group: militia who guarded city walls, a protected role that compensated for their battlefield vulnerability. From this, the use of the arquebus spread, but it is no accident that the weapon was most effective in the Italian Wars when employed in concert with field fortifications, as at Cerignola (1503).

Moreover, cannon initially were not very much more effective against stone walls than earlier siege machines, although they were very effective against wooden (ship) walls. Aside from a slow rate of fire, a short range, and recoil, cannon suffered from the poor casting techniques that led both to frequent accidents and to the need to tailor shot to particular guns.

The notion that cannon brought the value of medieval fortifications to an end requires qualification. Even when cannon were brought up to take part in sieges, itself a difficult process, they were frequently only marginally more effective than previous means of siegecraft. Indeed, cannon failed more often than they succeeded, and many times a castle fell to treachery or negotiation rather than bombardment; while stormings rather than sieges were also important, as when the French under Gaston of Foix stormed Venetian-held Brescia in February 1512. Despite the improvements in the design and manufacturing techniques of guns, other factors were still the main determinants of the outcome of sieges,[38] although, with the demise of the siege tower and the battering ram, siege operations in 1550 were different to those of a century earlier.[39] Thus, the introduction and effects of gunpowder weapons were gradual processes, more akin to evolution than revolution. Similarly, in response to gunpowder, there were a number of much cheaper ways to enhance existing fortifications than the *trace italienne*, and these other methods were used much more extensively.

Firearms eventually replaced bow weapons as their potential was grasped, but this learning curve also entailed learning to appreciate the limitations of firearms, both as individual weapons and tactically on the battlefield. Problems with the availability of muskets, powder and shot were important in helping ensure that mounted archers remained more important across much of Asia, while interlinked issues over range, accuracy and killing power guided the tactical use of handguns. Effectiveness was seen to depend on volume of fire, not individual accuracy and lethality. This emphasis lessened the need for lengthy training, which, in turn, increased the ease of use of muskets; but, to provide a volume of fire, musketeers were grouped together, creating, alongside their slow rate of fire, serious problems of vulnerability which ensured that pikemen had to be deployed for protection. Similar problems affected the use of cannon, and underlined the need for combined arms forces.

The British Isles

Firearms also played a role in the British Isles, the military history of which is worthy of consideration as it indicates the variety of military trajectories at issue in Europe in this period. In Scotland, the Douglas castle at Threave surrendered in 1455 in the face of a 'great bombard' [cannon], while James II of Scotland was killed in 1460 when hit by a flying wedge dislodged by the discharge of a cannon bombarding Roxburgh castle, the major English position in Scotland. The castle fell soon after. Yet, what is striking is that, whereas cannon were important in sieges, firearms played only a relatively minor part in battle. Thus, archers took a major role at Towton (19 March 1461), the largest, with up to 60,000 men involved, and bloodiest battle ever fought in England, and, as a battle in which Edward IV decisively defeated the Lancastrian forces, a key engagement in the (civil) Wars of the Roses.

This period in England and Scotland also showed the range of conflict involved in warfare, a range that helped ensure that the state-driven narrative of military development is only one among several that can be offered. Private warfare was an important alternative, with the numbers involved in feuds being considerable. For example, from 1453, two rival families, the Nevilles and the Percys, waged a small-scale war in the English county of Yorkshire. That year, the wedding party of Sir Thomas Percy was ambushed by a Neville band of 700 men.

Private and state warfare were not separate, however, but, instead different aspects of the system by which troops were raised. Payment was seen not only with mercenaries but also with troops raised from tenurial relationships. Lords tend to reward their followers and retain their services with an annual payment of money, rather than land, providing a dynamic of political and military power. Military professionalism was organised in terms of clientage within a society dominated by powerful nobles, whose willingness to raise troops was crucial to the ability of rulers to field armies.[40]

As elsewhere in the West, and more generally, the form of patronage and clientage described as 'Bastard Feudalism' was not necessarily a cause of civil conflict, but, in the event of a breakdown in relations between monarch and nobles, or in the ranks of the latter, it made it easier for the nobles to mobilise and sustain their strength. The course of the civil wars was affected by, and affected, aristocratic power bases. In some areas, powerful magnates dominated the situation, for example, in England, the Dukes of Suffolk in East Anglia, and the Stanleys in the North-West. These magnates played a major role in the wars, while the latter also laid low the magnates, which again repeated the situation elsewhere in the world. Thus, Leicestershire was dominated by the Beaumonts until 1460, when John, Viscount Beaumont was killed at the battle of Northampton, while William, Lord Hastings was established by the Yorkists as the local magnate. Hastings came to control government across much of the Midlands, and was thus able to raise troops, including a crucial 3,000 men for Edward IV in 1471 when he re-established his position on the throne. Aristocratic factionalism and royal government were interwoven: at least nineteen of Hastings' retainers became sheriffs, the representatives of royal government in the localities, in the counties of Derbyshire, Leicestershire, Staffordshire and Warwickshire between 1461 and 1487.

Again as elsewhere, tensions within states were related to conflict between them. Defeat by France in the 1440s and early 1450s, which led to the English crown losing all its French dominions bar Calais (which fell in 1558) and the Channel Isles, resulted in a crucial loss of royal prestige under the unimpressive Henry VI (r. 1421–61, 70–1). Defeat was followed by the Wars of the Roses, which also owed much to the war in France in the shape of battle-hardened veterans and nobles accustomed to military life. This was the lengthiest period of civil conflict in English history with warfare in 1455–64, 1469–71, and 1483–7 as a result of a dispute over the succession that reflected and triggered wider political problems.

The Wars of the Roses were a conflict of battles which were the centre-piece in short campaigns. A revival of fortified features in the houses of the élite testified to concern about safety,[41] but there were few sieges. As more widely in the West, moats and defensive walls encircled new manor houses of the period, such as Great Chalfield Manor in Wiltshire, which was completed in 1480. Two years later, Sir Edmund Bedingfield, an East Anglian landowner, was given a licence by Edward IV, to 'build, make and construct walls and towers with stone, lime and gravel, around and below his Manor of Oxburgh in the County of Norfolk, and enclose that Manor with walls and towers of this kind; also embattle, crenellate, and machico-late [create openings in parapets from where stones, etc. could be dropped on attackers] those walls and towers'.

Such features were a claim to status and a product of what it was thought a nobleman's residence ought to look like. They were also a testimony to the need of the propertied to rely on their own resources and local alliances, rather than on the power of royal government. The extent to which the fortified features in late medieval domestic architecture were defensive has been questioned, and it is clear that they were in part a mark of status, a theme that was important to military arrangements, but these features also affirmed strength in local politics. Landed families moreover built castles, that at Oxwich, a possession of the Mansels, one of the leading Glamorgan gentry families, being first specifically mentioned in 1459.

Similarly, in India, the town dwellings and rural centres of prominent families were fortified, with walled and gated compounds being a prominent feature in towns. If government could not provide safety, then it was scarcely surprising that others sought to protect themselves, and, however tenuously, this was a theme linking non-state tribal areas such as highland New Guinea, with the subjects of many states, although in China the central government proved better able to secure internal peace.

Despite factional disputes among the magnates, periods of actual conflict during the Wars of the Roses were fairly short, months or years rather than decades, there were limited funds available, and most of England was not threatened by foreign attack. As a result, there was no equivalent to the advances in fortification technique seen in Italy in the period, nor to the massive expenditure on urban fortifications in many parts of Europe. Town defences in England were useful, although they could not prevent trouble. Thus, Exeter was walled, but that did not stop Humphrey, Earl of Devon from occupying the city in 1455, ransacking the houses of opponents and breaking into the cathedral.

A key element of conflict in civil wars, also seen repeatedly in Japan, was that it led to the killing of leading opponents, and this killing was the most important aspect of successive battles. Thus, the first significant battle in the Wars of the Roses, the first battle of St Albans on 22 May 1455, was really a series of political assassinations, with the Yorkists picking off their rivals, but, because they were in the company of the king, Henry VI, this was shocking: the Dukes of Somerset and Northumberland were killed, and the king captured. Conversely, the Yorkist leader and claimant to the throne, Richard, Duke of York, was defeated and killed at the battle of Wakefield on 30 December 1460; while the defeat and killing of Richard Neville, Earl of Warwick, the 'King-Maker', at the battle of Barnet on 14 April 1471, was important, as was the killing of Henry VI's captured son, Edward, Prince of Wales, after Edward IV's victory at the battle of Tewkesbury on 4 May 1471.

Betrayal was an important aspect of politics, including on the battlefield. At the battle of Bosworth on 22 August 1485, Richard III, the last Yorkist king

(r. 1483–5) and the brother of Edward IV, was abandoned by the Stanleys, whose troops changed side, while the units in his army under Henry, Fourth Earl of Northumberland did not fight. The death of Richard gravely weakened the Yorkist cause and also reflected the extent to which leaders played a direct role in combat. Richard was killed when his attempt to overcome his opponent, Henry Tudor, and his bodyguard failed, but Richard came close, killing Henry's standard bearer. Henry's victory led to his becoming Henry VII (r. 1485–1509) and to his marrying Elizabeth of York, the daughter of Edward IV and niece of Richard III, thus greatly improving his dynastic position. This outcome was a prime instance of the extent to which victory had dynastic consequences. Another victory, Stoke (16 June 1487) over a Yorkist pretender, consolidated Henry VII's hold on the throne.

Scotland also indicated the importance of civil warfare based on aristocratic factionalism. In addition, there was the issue of control over extensive peripheral regions, an important element for many states. The strength of magnates in these regions restricted royal independence, and notably so in Scotland in the Borders with the Earls of Douglas, a family that had increased their possessions and power during wars with England. In 1452, James II stabbed William, 8th Earl of Douglas to death while the latter was under his safe conduct, and then went on to break Douglas power in the Borders. James III gained Orkney and the Shetlands in 1472, and the northern region of Ross in 1476, and in 1493 James IV (r. 1488–1513) destroyed the position of the Lord of the Isles and extended his authority to the Hebrides. The longstanding Viking/Norwegian interest in the maritime world of northern and western Scotland and the Irish Sea was broken.

Alongside this process, there was often bitter division in Scotland, with a politics of kidnappings and sudden executions, such as those of the members of the faction of Sir Alexander Livingstone in 1450. Foreign intervention played a role, with Scotland aligned to France and opposition stirred up by English rulers. After Henry VI was given shelter in Scotland following his defeat at Towton in 1461, Edward IV encouraged the rebellion of John, 11th Earl of Ross in 1462, while, in 1482–3, Edward sought to replace James III with the latter's brother, the Duke of Albany; as a result, Edward's brother Richard led an invasion of Scotland in 1482. From 1479, James III faced serious aristocratic opposition led by his brothers, and in 1488, unable to muster sufficient support, he was killed shortly after his defeat at Sauchieburn at the hands of rebels who took over the government, only themselves to face rebellion in 1489.

Similarly, tensions in the ruling house of Muscovy (Russia) in part reflected dissension over relations with foreign powers. Thus, Ivan III confiscated Uglich, the appanage of his brother Andrey the Elder, when he refused to participate in campaigns against the Kazan Tatars, and Tver' was annexed in 1485 when its prince attempted to ally with Casimir IV of Poland. The French supported opposition in the Low Countries to Maximilian, Archduke of Austria (later Emperor Maximilian I) the Habsburg who, by his marriage to Charles the Bold's daughter Mary, had inherited the Burgundian position. In 1487, the outbreak of a rebellion in Flanders saw the key city of Ghent negotiate a treaty with France and accept a French garrison, while, in 1491, the French supported a rebellion in Gelderland by Karel van Egmond who contested Maximilian's control of the duchy.

There was to be a consolidation of royal authority in Scotland under James IV, and, as in England, the strengthening of royal authority was linked to the enhancement of the military power of the state. Although Henry VII of England relied on some nobles, the private armed forces of the nobility was limited. At the same time, as so often, the military success and indeed power of the state in part rested on an ability to restrict exposure to the risks of sustained war. Thus, although he invaded France in 1492, Henry VII was careful not to become involved in lengthy hostilities abroad. Such a conflict would have challenged the consolidation of Tudor control.

The Italian Wars

Two years later, Charles VIII of France (r. 1483–98) invaded Italy and, the following March, captured Naples to which he had laid claim. A celebrated passage by the Florentine historian, and one-time Papal official, Francesco Guicciardini in the *Storia d'Italia* [*History of Italy*] (from 1494 to 1532) emphasised the impact of the French cannon which used iron shot, allowing smaller projectiles to achieve the same destructive impact as larger stone shot, which permitted smaller, lighter, more manoeuvrable cannon, that were mounted permanently on wheeled carriages. However, in fact in 1494, Charles deployed only about thirteen siege guns, while the key Tuscan frontier fortresses that were attacked by the French-Sarzana and Sarzanello – repulsed the attacks, and the French were able to advance only as a consequence of a treaty negotiated by Piero de'Medici. The following January, Montefortino near Valmontone was stormed and sacked, without any apparent use of cannon. A bombardment by French cannon did make a crucial breach in the walls of Monte San Giovanni, permitting its storming that February, but the bombardment of the Castel Nuovo in Naples was not as effective. Ten days of cannon fire inflicted only limited damage, the French ran short of iron balls and gunpowder, and the surrender of the garrison reflected exhaustion and division, rather than the inexorable pressure of cannon fire.[42] More generally, it is important not to underestimate the role in sieges of mining walls, digging under them and exploding gunpowder so as to cause breaches, rather than of using cannon to create breaches.

Charles VIII was unable to sustain his initial advantage in Italy. As a reminder of the crucial nature of the political context, his success aroused opposition, both within Italy, where there was growing suspicion that he aimed to seize, or at least dominate, the entire peninsula, and from two powerful rulers who had their own ambitions to pursue: Maximilian I, the Emperor (r. 1493–1519), who ruled Austria and the other Habsburg territories, and Ferdinand of Aragon (r. 1479–1516), ruler of Aragon (eastern Spain), Sicily and Sardinia, and husband of Isabella of Castile (r. 1474–1504), the other part of Spain. As a reminder that politics did not begin anew in 1494, Maximilian had inherited the Burgundian rivalry with the Valois rulers of France, while Ferdinand pursued longstanding Aragonese ambitions in the Mediterranean, which focused on southern Italy. Sicily, indeed, was a stepping stone to Naples.

Charles's troops were forced out of Italy in 1495, although an attempt to cut off his retreat failed at Fornovo on 6 July: the Italian forces of the League of St Mark had numerical superiority, but were poorly co-ordinated, and their cavalry was affected by the muddy nature of the terrain. The battle was largely a cavalry struggle, and suggested that French heavy cavalry still had a major role to play in achieving battlefield success, a lesson that was conducive to the French as it conformed with their force structure and doctrine, both of which, in turn, reflected the prominence, in French society and politics, of the nobility. In southern Italy, heavy cavalry and Swiss pikemen also brought the French victory in April 1495 at Seminara over a Spanish force sent by Ferdinand of Aragon: firearms were crucial in neither Fornovo nor Seminara. However, victory in battle could not bring success to the French. The Neapolitans largely deserted Charles, who was no longer able to command the tempo of operations. French forces left behind in southern Italy were defeated at Atella (1496), and their surviving positions were successfully besieged.[43]

Charles died in 1498. Rather than gains in Italy, his reign was to be important to France's acquisition of the independent duchy of Brittany. The crushing victory over the Bretons at St Aubin-du-Cormier on 29 July 1488 was followed by the fall of St Malo and by Duke Francis II of Brittany accepting harsh terms. His daughter and successor, Anne, married Charles VIII of France in 1491 and, after Charles' death, Louis XII in 1499, while her daughter, Claude, married the future Francis I in 1514 and ceded her husband the duchy in 1532.

The Discussion of War

While rulers carefully calculated or foolishly neglected the equations of aristocratic alignment and international backing, and their potential consequences for civil conflict or support in foreign war, there was a growing intellectual engagement with warfare. In part, this engagement reflected the possibilities created by the use of movable metal type by European printers from the 1450s by both writers and entrepreneurs seeking to create and define a market, but other factors also played a role. These included the interest in the Classics seen with the self-conscious revival in the Renaissance of Greek and Roman knowledge, and also with the determination of rulers to measure themselves against exalted Classical prototypes such as Alexander the Great. Thus, Kritovoulus compared Mehmed II's crossing of the Taurus mountains to that of Alexander in 333 BCE.

Prior to printing in Europe, there was already the production, translation and circulation of military manuals. These put an emphasis on expertise and, therefore, training, with the latter seen as contributing to the value of manuals. The fourth-century (CE) Roman writer Flavius Vegetius' *De Re Militari* was a major source for fifteenth-century manuals.[44] There was also a willingness to learn from personal experience. Philip of Cleves (1456–1528), who had an active military career from 1477 to 1506, wrote in about 1516 a manuscript treatise 'Instruction de toutes manières de guerroyer tant par terre que par terre', dedicated to the future Charles V, a work that survives in at least nine contemporary French manuscripts and sixteen German ones.[45]

Printing made earlier manuscript works more accessible. Thus, Leon Battista Alberti's *De Re Aedificatoria*, with its call for sloped and lower fortress walls, was written in the 1440s but first printed in 1485. The printing revolution was also followed by the widespread 're-discovery' and availability of Classical texts and prestige of ancient Rome was such that this 'return to the past' served to validate new emphases. The publication of military works became prominent from 1487 when the Roman writers Vegetius, Aelianus Tactitus, Frontinus and Modestus, the so-called 'Veteres de re militari scriptores', were published by Eucherius Silber in Rome. In turn, Julius Caesar's *Comentarii* were published in an Aldine edition in 1513, and this served as the basis for another Latin edition published in Paris in 1543. Guillaume Du Choul's study of Roman fortification and military discipline (as well as architecture and religion) proved so popular that, having been published in Lyon in 1554, new editions followed in 1555, 1556 and 1567. *Of the General Captain and of his Office* (1563) was Peter Whitehorne's translation, dedicated to the Earl Marshal, Thomas, Duke of Norfolk, of

Fabio Cotta's Italian version of Onosander's *Strategicus*. As an indication of the extent to which knowledge of the Ancient world was largely restricted to those who had direct access to Classical literature, Onosander's treatise on generalship, addressed to Quintus Veranius Nepos, Roman governor of Britain in 57–58 CE, was published in a parallel Greek and Latin text in Paris in 1598.

As a reminder of the eclectic nature of influences, and the extent to which current knowledge as well as the Classics provided a frame of reference, Whitehorne also translated Machiavelli's *Art of War*, his translation dedicated to Elizabeth I, appearing in 1560 and being subsequently republished in 1573 and 1588. Whitehorne, who had served in the Spanish army in North Africa and visited Constantinople and Italy, also published *Certain Ways for the Ordering of Soldiers in Battle* (1560). The prestige of Classical Rome was such that ideas and vocabulary associated with it were applied in the Western world in order to validate developments. For example, Battista della Valle's *Vallo Libro Continente Appertinentie à capitanij, Retenere e Fortificare una Città con bastioni*, a very popular work on fortifications that went through eleven editions from 1524 to 1558, drew heavily on Classical sources. The first French edition appeared in 1554, with a Classical title page depicting soldiers fighting without the benefit of firearms. In 1572, Francesco Barozzi's version of Hero of Alexandria's work of the first century CE on the mechanics of siege warfare, *Liber de Machinis Bellicis*, appeared in Venice. Philip of Cleves's treatise appeared in French, German and Dutch editions, the French editions being published in 1558, 1583, 1588 and 1596, and the Dutch one in 1579.

The Ottomans under Bayezid II

The importance of royal successions was repeatedly a theme in the politics of the late fifteenth century and not only in England. Ottoman expansionism declined under Mehmed II's successor, Bayezid II (r. 1481–1512), in part because his brother and defeated rival, Jem (or Cem), was able to take refuge in the West. This episode indicates the significance of the personal nature of rulership, and the monarchical character of states, in the face of the often misleading tendency to focus on an account of bureaucratic development. The absence of primogeniture was more generally a problem in Islamic states. Thus, following a revolt from 1452 to 1457, Uzum Hasan took control of the Aqquyunlu confederacy from his brother.

Defeated by Bayezid's forces in 1481 and 1482, Jem took refuge with the Knights of St John on the island of Rhodes. In 1483, however, Bayezid agreed an annual payment to the Knights, in return for Jem being kept in custody, and thus unable to challenge his position. In 1489, this payment was transferred to the Papacy when his custody was handed over. The threat posed by Jem's use by Christian powers led Bayezid to adopt a cautious stance in international relations, a classic instance of the impact of domestic politics on these relations, although the earlier defensive successes of the Christians at Belgrade and Rhodes were also a factor. Mehmed II's Italian gain of Otranto was abandoned in 1481, while there was no resumption of the Ottoman attack on Rhodes. Moreover, the 1479 treaty with Venice was ratified and, in 1483, Bayezid concluded a truce with his major rival in the Balkans, king Matthias Corvinus of Hungary, which enabled Matthias to focus on his third war against Emperor Frederick III which had started in 1481 and led to the successful siege of Vienna in 1485. Furthermore, in 1490, Bayezid promised not to attack the Papal States, Venice or Rhodes.

His options to the west, therefore, were largely closed although, in 1483, consolidating his position in the Balkans, Hercegovina was invaded and seized, while, in 1484, an expedition into Moldavia led to the capture of its ports, Kilia and Akkerman, which strengthened the Ottoman position on the Black Sea. The following decade, much effort was devoted to suppressing rebellion in Albania.

In 1494, Charles VIII gained custody of Jem on his invasion of Italy, and, the following year, he announced a crusade against the Ottomans, which both linked Charles to the prestige of an earlier king, Louis IX, St Louis, who had led the Seventh Crusade in 1248 and died on a new crusade in 1270; and enabled him to claim prestige as a leader of Christendom. The prospect of a French-imposed prince caused grave concern in Constantinople. In the event, in 1495, Charles' position in Italy collapsed, and Jem died. Once his body was returned in 1499 and buried publicly, the rumours that he was alive were stilled, which left Bayezid in a stronger position.[46] He used this as an opportunity to declare war on Venice that year.

The Jem episode indicated concern not so much about the legitimacy of Bayezid's rule but rather about its stability. Jem posed this question in an unusual fashion as he could be exploited by Christian powers. In contrast, issues of legitimacy and prestige, as well as stability, were posed by relations with other Muslim rulers. These issues brought together dynastic, ethnic, political and religious concerns. Under Bayezid, the point of concern was relations with the Mamluks, with whom there was a common frontier as a result of the Ottoman conquest of the emirate of Karaman in southern Anatolia in 1468–74. As in other cases of imperial tension, the removal of buffer states brought issues over borders and allegiances in uncertain frontier zones to the fore, and war with the Mamluks broke out in 1485. Jem played a role, as, seeking to weaken Bayezid, the Mamluks sought Jem's release from custody in the west. Having advanced into Cilicia (south-east Anatolia) in 1485, the Ottomans were driven back in 1486 and challenged by a rising in the Taurus mountains. A fresh Ottoman advance was defeated in 1488, and in 1491 the Ottomans had to accept peace on the basis of the pre-war border.

This war indicates the importance of not focusing solely on major conflicts with dramatic outcomes and using them to establish relative capability. With Mamluk troops, some armed with handguns, besieging Kayseri in 1490, Alaeddevle, ruler of Dhu'l-Kadr in south-eastern Anatolia, a weathercock in his pursuit of a powerful ally, defected to the Mamluks. With Bayezid thinking it necessary to prepare to march in person, there was no sign that the Ottomans would be able to crush the Mamluks, as they were to do in 1516–17 (see pp. 62–3). The later outcome cannot be used to explain the earlier situation and, correspondingly, it is necessary to be cautious in reading from the Ottoman force-structure, specifically the use of firearms, to some apparently obvious outcome. Although the financial cost was serious, the Mamluks did well in the war of 1485–91.

Babur and Mughal Power

Another instance of the same problem is provided by Zahir-ud-din Muhammad Babur, the founder of Mughal power in northern India, who overthrew the Lodi sultanate of Delhi in 1526. As with the Ottomans, this success is frequently discussed in terms of the rise of gunpowder empires, and Mughal power is the central theme in South Asian history in the sixteenth and seventeenth centuries. Yet, from the perspective of the 1490s and the first years of the following century, this was far from an obvious outcome. Indeed, not only were the Lodis still an expanding power in northern India, but the key force in the Mughal heartland of Central Asia were the Uzbeks, whose dynasty were descended from Chinggis Khan's son Jūjī, and not the Mughals. Born in 1483, Babur succeeded his father as ruler of the principality of Fergana (in modern Uzbekistan) in 1494, and in 1497 occupied the city of Samarqand, but he was driven from both by the Uzbeks, being defeated at Sir-e-pul in 1501 in one of the cavalry battles that were so important in Eurasia.

Conclusions

Such cavalry battles tend to be ignored if they seem to be without conse-quence, such as the Mamluk victory over the Ottomans at Aga-Cayiri in 1488, but Sir-e-pul was to be important to the change in direction of

Mughal policy. Moreover, the Uzbek victory indicated the ability of cavalry battles to deliver a decisive verdict.

Firearms were to fit into this established pattern of warmaking, rather than to transform it, in large part because they represented a new iteration of the firepower already offered by archery. The same was true of infantry, as the ability of archers in well-prepared positions to see off cavalry attacks had already been indicated in the Anglo-French Hundred Years' War. In contrast, artillery offered an enhancement of capability, and notably against fortifications.

A century divide may appear an arbitrary use of the Christian calendar, and there were certainly no major developments in weaponry or warmaking at that juncture. Nevertheless, there were important developments close to 1500, notably the rise of the Mughals and also of the Safavids, developments that were to reshape the geopolitics of South Asia for over a century. A different trajectory was offered by the arrival of (Christian) European power in Asian waters, and, in 1502, Portuguese warships destroyed the fleet of Calicut on India's Malabar coast. The respective importance of these developments is a topic that hereafter in this book will command greater attention.

3 Conflict, 1500–1535

In Eurasia, where the majority of the world's population lived throughout the period covered by this book and where most of its trade was conducted, the dramatic expansion of Mughal, Safavid and Ottoman power provides a central theme in the first third of the sixteenth century. In contrast, there was nothing of comparable significance or scale in sub-Saharan Africa, nor, within Eurasia, in East Asia. Indeed, China was less affected than other major Asian states by external challenges, and this situation may help explain its limited military development in this period. Nor within Christian Europe was there anything to compare with the dramatic expansion of Mughal, Safavid or Ottoman power. However, at the global scale, and linking Christian Europe with the outer world, the rise of Habsburg power under the Emperor Charles V (r. 1519–56, Charles I of Spain) was unprecedented. By 1535, he had an empire stretching from newly-conquered Peru, where the Inca capital, Cuzco, was captured in 1533, to Germany and Austria; and the causes and implications of this success for the military and political history of the sixteenth century were highly significant.

The warfare of the period owed something to the widespread recovery of Asian and European populations from the fourteenth-century epidemic of bubonic plague known as the Black Death. This recovery led to economic growth, as there were more producers and consumers, and also ensured that there was more manpower available for conflict. At the same time, while economic growth produced the wherewithal to support military activity, and thus territorial expansion and political consolidation, the extent to which it was tapped by rulers varied, and not least where they failed to accommodate religious differences and other challenges to authority. Such accommodation was a major issue in Western Europe, the Near East, and India; although, conversely, not so in China, which helped explain the limited extent of civil warfare there.

Mughal rise

Northern India saw one of the most dramatic changes of the period. Pushed out of Fergana and Samarqand by the Uzbeks, Babur captured the cities and regions of Kabul and Ghazni in modern Afghanistan in 1504, and his control of them was to be the basis of his subsequent intervention in the Punjab and northern India. Nevertheless, as a sign of the key role of Central Asia and of the significance of maintaining areas of family power, Babur continued to seek to recover his earlier position, and his struggle with the Uzbeks rose to a height in the early 1510s. However, after a final victory by the Uzbeks at Ghajdewān near Bukhara in 1514, in this case largely over his Safavid allies, Babur came to concentrate on the prospects offered by the wealthy agricultural zone of the Punjab in north-west India. Notions of legitimacy played a role as he saw the region as his rightful heritage as a descendant of Timur, who had conquered it prior to capturing Delhi. Babur's conquest of the Punjab helped compensate psychologically and in prestige terms for the loss of his homeland.

Raids on the Punjab initially provided wealth that strengthened his position, and Babur benefited from the growing weakness of the Lodis as they were affected by internal strife, with the Afghan emirs in rebellion and with east Punjab, under Ala al-Din 'Alam Khan Lodi, in particular in revolt against Ibrahim, the Lodi sultan of Delhi. Babur intervened, annexed the entire Punjab in early 1526, and then moved on to attack Ibrahim, as the overthrow of the sultanate seemed necessary in order to consolidate his new position in the Punjab. Babur's invasion was encouraged by opponents of Ibrahim who provided him with important manpower, although the promised supporting attack by rana Sanga of the Rajput state of Mewar did not materialise.

At the first battle of Panipat near Delhi on 21 April 1526, Babur employed both matchlockmen and field artillery successfully against the Lodi cavalry, whose far larger army did not use firearms.[1] Nevertheless, the challenge posed by the approximately 100,000-strong Lodi army was magnified by the mobility and speed of its cavalry, and by the slow rate of fire of the Mughals' firearms. As a result, Babur planned his victory by selecting a battlefield that would limit the mobility of the Lodi cavalry and delay its advance, as well as countering both Lodi numbers and the Lodi war-elephants. As with the English against the French at Crécy in 1346, Babur selected a position for his 12,000 troops between two blocks of forest, which channelled the Lodi advance, and, to delay it, deployed a line of wagons linked by ropes of hide and breastworks. Digging a ditch strengthened the forest cover for his flanks. Similarly, at Mohacs, four months later, the possibility of the Ottomans outflanking the Hungarians was countered by the latter choosing a defensive position that benefited from the Danube and its tributaries.

The Lodis did not initially attack, but the large number of their army posed a logistical challenge that finally led them to advance. This was a classic instance of the dependence of tactics on logistics, a dependence that tends to be underplayed because of our limited knowledge of logistics in this period. Frightened by Babur's cannon the war elephants in the van, about 100 strong, stampeded back through the Lodi army, and the Lodi cavalry attack that followed failed to pass the wagons while also being cut down by Mughal fire at close quarters. With the Lodis hit hard, Babur had gaps made in his wagon line, and his cavalry, held in reserve, then attacked, wreaking havoc. Underlining, however, the difficulty of establishing the precise course of events, it is unclear whether the divided nature of the Lodi regime helped account for battlefield deficiencies. Moreover, Babur's account acknowledged the role of his cannon, but also put much emphasis on his mounted archers who succeeded in passing the Lodi flanks and attacking the Lodi army in the rear:

> Ustād Ali Kuli discharged his guns many times in front of the line to good purpose. Mustafa, the cannoneer on the left of the centre, managed his artillery with great effect. The right and left divisions, the centre and flankers having surrounded the enemy and taken them in rear, were now engaged in hot conflict, and busy pouring in discharges of arrows on them. They made one or two very poor charges on our right and left divisions. My troops making use of their bows, plied them with arrows, and drove them in upon their centre.[2]

As for the Spaniards against the French at Cerignola in 1503 (see pp. 78–9), a pursuit after victory was necessary in order to gain full advantage. The death of Ibrahim and most of the Lodi élite at Panipat helped greatly in the establishment of Mughal power. Agra (the capital), Delhi, and much of the sultanate rapidly fell after the battle, and, in 1527, Babur pressed on to defeat the Rajput Confederacy at Kanua on 16 March.

Mughal firepower played a role in this defeat of the frontal attack by Rajput cavalry and war elephants on Babur's fieldworks; although the flexible enveloping tactics used by Babur's cavalry were also effective, and mounted archers were probably at least as important as the infantry matchlockmen in the course of the battle. Firearms, however, joined leadership and tactics in providing a necessary force-multiplier, and were significant in the early stages of the battle. The Mughal position was fortified with a ditch and wagons linked by chains, and the matchlockmen, placed in the front of the force, 'broke the ranks of the pagan army with matchlocks and guns like their hearts': the latter were allegedly black and the soldiers covered with smoke. At Kanua, Babur had only about 12,000 troops, whereas the Rajputs, allegedly, had 80,000 cavalry and 500 war elephants. After his victory, Babur, on the pattern of Timur, built a tower of the skulls of the dead 'infidels': the Rajputs were Hindus.[3]

The Afghans, the basis of Lodi strength, however, continued resistance in northern India. Babur defeated Afghan resistance in the region of Bihar, but

Ibrahim's brother, Mahmud, was established as an independent king; only to be defeated at Dadra, near Lucknow, in 1531. Resistance to the Mughals, nevertheless, continued under Sher Khān Sūr, an Afghan noble based in southern Bihar who had survived Panipat. This continued resistance indicated the contrast between the initial victory that so often attracts attention, in this case Panipat, and the difficulties of grounding a new system, a situation also seen for example with the aftermath of the Moroccan victory at Tondibi in 1591 (see p. 127).

It is also necessary to note the range of military narratives in India in this period, for they help to explain the difficulties that the Mughals were to face in consolidating and expanding their gains. For example, the Arghūns of southern Afghanistan, with their capital at Kandahar, who were descended from the Īl-Khāns of Persia, and thus from the Chinggisid Mongols, conquered the city of Quetta and part of the region of Baluchistan in the 1490s, and later overran the Sammas of Sind in 1518–22 and the Langas of Multan in the middle Indus in 1526–7, creating what, however, turned out to be only a short-lived empire in modern Pakistan.

As a sign of Mughal expansion, the Arghūns, indeed, lost Kabul (1504) and Ghazni (1504) to Babur. Moreover, they held Ghūr and Zamīndāwar in central Afghanistan as Timūrid vassals, but were driven out by Babur in 1522, while Multan was turned over to Babur in 1527, and Sind was to be conquered by the Mughals later in the century. This rush of names may appear confusing, but it serves to show the extent to which the military history of the period cannot be thought of solely in terms of the powers that subsequently emerged as prominent, let alone of the Europeans. Instead, each of the campaigns mentioned is worthy of detailed discussion, although the sources are limited and make it difficult to offer observations about changes and relative capability. This situation can make it dangerous to treat the sources that do survive as if they were symptomatic of the wider situation.

Iran and the Safavids

As an instance of the interaction of developments in different areas that are frequently treated separately, Babur benefited from the rise of the Safavids in Iran, because the latter proved both enemies of the Uzbeks and willing to align with the Mughals. In Eurocentric accounts, an emphasis on the Ottoman threat to Christendom ensures that the role and importance of the Safavids are generally minimised, but this approach is far less pertinent from the perspective of South and Central Asia. The Safavids, a militant Shi'a Muslim religious order that developed a powerful military dimension, were led by Isma'il, who was seen as having divine attributes and deserving absolute obedience. He was regarded as the reincarnation of Imam Ali, Muhammad's son-in-law and the founder of Shi'a Islam, or as the hidden Imam, a millenarian figure. Conversion to Shi'ism helped provide coherence to the tribes supporting Isma'il.

With his nomadic Türkmen followers from Azerbaijan, Isma'il conquered the neighbouring province of Shirwan in 1500, Isma'il defeating the Shirwan shah, Farrukh-Yasār, at Jabani in December. He pressed on, the following year, to defeat the Aqquyunlu at Sharur and to capture the city of Tabriz, where he had himself proclaimed shah. Isma'il benefited greatly from Aqquyunlu disunity. The sudden death of sultan Ya'qūb in 1490 had led to struggle for power among the Türkmen princes, the grandsons of Uzun Hasan. Ya'qub himself had defeated his elder brother Khalil in 1478 in order to gain the throne. Isma'il considered himself a legitimate heir of Uzun Hasan who was also his grandfather.[4] Isma'il continued by defeating the Aqquyunlu under sultan Murād totally at Alme-Qulaq near Hamadan on 20 June 1503, one of the most decisive battles of the century. Divisions among the Aqquyunlu undermined their attempt to unlimber cannon behind a wagon fort and the Safavids won the cavalry conflict. As was frequently, but not invariably the case, victory in battle was followed by the rapid fall of cities as the existing regime was discredited as well as decimated by its defeat. Thus, most of the Iranian plateau, including the cities of Isfahan, Shiraz, Yazd and Kirman, was rapidly overrun. Mardin in Mesopotamia, the last Aqquyunlu stronghold, fell in 1507 and Murād then took refuge with the Ottomans. Baghdad fell without resistance in 1508.

The capture of these cities ensured that the new regime gained both prestige and control over resources, each of which helped ensure that the Safavids were able to ground their position and system. Conversely, their opponents lost both prestige and resources. Iraq brought the particular prestige of gaining major Shi'a shrines, notably Karbala, Kazir, Najaf and Samarra. The religious dimension of the struggle was also seen in the desecration of Sunni shrines and the slaughter of prominent Sunni figures. Moreover, the Christian community in Baghdad was destroyed. By 1510, modern Iran and Iraq were under Isma'il's control.

As a reminder of the mistake of reading the history of Asia, and more particularly the Islamic world, from west to east, the Safavids were initially concerned more about the Uzbeks to their north-east than the Ottomans to the west, which again underlines the importance of Central Asia. Uzbek success reflected the potency of light cavalry, specifically mounted archers. Having seized Bukhara in 1499, Samarqand in 1500, Tashkent in 1503, Fergana and Kunduz in 1504, Balkh in 1506, and Herat in 1507, the Uzbeks, who were both a steppe and a non-steppe people, were a dynamic force and in an important and prestigious area. As elsewhere, the pattern of expansion was not simply that of conquest, as Uzbek concerns interacted with those of local interests. Thus, in Herat, the death in 1506 of the ruler, Husain Baiqara, was followed by a dispute over the succession between two of his sons which left Herat vulnerable to Uzbek attack. Success in sieges also owed much to famine, as with Balkh in 1506.

Although Iran might appear as a unit, the region of north-east Iran known as Khurasan (in which Meshed was a key city) had been a Timurid dominion not under Aqquyunlu control. With their prosleytising mission, the Safavids had no intention of accepting Aqquyunlu limits, and they competed with the Uzbeks to rule the region. It was long unclear which would be the dominant power in a struggle that had implications for the control of surrounding lands. Badi'al-Zaman, one of the sons of Husain Baiqara of Herat, had taken refuge with the Safavids after the fall of Herat to the Uzbeks, and he urged Isma'il to intervene in Khurasan.

In a major battle between cavalry forces, one that indicated the marginality of gunpowder weaponry at this stage, Isma'il defeated the Uzbeks on 2 December 1510 near the fortified city of Merv to the north-east of Meshed in modern Turkmenistan. A feint retreat by the Safavids, a tactic often used in steppe warfare, led the Uzbeks to advance from Merv. The Safavids then attacked when the Uzbeks were in a vulnerable position, just after they had crossed a river. An equivalent vulnerability was to fight with one's back to a mountain pass. After a Safavid contingent had broken down the bridge in the Uzbek rear, the main body of 17,000 Safavid cavalry attacked. Babur's account stressed the value of discipline when he wrote that their 'regulated valour … speedily prevailed'. In the discussion of military history, discipline is a factor overly focused on infantry rather than cavalry for which it was also very important. The skin of the head of the slaughtered Uzbek ruler, Muhammad Shaybni, was stripped off, stuffed with hay, and sent as a warning to Isma'il's other major enemy, Bayezid II, while his skull, set in gold, was used as a drinking cup, a longstanding practice.[5]

Victory enabled the Safavids to take Herat, to the south-east of Meshed, from the Uzbeks, increasing the area of the Timurid legacy they controlled. They pressed on to capture Balkh in modern northern Afghanistan and the province of Sistan in modern south-west Afghanistan; and a treaty in 1511 with Shaybni's cousin, Jani Bey, fixed the river Amu (Oxus) as the boundary between the Uzbeks and the Safavids and included a superficial submission to Isma'il.

The regional consequences were far-reaching and included an important religious dimension. Babur looked to the Safavids, allying with Isma'il after his victory at Merv and professing the Shi'a creed of the Safavids in order to ensure their support against the Uzbeks. The Safavid position in western Afghanistan, however, showed the difficulty of moving from conquest to incorporation. Herat had not resisted after the battle near Merv, but, when Isma'il subsequently tried to introduce Shi'a rites, he faced much opposition which even executions could not end.

Isma'il had earlier used force in Arabistan in south-west Iran against the Musha'sha, Shi'a sectarians who saw their leader, Sayyid Fayyāz, as the incarnation of God. After he was killed in battle, his brother was established by the Safavids as their vassal in Arabistan, a frequent pattern when trying to bring a semblance of control over border areas. This method, however, was not without problems. Further north, leaders of the Kurdish Mawsillu were made governors of Baghdad, only for a rival Mawsillu leader to defeat the Safavid governor in 1526 and declare his support for the Ottomans. However, in 1529, shah Tahmasp regained Baghdad, bringing it under direct Safavid control. In turn, Süleyman the Magnificent occupied the city in November 1534, promising tolerance to the Shi'a.

Meanwhile, conflict continued further north in Central Asia, with a fresh Uzbek invasion of Khurasan in 1512 being initially successful but followed in 1513 by a withdrawal when Isma'il advanced. There were features different to the contemporary Italian Wars in Christian Europe, notably the far more major role of cavalry, but there were some similarities, including the relationship between battles and sieges. Thus, on 22 October 1514, the attempt by an Uzbek relief army to end the Safavid siege of Ghajdewān west of Bukhara led to a Uzbek victory. Babur recorded that 'the Uzbeks by a resolute charge broke their centre', and the wounding and unhorsing of Bairām Khan, the ablest Safavid general present, led to the army's rout. Disaffection, as so often, was important, with many of the Safavid chiefs opposed to the commander, Amir Najm, while the Safavids also accused their ally, Babur, of providing insufficient support.[6] The Safavids themselves were under great pressure from the Ottomans at this juncture.

War between the Uzbeks and the Safavids resumed with a new Uzbek invasion in 1521 and continued for most of the period until the late 1530s, benefiting the other opponents of each, notably the Mughals and Ottomans respectively. The unstable situation in Iran after the accession of the ten-year-old Tahmasp I (r. 1524–76), both encouraged Uzbek attack and weakened the resistance to it. A large-scale Uzbek attack launched in 1524 culminated in a lengthy, but failed, siege of Herat in 1525–6, but as the Türkmen tribes of Iran fought over who should run the government, attacks continued. The Uzbeks regained Khurasan in 1528, occupying Meshed and Astarab and besieging Herat, only for a Safavid relief force to relieve the city thanks to victory at Jam on 24 September 1528. Safavid artillery played a part in the shah's victory: he had four cannon there. Nevertheless, the traditional tactics and fighting styles of steppe warfare, such as feints, continued to be valuable, and were important in clashes between the Safavids and the Uzbeks.

The interaction of operations on different fronts was shown in 1529, as the Safavid focus that year on the suppression of the revolt in Baghdad enabled the Uzbeks to attack again, taking both Meshed and Herat. In turn, in 1530, with no conflict to the west, the Safavids re-established their position in Khurusan, regaining Meshed and Herat, although the problems of supplying their large army over-winter may have led to a decision to withdraw it that November. In 1532, another Uzbek invasion led to the conquest of Khurasan with the exception of Herat. It was besieged for a year and a half in 1532–3 before the Uzbeks withdrew: they lacked the capability for breaching walls shown by the Ottomans. In 1533, the Safavids relieved Herat, and in 1534 Tahmasp pressed on to attack Balkh (in northern Afghanistan) only to turn west in response to an Ottoman invasion which does not appear to have been coordinated with the Uzbeks. However, the Ottomans were linked to Alqass Mirza, Tahmasp's rebellious brother who was also governor of Herat. In late 1535, the Uzbeks attacked anew, allied with these rebels, and Herat fell to them as a result of support for the rebellion. In turn, Tahmasp advanced in early 1537, seizing first Herat, which was abandoned by his opponents without fighting, and then Kandahar.

The Ottomans

Religion was also a key factor in the rivalry between the Shi'a Safavids and the Sunni Ottomans. Support among the peoples of eastern Anatolia for the Safavids and for their millenarianism threatened Ottoman control and security and their sense of religious identity. Already, in 1502, people known to have Safavid sympathies were branded in the face and deported, mostly to Moron and Coron in the Morea, which had been conquered from Venice in 1500. That support prompted a serious rebellion in the area in 1511–12, led by shah Kulu, a Safavid proselytiser. In addition to the general challenge to the Sunnism of the Ottoman sultans from Shi'ism, in 1505, Isma'il claimed Trebizond, and thus a coastline on the Black Sea. In 1507, moreover, he campaigned against the emirate of Dhu'l-Kadr which was a buffer zone covering the Ottoman sphere of influence in south-east Anatolia.

The shah Kulu rebellion was more immediate. The rebels occupied the city of Antalya, defeating and killing the Governor-General of Anatolia (and allegedly roasting his corpse), advancing on Bursa, towards Constantinople, and defeating and morally wounding the Grand Vizier, Khadim 'Ali Pasha, near Sivas on 2 July 1511. As Kulu was killed in the battle, while the rebels took heavy losses, the rebellion was greatly weakened; but it continued. Moreover, the seriousness of the shah Kulu rebellion discredited Bayezid, providing an opportunity for a rising by his son Selim, who also benefited from the extent to which his brothers Ahmed and Korkud had lost prestige as a result of their failures against the shah Kulu rebels. Selim advanced into Constantinople in April 1512 and Bayezid was soon forced to abdicate in his favour.

Selim I, 1512–20

To consolidate his position, Selim the Grim (r. 1512–20) had to kill his brothers and also defeat the Safavids, not least as a Safavid force under the governor of Azerbaijan had defeated an Ottoman army in Anatolia in 1512. Moreover, the Safavids had backed Ahmed against Selim. To ensure that the Ottoman claim to defend orthodoxy was clear, Selim obtained a *fatwa* declaring his opponents heretics. In 1514, Selim invaded the upper valley of the Euphrates and advanced deep into Armenia. In response, the initial Safavid scorched-earth strategy, a strategy that the economic system, the role of distance, and political culture all encouraged, created serious logistical problems for the Ottoman forces, but, rather than relying on these, Isma'il chose to fight his far more numerous opponents at Chaldiran in Azerbaijan on 23 August. The Safavid army was of the traditional Central Asian type, mounted archers, but the Ottomans had made the transition to a more mixed force, combining their janissary infantry with the cavalry. Although the Safavids had used cannon in siege warfare, they had none at Chaldiran. Cultural factors were important: the Safavids thought firearms cowardly and, initially, adopted cannon with reluctance, preferring to use them for sieges not battles.

Thanks to their numerical superiority and firepower, the Ottomans won a crushing victory at Chaldiran over the Safavid cavalry. The roughly 500 Ottoman cannon were important not only for firepower but also because, chained together, they formed a barrier to cavalry charges. Ottoman tactics at Chaldiran were similar to those at Baskent (1473) and Mohacs (1526), as well as to the Mughal tactics at Panipat (1526) and Kanua (1527), and the Safavid tactics at Jam (1528). The winning side employed a deployment known in Turkish as *tábúr cengí*: a row of carts linked by chains was arranged across the centre to block the advance of the opposing force, and, behind it, both artillery and infantry were deployed. Mounted archers were placed on the wings. The vital Ottoman addition to the notion of a wagon fort familiar to the Turko-Mongols of Central Asia was firepower. At Chaldiran, the Safavid cavalry failed to penetrate the Ottoman line.

Babur borrowed the tactic, as did Ivan IV (the Terrible) of Muscovy, helping the Russians to defeat the Crimean Tatars at Molodye in 1572. Yet, it would be misleading to explain victory simply in terms of this one tactic. In practice, a number of tactics were used, and there were victories, such as the Mughal one at second Panipat in 1556, without the use of *tábúr cengí*. In response to the Ottoman use of firepower, the Safavids created a small unit of musketeers and gunners in 1516.

Selim's success was followed in the West, for example with a newsletter *Von der Schlacht geschehen dem Turcken von dem grossen Sophi*... published in Nuremberg in 1514, and with a German edition and Latin version also published in Augsburg. Concern over the Ottoman advance led to the publication of tracts later in the decade pressing for a countervailing crusade.

Unlike Baskent in 1473, which was not succeeded by any significant Ottoman territorial advance, Chaldiran was exploited with the capture of the Safavid capital, Tabriz, in 1514. However, an Ottoman-backed advance by the Aqquyunlu leader, sultan Murād, was defeated near Ruha, and Murād was killed. Furthermore, logistical problems, exacerbated by Safavid scorched-earth tactics and the coming of winter, as well as the janissaries' unwillingness to spend the winter there, meant that Tabriz was not retained. Instead of campaigning further to the east next year, as he had intended, Selim had to retreat. Thus, Chaldiran did not have an equivalent effect to the Safavid and Mughal victories at Alme-Qulaq and Panipat. The Ottoman attempt to produce a decisive outcome by backing Murād, a key asset, had been unsuccessful, but underlines the political dimension of conflict, not least the Ottoman preference for client rulers in border regions.

Nevertheless, victory over the Safavids in 1514 moved the frontier to the east, took much of the initiative and impetus from Isma'il, who had fought badly at Chaldiran and been shown to be vulnerable, and was a crucial precondition of subsequent Ottoman success. First, Selim consolidated his position in eastern Anatolia in 1515–16, winning over key parts of the population including the Kurdish chiefs, and defeating the Safavids. This process was indicative of a more widespread means of warfare and empire-building, that of success through alliance. Forced to choose, the Kurdish chiefs viewed Selim with greater favour, as Isma'il, distrusting them, had tried to rule directly by means of governors from his loyal Türkmen. The latter were driven out by the Kurds in 1514–15, but then, in 1515, besieged the key city of Diyarbekir, only for the position to be relieved in September 1515 by a joint Kurdish-Ottoman army after Safavid reinforcements for the besiegers had been routed. In 1516, near Qochīsar, Kurdish forces heavily defeated the Türkmen.[7] This victory in battle led to the fall of the surviving Safavid positions in the region.

Secondly, the Ottoman advance to the north of the Mamluk territories in Syria resulted in the annexation of the emirate of Dhu'l-Kadr in 1515, which destroyed the buffer zone between the two empires and led Sultan Qansuh al-Gawri of Egypt (r. 1500–16), the nominal overlord of the Dhu'l-Kadr emirate, to respond favourably to Shah Isma'il's approach for an alliance. Threatened by concerted action, Selim marched east in 1516, unsure which of his opponents to attack, but Qansuh's advance to the city of Aleppo in northern Syria, under the pretext of mediating between the Ottomans and the Safavids, led Selim to turn against him as he would have been unable to fight Isma'il with the Mamluks threatening his rear. Moreover, there may well have been economic motivation for war with Egypt in the shape of its position in the lucrative spice trade, and a wish to resist the Portuguese advance in the Indian Ocean and Red Sea, as well as a desire to strengthen legitimacy by gaining control over key Muslim sites.[8]

Firepower was significant in the defeat of the Mamluk heavy cavalry at Marj Dabiq north of Aleppo on 24 August 1516, but other factors were also important. Moreover, the initial Mamluk onslaught was successful, with the cavalry manoeuvring round the Ottoman artillery and cutting down their musketeers so that victory seemed close. However, the death of Mamluk commanders in the front line was accompanied by dissension, not least with the sultan's call for the new recruits to fall back, so that the veterans could bear the brunt of the fighting, leading the angry latter to hold back. Furthermore, in part due to the impact of plague attacks in 1505 and 1513 and in part to the dispatch of Mamluk handgunners to the Red Sea in 1513, (see p. 148), the Ottoman army was far larger, and Selim had made a secret agreement with Khayrbak, the governor of the province of Aleppo, the commander of the Mamluk left flank, and his troops, to abandon the battle at its height. The struggle was swiftly over, the 75–year old sultan dying, probably of a stroke.

Ottoman victory and the flight of the defeated Mamluk army enabled Selim to occupy Syria and Palestine with scant resistance. The citadel of Aleppo was abandoned after the battle, and, although the governor of Damascus won Bedouin support against the Ottomans, Selim entered the city with few problems on 3 October. The Mamluk army had been accompanied by al-Mutawakkil, who claimed to be the heir to the prestigious Abbasid caliphate, which had been destroyed by the Mongols in 1258; he switched to Selim after the battle.

Selim did not intend to invade Egypt, because he was concerned about Isma'il in his rear, as well as the hazards of crossing the Sinai desert. However, Tumanbay, the new Mamluk sultan, executed Selim's ambassador and mounted a counter-attack in Gaza, only to be defeated on 22 December. The Ottomans then advanced across the Sinai and swiftly defeated Tumanbay, at Raydaniyya outside Cairo, on 23 January 1517. The Ottoman attack proved more successful than that of the Mamluks who had failed to break through the Ottoman *tabūr cengi* and were driven off by the Ottoman field guns. In contrast, although the Mamluks had about 100 brass cannon mounted on carts as well as handguns, their positions were outflanked by the more mobile Ottomans, who then successfully attacked the gun emplacements from the rear.[9] Surviving resistance in Egypt was rapidly overcome, and Tumanbay was captured, and then executed at the Bāb al-Zuwaylah gate in Cairo. Having established his authority, Selim left a garrison of 5,000 cavalry and 500 arquebusiers.

The defection of Khayrbak in 1516 was an aspect of a more general collapse of Mamluk solidarity which greatly weakened the Mamluk response to the Ottomans, encouraging the switch of units in 1516 and 1517 to back the latter. This lack of solidarity was a reflection of a longstanding Mamluk weakness in the shape of serious rivalries between the Mamluk leaders and their household forces.[10] The Mamluks also suffered in 1516–17 from the lack of Safavid and Venetian co-operation against the Ottomans.

From Egypt, the Ottomans extended their power along the coast of North Africa, where Hayreddin, 'Barbarossa', increasingly the de facto ruler of Algeria, accepted Selim's authority in 1519. Ottoman authority was also extended down the Red Sea, as Selim succeeded to the Mamluk position in the Hejaz. Barakat II, the sharif of Mecca, accepted Ottoman overlordship in 1517, which brought Selim control over Mecca and Medina. Joined with that over Jerusalem, this control was a major boost to Ottoman prestige and strengthened the claim to be the protector of Muslim orthodoxy, which provided another rationale for the invasion of Egypt.

This claim was important in the struggle with the Safavids, but also helped ensure that this struggle became even more important to the Ottoman sense of mission. Selim assumed the title of Servant of the Two Noble Sanctuaries, and thus became responsible for protecting the annual *haj* pilgrimage to Mecca. The new direction of Ottoman interest was shown in 1519 when a naval expedition to Yemen was planned, although Selim's death in 1520 led to it turning back.[11] Control of Yemen offered a way to protect Mecca and Medina.

Another aspect of legitimacy was also catered for as, just as the Mamluks had sought to use Jem against Bayezid II, so Egypt had provided a refuge for Ottoman princes fearing slaughter at the hands of Selim as he sought to remove potential challengers. One nephew had taken refuge in Egypt in 1513, while another, Qāsim Bey, who had been treated by the Mamluks in 1516 as an Ottoman ruler, was unsuccessfully searched for by Selim once he seized Egypt. Qāsim was later arrested and killed.

Selim's plan to resume operations against Isma'il in 1518 was thwarted by the refusal of his troops, but, when Selim died in 1520, he was building up a fleet, presumably against the island of Rhodes, which threatened the sea route between Constantinople and Egypt. The conquest of the latter had made power in the eastern Mediterranean a far more significant factor in Ottoman geopolitics as well as greatly increasing the number of Muslims under Ottoman control; in contrast, earlier Balkan conquests had reduced the percentage of Muslim subjects. Syria and Egypt produced about a third of the empire's income, and the Arab influences they encouraged led the Ottomans to become more clearly Muslim in their practice of statecraft.[12]

Süleyman I

Selim was succeeded by his only son, Süleyman I (Suleiman the Magnificent, r. 1520–66), and he established his position by seeking and gaining victory. Appreciating the difficulties of operating against the Safavids, and responding to the army's preference for conflict with the Hungarian 'infidels' and the loot they offered, Süleyman focused on war in Europe. Weakly-defended Belgrade was captured in 1521, the small garrison capitulating after a short siege, and the contrast with earlier Ottoman failures serving notice of a new situation.[13] In 1522, a longer siege of five months led to the capitulation of Rhodes, a major demonstration of Ottoman amphibious power, albeit one assisted by the refusal of Venice, mindful of its relations with the Ottomans, to permit the dispatch of supplies. The Knights of St John, their fortifications strengthened by bastions, resisted assaults and bombardment, inflicting very heavy casualties on attacking forces, before accepting reasonable terms of capitulation when their supplies of gunpowder ran out.[14]

These successes had eluded Süleyman's great-grandfather, Mehmed II, and comparative success within the dynasty was important to fame, with such fame serving as a lubricant of obedience. The Knights still held the fortress of Bodrum on the Anatolian mainland, but it was evacuated in 1523 as, without Rhodes, the logistical burden of supporting the position was now much greater.

Foreign conquest was not the sole challenge facing Süleyman. Indeed, repeatedly, the Ottomans also had to confront rebellions, and not only by subject peoples but also by members of their governing system. This situation was not true of all empires to the same extent, with the Chinese in particular having fewer rebellions by members of the governing system, but it was a common element for most empires. These rebellions underlined both the range of tasks that the military had to confront, and the need to place a greater emphasis on civil war when discussing the military history of the period.

Thus, in 1520–1, it was necessary to put down a rebellion by Janbirdi Ghazālī, a Mamluk whom Selim had made governor of Damascus. Opposition in Syria and Palestine had been quietened by Selim's victory in Egypt in 1517, but, after he died, al-Ghazālī rebelled, declaring himself independent and seeking thus to derive his own benefit from the conquest of Syria. Al-Ghazālī's army was 12,000 strong, of whom 500 had handguns, and had about twenty cannon. In December 1520, al-Ghazālī besieged Aleppo, a key point if an Ottoman counter-offensive from Anatolia was to be blocked. The cutting off of the water supply was a typical tactical move in sieges in the Islamic world in this period. However, al-Ghazālī had to raise the siege and return to Damascus in order to repel a force en route from Egypt where the governor had refused to rebel in support of him. Deserted, moreover, by his supporters and faced by an Ottoman army of 34,000 troops and about 180 cannon[15] under Farhād Pasha, al-Ghazālī was defeated and killed outside Damascus on 6 February 1521, and the city then fell.

In 1523, Ahmed Pasha, the ambitious governor of Egypt, sought to do the same as al-Ghazālī, although the local garrison ended his attempt. The previous year, his predecessor, Mustafa Pasha, had to defeat a Mamluk rebellion having bought off their allies among the Arab sheykhs with tax cuts. The rebel heads rolled around Cairo by Mustafa Pasha, and the executions that Ibrahim Pasha, the Grand Vezir, ordered there in 1525, demonstrated the reliance of the regime on force, its use in an exemplary fashion, and the extent to which it had to be turned to repeatedly. However, this was the last Mamluk rising until the soldiers' riots motivated by dissatisfaction over pay that began in 1589.

Internal opposition tends to be underplayed in the discussion of the military history of the non-West, in large part because the domestic political history of its states is not generally integrated with its military history. However, the interplay between foreign and domestic foes was amply illustrated by Süleyman's campaigning later in the decade.

His campaigns in Europe attract attention. Once Belgrade had fallen in 1521, Hungary represented an opportunity, and *janissary* complaints in 1525 about a lack of campaigning, and thus of plunder, were a spur to action, as were Hungarian successes in 1522 and 1523, notably the installation of a sympathetic voivode in Wallachia in 1522. Süleyman set off in April 1526, but bad weather delayed his crossing of the river Drava until late August. The Hungarians were to be heavily defeated, and there has been a tendency as with the Lodis at Panipat four months earlier to present their defeat as inevitable. It has been suggested that in part due to slow preparations, an inadequate logistical infrastructure, and a shortage of sufficient recent experience in fighting the Ottomans, the Hungarians were divided, poorly led, and short of infantry. The Hungarians certainly failed either to contest the Drava crossing, or to retire to Buda (now part of Budapest) and to allow the Ottomans to exhaust their resources in a siege. Instead, the Hungarians, with about 13,000–15,000 cavalry, 10,000–12,000 infantry (including 500 handgunners) and 85 cannon,[16] deployed behind the Borza, a small tributary of the Danube, but, rather than waiting on the defensive, their heavy cavalry advanced on 29 August.

In some respects, the battle of Mohacs was similar to that of Nicopolis in 1396, although, far from being anachronistic, the Hungarian army was well-equipped and up-to-date. At Mohacs, the Hungarian charge pushed back the Ottoman *sipahis* (cavalry) of Rumelia, but halted when Ottoman troops advanced on their flank. King Louis then led the remainder of his cavalry in a second attack which drove through the *sipahis* of Anatolia, but was stopped by the *janissaries* and cannon, the latter about 240 to 300 strong. Their fire caused havoc, and the Hungarians, their dynamism spent, were then attacked in front and rear in a sustained counter-offensive by the far more numerous Ottoman forces. Louis and most of his aristocracy died on the battlefield or in the nearby Danube marshes, Louis drowning while trying to swim across a river in armour, always a limit to mobility, and about 16–18,000 Hungarians were lost. After what he presented as a hard-won battle, Süleyman swept on to Buda, which fell ten days later.[17]

The standard narrative then continues by explaining that, as Louis had no children, there was a clash to control Hungary between John Szapolyai, Prince of Transylvania, an autonomous part of Hungary now north-west Romania, and Archduke Ferdinand of Austria, the brother of Charles V and the brother-in-law of Louis of Hungary; and that this clash provoked renewed Ottoman action in 1529.[18] While correct, this account fails to help explain the chronology by noting the problems created for Süleyman by major rebellions in Anatolia in 1526, 1527, and 1528. As with the Protestant challenge facing Charles V in Germany, religion played a role in these rebellions, with Safavid supporters proving a major problem.

The 1527 rising was led by Kalenderoghlu, a millenarian dervish, and initially defeated the Ottoman army sent to suppress it. In a parallel to the problems that were to confront Christian rulers, for example Philip II in the Low Countries (Netherlands) from the 1560s, the rebellion involved both religious opponents and disaffected landowners, in the case of 1527 those who had lost fiefs when the territory of Dhu'l-Kadr was annexed in 1522; and, as with a standard response, for example by Philip II in the 1580s, the landowners were won back, with their fiefs restored, and conflict then focused on the religious opponents. Meanwhile, Mohacs had helped advance Ottoman power in the Adriatic. Preserving its position by responding to developments, the city-state of Dubrovnik became a vassal in 1526, while the spread of Ottoman power in Croatia threatened the hinterland of Venetian-ruled Dalmatia.

John Szapolyai, elected king of Hungary by the Estates, was accepted by Süleyman in return for an acknowledgement of Ottoman suzerainty and a payment of tribute. Ferdinand, in return, seized Buda, which led Süleyman in 1529 to advance on Ferdinand's capital, Vienna, taking Buda en route. However, Vienna proved the limit of the Ottoman range. Süleyman did not reach the city until 27 September, and a determined defence was able to resist assaults until the Ottoman retreat began on 14 October. Campaigning at such a distance from their base caused major logistical problems, as troops and supplies had to move for months before they could reach the sphere of operations, and the onset of winter limited the campaigning season. During the campaign, Ottoman raiders reached as far as Regensburg (in modern Germany) and Brno (Czech Republic). Vienna was not besieged again by the Ottomans until 1683, but, unlike in 1683, Ottoman failure in 1529 was not due to defeat by a Christian relief force.

The campaign also failed to intimidate Ferdinand, who besieged Buda anew in 1530. Süleyman, in response, mounted a fresh invasion in 1532, hoping that he would provoke the main Habsburg army into battle, and thus repeat his triumph at Mohacs. Such a triumph would lessen the need to face lengthy sieges in order to capture fortresses, and would also make it more likely that Ferdinand would heed Ottoman wishes over Hungary. This battle and outcome, however, were not to be, although the widespread devastation achieved by Ottoman raiders was matched by the capture of fortresses to the south-east of Vienna, but not of Güns which was unsuccessfully besieged. Moreover, the size of the Habsburg army, possibly 210,000 strong[19], was a powerful deterrent.

The campaign was followed in 1533 by a truce confirming the status quo, which meant that much of Hungary was under a degree of Ottoman control via Szapolyai's tributary status.[20] Peace on one frontier ensured war on another, and Ottoman campaigning against the Safavids began in 1533. Tabriz and Baghdad fell to the Ottomans the following year with limited resistance.

The Mediterranean

In 1535, however, pressure was registered on another front when Charles V launched a successful expedition against Tunis in response to the capture of the city by Hayreddin ('Barbarossa') from Mulay Hasan, the pro-Spanish ruler, the previous year. This was a peripheral sphere as far as the Ottomans were traditionally concerned, but seapower was of growing concern to Süleyman, and he was also increasingly aware of Habsburg power, not least rivalry with Charles, who appeared a competing imperial figure. Charles responded with a successful expedition mounted with 82 war galleys and over 30,000 troops, an expedition in large part paid for with Inca gold from South America which repaid loans from Genoese bankers. Mounted in ferociously hot conditions, this expedition displayed amphibious capability and success in fighting on land. The fortress of La Goletta at the entrance to the Bay of Tunis, though defended by a large Ottoman garrison, was successfully besieged, falling on 14 July. A week later, Tunis was captured and sacked. Thousands of Christians were released from slavery while thousands of the local population were slaughtered and large numbers sold as slaves. This victory was celebrated in a magnificent series of tapestries hung in the royal palace in Seville, Charles installed a pro-Spanish Muslim ruler in Tunis in 1535 and Spanish troops remained at Goletta until 1569. Hayreddin, however, escaped and this campaign marked an accentuation of the struggle in North Africa, one that was increasingly linked into the general contest for naval predominance in the Mediterranean, and with the rivalry between Ottomans and Habsburgs the more central theme.[21]

Already, prior to that, the struggle in North Africa had played a major role, one moreover that is unreasonably neglected in favour of trans-oceanic expansion by Portugal and Spain which, at this stage, in fact commanded fewer resources. Portuguese expansionism on the Moroccan coast had continued, with the town of Agadir falling in 1505, followed by Safi in 1508, Azamor in 1513, and Mazagão in 1514, although the Portuguese were defeated in 1515. Further east, the Spaniards enjoyed much success. Their military machine had been well honed by the long war for Granada, and their opponents were weak and divided. The town of Melilla was gained in 1497, Mers-al-Kabir (where the Portuguese had failed in 1501), in 1505, Oran in 1509, and Bougie, Tripoli, and the Peñón d'Argel position dominating Algiers in 1510.

Spanish interest in North Africa was further aroused by religious concern. The conquest of Granada raised anxiety about the loyalty of the Muslims in Spain and the spectre of foreign intervention on their behalf, while the refusal to observe the terms on which Granada had surrendered resulted, in 1500–1, in a rebellion that was suppressed with great brutality. This rebellion led to the forcible conversion of the Muslims of Granada[22], which was followed, in 1502 and 1525, by decrees insisting on baptism or exile for the Muslims of Castile and Aragon respectively. However, Spain was left with a substantial minority of *moriscos*, converts whose loyalty, in turn, was suspect. Already in Portugal, religious tolerance had ended in 1496–7 with the introduction of harsh anti-Muslim policies.[23]

The situation in North Africa and the Mediterranean deteriorated in the 1520s as Charles V, though Charles I of Spain, devoted more resources, instead, to war with Francis I of France, especially in northern Italy, which helped the Muslims, in part strengthened by the Ottoman conquest of Egypt, to seize the initiative in North Africa. This process began with corsairs, especially Hayreddin, 'Barbarossa', and his brother Uruj, but, from the 1520s, Süleyman took a greater interest in North Africa. In 1516, the rulers of Algiers had called on the brothers to recapture the Peñón. By the time Hayreddin did so, in 1529, he had also gained control of Algiers and its hinterland, displacing local Muslim rulers, especially the Zayanid sultanate of Tlemcen. Uruj had captured Tlemcen in 1517, but was killed by the Spaniards in 1518. As elsewhere, an emphasis on the struggle between the Muslims and Christian powers can lead to a failure to devote sufficient attention to conflict between Muslim powers.

Hayreddin's submission to the Ottomans extended their power, and Süleyman's commitment to North Africa and the Mediterranean was shown in 1533 when Hayreddin was appointed Kapudan Pasha, the admiral of the Mediterranean fleet, as well as the Governor-General of the new province of the Archipelago: the Aegean islands and coasts. Already, the Spaniards had lost the port of Bougie in North Africa in 1529 and, in 1534, Hayreddin drove the Spaniards from the fortress of Coron in the Morea (which they had captured in 1532), attacked the coasts of southern Italy, and also occupied Tunis, overthrowing the semi-independent Hafsid dynasty. Alongside the Spanish position in North Africa, maritime links between Spain and Italy, especially between Barcelona and Genoa, and, with them, the basic axes of Habsburg power, were threatened. Whereas the Ottomans were able to ground their North African position on strong economic underpinnings, especially the agriculture and commerce of Egypt, the Spanish and Portuguese positions in North Africa entailed continual infusions of funds. The same was true of the Venetian bases in Greece.

Russia

The struggle between Habsburgs and Ottomans was to be a leading theme until the 1570s, but it did not exhaust the subject of Christian-Muslim conflict. Indeed, the latter became more prominent as a result of Portuguese expansion into the Indian Ocean, a subject addressed in chapters six and seven. Moreover, two established areas of rivalry saw fresh conflict, which underlined the extent to which warfare across cultural divides remained important while demonstrating, in practice, that such warfare could also involve co-operation across what could turn out to be porous boundaries. Vassily III (r. 1505–33) of Muscovy (Russia) initially maintained good relations with the neighbouring Muslim khanate of Kazan, but the Crimean Tatars organised a pan-Tatar league which ousted the pro-Muscovite ruler of Kazan in 1521, replacing him with Sahib, brother of the Crimean khan. In the same year, in a demonstration of the significance of Kazan, the Crimean and Kazan Tatars advanced on Moscow from the south and east, and the city was saved only by an attack on the Crimea by the Tatars of Astrakhan. In 1524, the khan of Kazan acknowledged the suzerainty of Süleyman, but, in 1532, Vassily succeeded in installing another pro-Muscovite khan, Djan Ali. This process was similar to the rivalry between Ottomans, Mamlūks, Aqquyunlus and Safavids for control over southern and eastern Anatolia and the Caucasus, a rivalry pursued by supporting client rulers, who, in turn, used such support in order to pursue their own interests, both within their principalities and externally.

Africa

In the Horn of Africa, Iman Ahmäd ibn Ibrahim al-Ghazi, the son-in-law of the emir of Zeyla, conquered Adal (centred on modern Dijbouti) in the mid-1520s after a difficult struggle with the sultan of Harar who was killed in 1525. Ahmäd then launched a holy war against Christian Ethiopia which had long expanded into Muslim lands, forcing conversion on local people. Thus, as in Christian Europe, conflict in the sixteenth century continued the pattern and dynamic of earlier rivalries[24]; a situation also seen in Mexico where the native allies of the conquering Spaniards joined them in campaigning into areas of traditional expansion. At the same time, holy war was not the sole element. Ahmäd's attempt to stop the Muslim towns paying tribute to Ethiopia was part of the economic motivation which included a search for loot and slaves.

Ahmäd trained his men in the new firearms and tactics introduced into the Red Sea region by the Ottomans after their conquest of Egypt in 1517, and better weapons were partly responsible for his victory over the Ethiopian emperor, Lebna-Dengel, at Shimbra-Kure in 1528, but he was unable to follow it up in 1529 because the tribal confederation he had built up collapsed. In 1530, however, Ahmäd spent loot from his 1528 campaign to buy cannon, and recruited foreign experts to use them; although he also hired a force of Arabian archers while Lebna-Dengel used Mayas, a local tribe skilled in the use of poisoned arrows. Whereas Ahmäd had initially attacked the mountainous hinterland in order to consolidate his control of the coastal littoral, now he sought to replace the Christian empire.[25] Ahmäd's cannon apparently helped lead to victory over the Ethiopians at Antika in 1531, and Ahmäd's forces then raided far into Ethiopia.

Another Christian civilisation seemed under serious threat. Ahmäd's success owed much to half a century of political strife among the Christian warlords of Ethiopia, but also to the very nature of the state as a highly heterogeneous polity composed of numerous linguistic, ethnic and religious communities that lacked the cohesion achieved by cultural assimilation or political integration. This was similar to the fate of Lodi-dominated northern India at the hands of the Mughals, of the Aqquyunlu empire at the hands of the Safavids, and of the Aztec and Inca empires at those of the Spaniards.

To the north-west of Ethiopia, in the early decades of the century, the Funj kingdom was established on the upper Blue Nile, probably by pagan cattle nomads moving down the river; while the kingdom of 'Alwa on the lower Blue Nile and along the nearby White Nile was overrun by Arab immigrants. The latter were defeated by the Funj in 1504 near Arbaji, and the Funj kingdom which was a form of high kingship over subordinate rulers then dominated 'Alwa appointing the Arab king. The early Funj period was one of territorial expansion, while there was no clash with Egypt as upper Egypt was for long beyond effective control from Cairo, and 'Alwa was only loosely dependent on the Funj. However, in the 1550s, the Ottomans were to intervene in the tribal struggle in 'Alwa.[26]

In much of sub-Saharan Africa, the military history of this period is largely obscure, in part because of problems with sources but also due to limited research. In West Africa, the key theme was the continuation of the wars of Songhai expansion by Askia Muhammad (r. 1493–1528). Muhammad exemplified the extent to which the military could challenge the control of states, a process constrained in most empires by an emphasis on dynastic continuity. A leading general under Sonni Ali (r. 1464–92), Muhammad launched a bid for the throne after he died and, on 12 April 1493, although outnumbered, defeated the forces of Sonni Ali's son, Sonni Baru, at Anfao. Muhammad revitalised the Songhai state, including the government and the military, establishing a standing army and a fleet of war canoes on the River Niger. The latter reflected the extent to which naval power was not solely a matter of deep-draught ocean-going ships.

After his pilgrimage to Mecca, a display of piety and a means to prestige, Muhammad launched a wide-ranging series of campaigns in which he conquered the Mossi of Yatenga (modern northern Burkina Faso) in 1498–1502, and defeated the Tuaregs of the Air massif (near Agadez, modern Niger) in 1505–6. Later campaigns against the Fulani to the west and the Borgu to the south between 1507 and 1514 were less successful, although Bornu (northeast Nigeria) was conquered. In turn, Muhammad was challenged by a rebellion by one of his generals, the Karta of Kabi (northwest Nigeria), and a campaign against the latter proved unsuccessful. Quarrels between Muhammad's children also became a problem, and Songhai expansion ceased. In 1528, Muhammad was deposed by one of his sons, his fate reminiscent of that of the Ottoman ruler Bayezid II in 1512 and prefiguring that of Muhammad Khudabanda of Iran in 1587.

The Songhai campaigns indicated the operational and tactical value of cavalry, as well as the strategic ambition to which it could give rise.[27] Linked to this, the campaigns demonstrated the potential of the *sahel* environment for the creation of a far-flung empire. The jungles of coastal West Africa had a very different politics, with much smaller states deploying infantry forces. Songhai history also demonstrated the challenges posed by different environments, for there were the problems of controlling the Sahara desert to the north and operating into forest terrain to the south, and, linked to the latter but extending into the *sahel*, were the serious difficulties posed by disease, notably the tsetse fly, to the use of horses.[28]

Moreover, there was the issue of reconciling the Islamic character of the Songhai inheritance with the pagan beliefs and practices of many of their subjects, a tension that reflected both the long-standing southwards movement of Islam in Africa, and the relationship between Muslim urban merchants in centres such as the Songhai capital, Gao, and pagan pastoralists. Sonni Ali had continued the syncretic blend of Islam and paganism of his ancestors, but Muhammad moved in a far more orthodox direction. There is a parallel with the process by which Spain grounded its control in Latin America before lessening its tolerance of non-Christian practices, while the rivalry between the Safavids and, on the other hand, both Ottomans and Uzbeks also reflected the serious tensions within Islam.

South-East Asia

Islam also continued to spread in South-East Asia, with trade, as in the *sahel* belt, proving an important medium for extending influence. The commercial centre of Malacca (Melaka) was a centre of Islam from 1414 and also, due to the narrow Malacca Straits between Malaya and Sumatra, the key entrepôt between the South China Sea and the Indian Ocean. Chinese patronage and trade with India assisted Malacca in resisting vassalage to the Thai state of Ayuthia (with conflicts between Malacca and Ayunthia in 1445 and 1456), and then helped to end the vassalage in about 1490. Chinese patronage also assisted in the spread of Malacca's commercial network, and thus of Islam. The latter was encouraged by Sufi mysticism from India, and Islam became much more influential in South-East Asia and the East Indies, both limiting Hinduism, which itself was greatly affected by the Islamic conquest of much of India, and challenging Buddhism. However, in a significant sign of a major change in Chinese power projection, there was no attempt to assist Malacca against the Portuguese conquest in 1511 nor, subsequently, to back the numerous regional attempts to drive the Portuguese out.

Earlier, Malacca was not the sole source of spreading Islamic power. Achin, at the north-west tip of the island of Sumatra, became a sultanate in about 1496 and, under sultan Ali Mughayat Syah, had conquered northern Sumatra by 1524, contesting Portuguese power in the area, as two expanding forces came into conflict. Islam's spread in the early decades of the sixteenth century was also particularly important in the coastal areas of the island of Java, where Demak became an important trading state. Islam helped the coastal cities unite to overthrow the power of the inland state of Majapahit, which had dominated eastern Java.

This world was confronted by Portuguese expansion, notably the capture of Malacca in 1511. The city had numerous bronze cannon, but the decisive clash was between the sultan's war elephants and a well-coordinated and determined Portuguese force reliant on pikes as much as firepower; moreover, Portuguese cannon were superior to those of their opponents.

A dramatic episode, but the extent to which Western power transformed the situation should not be exaggerated. First, to be successful, the Westerners, to a considerable extent, had to fit into existing commercial and political networks. Thus, in the spice-rich Moluccas, Spanish and Portuguese activity in large part rested on the existing rivalry between the sultanates of Tidore and Ternate, with which they formed alliances respectively in 1521 and 1522. Secondly, the local powers were capable of defeating Western forces, as when Ali Mughayat Syah of Achin defeated a Portuguese fleet in 1524 and ended the Portuguese presence in northern Sumatra. Thirdly, the Europeans were scarcely alone among external forces affecting existing states. Thus, Ava, the major state in the middle-Irrawaddy valley in Burma was repeatedly attacked by the Maw Shan states to the north, with its capital, Ava, captured in 1527. This was also the year of the Sack of Rome by forces of Charles V that were out of control, although the extent to which coincidences in time constitute a helpful parallel can be queried. In Burma, a new line of Shan rulers then took power in Ava.

Lastly, aside from external conquest by other non-Western powers, most states were more affected by domestic divisions than by Western pressure. Thus, Dai Viet (Annam), the major state in northern Vietnam was affected by rivalry between competing dynasties in the early decades of the century, leading to its division by 1533. As a result, Dai Viet was unable to serve as the base for expansion, whether in Indochina or overseas.

New World

The Westerners were more effective in the New World than in South Asia. Christopher Columbus' arrival in 1492 in what he thought were the outliers of Asia, was rapidly followed by the spread of Spanish power. Initially, this expansion was a matter of the conquest of islands in the Caribbean, especially Hispaniola and Cuba although not many of the smaller islands, but the Spaniards then expanded onto the mainland. The conquest of the Aztecs of Mexico in 1519–21 and the Incas of Peru in 1531–3 ensured the destruction of the only major states in the Americas.

These conquests are frequently discussed in terms of the impact of a military new world, and explanations of them in terms of weaponry are particularly pertinent for those who link technology with military success. In turn, possibly, the importance of the horse to the conquest was exaggerated by Spanish contemporaries, in large part because of the cultural context, specifically the association of cavalry with honour and social status.[29] Certainly, neither Incas nor Aztecs had firearms or horses, and their societies were reliant on wood and stone, not the iron and steel used by the Spaniards. As with much explanation, there is a mixture of realist and cultural factors, both at the time and subsequently. Slings, wooden clubs and obsidian knives were no match for the Spaniards' arms. The cannon, firearms and crossbows of the Spaniards all had a greater range than their rivals' weapons, while, in hand-to-hand combat, the Spaniards also benefited from armour, made of either steel or iron, as well as helmets. Moreover, these weapons promised those who allied with them a good chance of victory. However, as will be discussed in chapter seven, other factors played a more important role.

A focus on Portuguese and Spanish expansion has taken attention from the military history of the rest of the Americas, and this is particularly serious for North America where European contact in the first third of the century was very limited. Conflict there seems to have focused on rivalry between tribes, with the need for males to prove their masculinity through fighting being particularly important. There was also an overlap between hunting animals and fighting other tribes, each seen as a response to what was different.

Oceania

The same was the case in Oceania and Australasia. New Zealand had been settled from the Pacific islands of Polynesia, introducing Polynesian practices of warfare and methods of fighting. Fortified *pā* settlements, as opposed to *kāinga* or open settlements, spread, particularly on the North Island of New Zealand, and their number suggests serious competition for the resources of land and sea. Although they are difficult to date, and many would not have been occupied at the same time, over 6,000 *pā* sites have been found, and it has been suggested that there may have been about twice that number. In contrast, in Hawai'i and Tahiti, there was a preference for fighting in the open, and the Hawai'ians used projectiles, such as sling and stones, while the Maori made little use of projectiles.[30] Bellicosity was not restricted to the world of the gunpowder empires. War greatly affected social relationships, bringing status or the stigma of defeat, with the weak seeking shelter with stronger kinsmen or, if captured, being incorporated into the victors' kinship network.[31]

Christian Europe

Far more is known about conflict in Europe than the Antipodes, the Americas and Africa combined, and that poses three related problems. First, it is all too easy to let a focus on Europe drown out attention to the remainder of the world. Secondly, it is too easy to allow European developments to set the paradigm for analysing changes elsewhere. Thirdly, it is far from clear how much space to devote to Europe and, within that, what to cover. One possible analysis, and thus narrative, is based on new technology, with firearms and fortifications both vying for attention and being integrated with the argument that new styles and expenditure in fortification reflected the transformative demands created by the destructive impact of cannon fire on traditional stone walls.

This approach is linked to a diffusionist approach to the spread of new techniques. Thus, at the battle of Orsha in 1514 in the upper Dnieper valley west of Smolensk, the Poles scored a decisive victory over a larger Muscovite army by using artillery and arquebusiers, although the Muscovites had deployed arquebusiers already by 1480. Orsha was the first significant Muscovite defeat attributable to superior enemy gunpowder firepower. This defeat pushed Vassily III to focus attention on developing an arquebusier infantry force from volunteers at Novgorod and Pskov. His predecessor, Ivan III, had felt it necessary to recruit Italian cannon-founders, and, by 1494, they had established a cannon-casting yard and powder yard in Moscow. However, it was not until the siege of the major Polish-held fortress of Smolensk in 1514 that Muscovite artillery was sufficiently powerful to help determine the fate of a siege. The city was held thereafter until regained by the Poles during the Russian Time of Troubles early in the following century.

Yet, as will emerge repeatedly in this work, technology and its spread was not the sole narrative. Organisational, social, and cultural factors were also important, as were the goals of the military and of warfare. In Russia, the cavalry increasingly did not employ the bow, but the switch was largely to swords, not handguns. Moreover, whatever the significance of firepower, it did not have the consequences that might have been anticipated. Promotion to *boyar* (noble) rank in sixteenth-century Muscovy depended in part upon service in the field army, but in the case of Muscovy, as elsewhere, the social order was not dominated by those who used firepower. The cavalry was more significant.

Rather than beginning with war-fighting, it is more pertinent to start with the purposes of military strength and activity. There is a tendency to view conflicts in terms of modern concepts such as state-building and the pursuit of resources, not least because there is only limited work on the contemporary strategic cultures that framed strategic and operational goals. Excellent work on Philip II of Spain[32] has not been matched elsewhere.[33] It is particularly necessary to consider these cultures in contemporary terms rather than with anachronistic modern concepts. The role of the search for prestige, not as an 'add-on', but as a crucial component of international and domestic power emerges clearly from some important studies.[34] Rulers sought not only to defend dynastic interests, but also to ensure that they were exemplary members of the royal clan, and that they were regarded accordingly.

These considerations played a major role both in strategic objectives, such as the acquisition of territory, notably territory that was significant in dynastic terms, for example his homeland of Fergana for Babur. These considerations also played a role in operational methods, with rulers seeking to secure triumphs that were as much symbolic as real, particularly sieges that culminated in stage-managed surrenders and ceremonial entries, such as that of the Christian monarchs of Spain (Ferdinand and Isabella) into Granada in 1492. However, for most rulers, there is a lack of detailed work on the range of pressures and goals affecting their conduct, and the nature of the sources is, often, at best suggestive as to motivation. This ensures that it is still possible to debate the causes of many conflicts, an issue that is not separate from military history, as these causes are a basis for the assessment of military effectiveness. Uncertainty as to goals makes it difficult to make qualitative judgments on strategic and operational policies, but the value of war in winning prestige and glory, and asserting and affirming rank and privilege, are readily apparent.[35]

Heroic conceptions of conduct in warfare ensured that the latter was crucial to individuals and families gaining glory and honour. This importance was a matter not only of engaging in war but also of the method of conflict. In particular, heroic conceptions led to an emphasis in Christian Europe on hand-to-hand conflict and on officership in the more socially distinguished cavalry, and the equivalents were also the case in the Islamic world. The nature of exemplary military conduct was very different in China where, indeed, the social and cultural context led to far less of an emphasis on military service, a situation seen with the lack of such activity by most emperors and with the extent to which senior advisors had no experience of such service. Many, moreover, were eunuchs.

If the ambitions of rulers were the key element in causing wars, these frequently focused on concepts of honour (then a legal, not a moral, category) and glory, and, if in China, this did not require personal service against barbarians on the part of the emperor, most other rulers campaigned in person. For example, Maurice of Nassau led a cavalry charge against the Spaniards at the battle of Turnhout in 1597. Yet, the willingness to serve varied. Süleyman the Magnificent died on campaign in Hungary in 1566, but his son, Selim II, lacked this commitment, and it was not revived until Mehmed III campaigned in Hungary in 1596.

The choice of where and how to campaign was often greatly influenced by political considerations. Thus, Charles V's reputation played a major role in the choices he made, not least in resolving the conflicting priorities of his various dominions. Far from being a mere chivalric fantasy, this concern with reputation was 'the keystone in a conceptual arch forming the grand strategy that guided Charles and his advisers'. Charles risked his own person in defence of his honour and reputation, which both increased the cost of his wars, and made it easier to elicit aristocratic participation in his campaigning.[36]

The attraction of imperial aspirations led a number of rulers to entertain such claims, and to sponsor artistic and other comparisons with great emperors of the past. Henry VIII claimed that England was a sovereign empire and asserted his kingship over Ireland as well as his claim to the French throne; while, in Russia, the theme of the Third Rome was increasingly deployed. The fall of Constantinople in 1453 enabled Russia to claim the leadership of Orthodox Christianity and this encouraged a policy of 'gathering of the lands of Rus''. Islamic rulers claimed descent in religious and dynastic terms, for example emphasising a link with past caliphs or with Chinggis Khan. The rulers of Morocco claimed a caliphal status to rival that of the Ottomans.

The individual background to such claims varied, but they shared a sense that authority and power were hierarchical, with the hierarchy presided over by emperors, not kings. There was no understanding of the equivalent rights of all states and rulers, which did not become an important concept until after the Peace of Westphalia in 1648, and then only in Christian Europe.

Instead, there was a leading position in Christian Europe, the Emperor, and that position was enhanced in practice after the election as Emperor of Charles V in 1519 as he brought together four inheritances, the Habsburg, Burgundian, Aragonese and Castilian. Joining Spanish resources to Imperial pretensions was a key development, and the Habsburg position was further exalted when, after the death of king Louis of Hungary at the battle of Mohacs in 1526, Charles's brother Ferdinand was elected king of Bohemia, and, more contentiously, advanced a claim to the crown of Hungary, being crowned king.

Charles' predecessor as Emperor, his paternal grandfather Maximilian I (r. 1493–1519), pursued an ambitious foreign policy, but lacked the resources to give it sufficient force, not least as he had no equivalent to the great wealth Charles V was to derive from Italy, Spain and the New World. At the beginning of the century, Maximilian faced the resumption of the Italian wars when Charles VIII of France's successor, Louis XII (r. 1498–1515), overran the duchy of Milan with Venetian support in 1499, and conquered Naples in 1501.[37] Louis and Ferdinand, king of Aragon, another of Charles V's grandfathers, partitioned the kingdom of Naples, but disputes with Ferdinand in 1502 led the French to try to take the entire kingdom.

In turn, Spanish opposition resulted, at the battle of Cerignola on 28 April 1503, in a striking demonstration of the value of new weapons. The greatly-outnumbered Spaniards were commanded by Gonzalo de Córdoba, the 'Great Captain', a veteran of the conquest of Granada[38] in which firearms had played an important role. At Cerignola, he held his men in defence behind a trench and earth parapet, which stopped three attacks by the French cavalry, exposing them, and the Swiss pikemen in support, to heavy Spanish fire from arquebuses: handguns in which the powder was ignited by a length of slow-burning match. In a parallel to the use of wagon-camps (see pp. 35, 60), Córdoba's revival of the art of field fortification was used to devastating effect, transforming tactical possibilities; although, as a reminder of the difficulty of judging success, this was possible largely because the French attacked rapidly and without due care, failing to bring up their artillery against the Spanish fieldworks, which would have been vulnerable to cannon.

The effectiveness of firearms was linked to their mobility and rate of fire, and, as a result, cannon fire was most effective against a static defence, both fortifications and in the field.[39] In contrast, cannon offered particularly little against rapidly-moving light cavalry of the Central Asian type. Underlining the importance of the tempo of a battle and of seizing the initiative, the Spaniards at Cerignola then mounted a successful counterattack, with infantry providing fire and movement, and then cavalry, and thus completing the victory.

Cerignola was the first in a series of battles, in Italy and more generally in Western Europe, that involved the testing of a variety of weapons, weapon systems, and tactics, in the search for a clear margin of military superiority[40]; with different combinations of infantry, cavalry and artillery owing much to the precedents created by the organisation and sophistication of combined arms systems in the late fifteenth century, notably by the Burgundians. In this testing, there was no clear model of good practice. Thus, although their force structure was far from identical, English armies were not intrinsically backward nor less tactically capable than their western European counterparts.[41]

Contemporary Western warfare could be understood in Classical terms: the Greeks, Macedonians and Romans did not have gunpowder weapons, but their forces did have a mixture of infantry and cavalry, cold steel and projectiles. In his *Libro dell' Arte della Guerra* [*Art of War*] (1521), which was frequently reprinted until it was placed on the (Papal) Index of Prohibited Books in 1559, the Florentine thinker Niccolò Machiavelli tried to update Flavius Vegetius' fourth- or fifth-century *Epitoma Rei Militaris* [*On Military Matters*] by focusing on the pike and treating the handgun as similar to missile weaponry. Indeed, the value of the latter comparison was such that the major problem in comparing Renaissance with Classical warfare was seemingly set by the important role of French heavy cavalry in the fifteenth and sixteenth centuries, not by that of firearms. As the large-scale use of the pike in the early sixteenth century in Western Europe in many respects represented a revival of the Macedonian phalanx, the key development in Western infantry warfare of the period was apparently organisational, rather than technological.[42]

Close-proximity action remained the crucial nature of conflict in both battle and small war. Firearms did not greatly lessen that as they were not sufficiently effective to clear the battlefield. Although firearms could do considerable damage, hand-to-hand combat and cold steel remained important in both infantry and, even more, cavalry fighting, although less scholarly attention has been devoted to hand-held weaponry than to firearms. The same was true at sea, particularly in galley warfare: firepower alone could not determine battles, not least because wooden warships were difficult to sink. It was easier to board and capture them, but that required hand-to-hand fighting.

More significant in the Italian Wars (1494–1559) than changes in weaponry was the extent to which France and Spain increasingly dominated Italy, in large part because they were the only powers with the resources to support and sustain a major military effort. The weakness of the Italian powers did not indicate any inability to respond to the changing nature of battle, and, in particular, the Italians built up artillery parks (forces), used cannon in conjunction with field entrenchments, adopted both arquebuses and pikes, and produced effective military units.[43] However, at Agnadello on 14 May 1509, the weakness of a major Italian power, Venice, was to be clearly exposed with a heavy defeat by a much larger French army with stronger cavalry: the Venetian cavalry broke and fled, while the infantry was crushed, although the arquebusiers in Venetian service inflicted heavy casualties on the French cavalry before being defeated.

As a reminder of the way in which conflict could expose the fragility of political sway, a lesson also seen with the Aztecs in 1519–21, much of the Venetian *terraferma* (mainland territories) then rebelled and was occupied by Venice's opponents. The campaign also demonstrated the value of fortifications, as the impact of the French victory was lessened by the Venetian success in recapturing Padua in July and then successfully resisting a siege in September and October: the city, besieged by about 50,000 troops, was strongly protected by recently-built outlying bastions while it took a long time to assemble the large siege train of about sixty heavy cannon. Defeat in 1509, and again by the Duke of Ferrara, a weaker power, in 1510, however, led Venice to adopt a more cautious stance in foreign policy, one in which it was reluctant to resist Spanish expansion in Italy.[44]

The Holy League, formed by Pope Julius II in 1511, was next to contest French dominance of northern Italy, but, as a sign of the importance of non-Italian powers, Spanish participation in this alliance was crucial. As a reminder of the value of cavalry, the key battle, Ravenna on 11 April 1511, was a French victory in which heavy cavalry and superior combined-arms coordination, including artillery and pikemen, maintained eventually successful pressure on the Spaniards. However, on 6 June 1513, the French were beaten at Novara by the experienced Swiss pikemen in Milanese service. Firepower had only limited impact in this battle, but the circumstances of the day played a key role in this: the French cavalry was not ready for combat in time, and the infantry had not time to entrench. Partly as a result, the French use of cannon and 500 arquebusiers made scant difference and, without cover, they were overrun by the Swiss. Morale was important, for casualties from French shot did not deter the Swiss from pressing home the attack.

A fresh French invasion under the new king, the young Francis I (r. 1515–47), led to the battle of Marignano (13–14 September 1515), a French victory that, in combination with the other recent battles, suggested that various conclusions could be drawn from the combination of arms and tactical formations. The French then occupied the duchy of Milan, the strategic core of northern Italy; but the election of Charles V as Emperor in 1519 resulted in Francis, unwilling to accept Habsburg primacy, declaring war anew in 1521. However, successive victories, notably Bicocca (1522), Pavia (1525), and Landriano (1529), left Charles dominant in Italy, and displayed the ability of armies to deliver a decisive result. In particular, Charles's combined-arms forces, with their combination of arquebusiers, pikemen and light infantry, proved especially effective. At Bicocca, defensive Spanish firepower caused heavy losses among the attacking Swiss. Like the Mongol victory of 1449 at T'u-mu, Pavia led to the capture of the defeated commander, and, as with that battle, it was the ruler, in this case Francis I. As a result, the victor, Charles V, was given an important strategic advantage, with control over Francis becoming an important political issue.

Francis apparently accepted his failure by the Treaty of Madrid with Charles (1526), which led to his release. However, Francis then created a new alliance, the League of Cognac, and resumed fighting. However, Charles V's forces were victorious, with the French unsuccessfully besieging Naples in 1528 greatly weakened by malaria, which led Francis to accept defeat anew with the Treaty of Cambrai of 1529. By this, Naples was left in Charles' hands and Milan in that of an ally. As a result of his power, Charles was able to restore his Italian protégés, notably the Medici in Tuscany, to their territories, Florence surrendering in 1530. Charles' strength in Italy, moreover, helped ensure that he was able to sustain his alliance with Genoa, and thus establish his naval position in the Mediterranean. Charles's power was also shown at Bologna in 1530 when Pope Clement crowned him Emperor. The sack of Rome three years earlier by Charles' unpaid mutinous forces had displayed the inability of the Italians to protect themselves. Charles' power was also shown in the formidable army he deployed against the Ottomans in Austria in 1532.

Conclusions

As protector of the Church against Protestants and Muslims, and its propagator in the New World, Charles seemed to represent a new caesaropapalism that was designed to defend and revive the Empire's sacred mission.

At the same time, the New World suggested a novel universality for the Holy Roman Empire.[45] With Aztec Mexico recently brought under his sway, and Inca Peru soon to follow, Charles had carried Habsburg power and the Crown of Spain to hitherto unsurpassed and unimagined heights. Indeed, the grandiloquent Latin inscription above the entrance to the royal mausoleum in the Escorial palace built near Madrid by his son, Philip II, was to refer to him as 'the most exalted of all Caesars'.

4 Conflict, 1535–1575

Nearly a century after the fall of Constantinople in 1453, another imperial capital came seemingly close to falling in 1550. On 26 September, Mongol raiders under Altan khan (1507–82) breached the Chinese frontier defences at the Gubei Pass, forty miles north-east of Beijing. On 1 October, the city was besieged and the suburbs looted. The demoralised garrison refused to sally forth, and there were no supplies for any reinforcements. On 6 October, the hapless minister of war was executed on the emperor's orders while the Mongols defeated a Chinese force in the open. In practice, there is no real comparison with Constantinople: the Mongols had no artillery to breach the walls of Beijing and, instead, swiftly left with their spoils. But the threat to Beijing, as well as the serious Mongol raiding of northern China over the following decade and a half, showed that major states were scarcely able to overawe their neighbours, and also revealed the extent to which the use of firearms, while capable of being employed to help achieve victory in certain contexts, could not necessarily do so.

The first third of the century had seen the establishment or expansion of major empires, notably the Mughal, Safavid, Habsburg, Ottoman and Songhai empires, but the following four decades was to see a more mixed position. There was still further expansion, notably by the Ottoman and Songhai empires, but, while Ming China and Safavid Iran, particularly the first, held off attacks with only limited losses, there were also serious challenges for empires, especially for the Habsburgs and, even more, Mughals. These challenges brought together the problems of external threat and the vulnerability of domestic control, indeed the artificiality of any division between them. Thus, success in overcoming external threats won monarchs the prestige necessary to maintain a controlling influence over the domestic sphere, notably their aristocrats, while, in turn, such influence helped provide the strength important to the winning of success.

The relationship between struggles in different parts of the world was often limited and at best indirect. Warfare between China and the Mongols had only a minor impact in India, while, although it affected trans-Saharan trade routes, the Songhai conquest of Mali did not influence greatly the struggle between Ottomans and Habsburgs in the Mediterranean. Yet, there were linkages, and sometimes they were close. Thus, the Habsburgs, Ottomans, Safavids and Uzbeks were involved in interrelated struggles, and these struggles spread to include a wide range of other forces, which were affected and/or influential, or were thought likely to be affected and/or influential. These forces and settings ranged from combatants across Europe, such as Irish Catholics unsuccessfully resisting the Tudors and encouraged to do so by the Papacy, to the steppes of Russia, and from East Africa to Sumatra.

This range helped give a particular character to the warfare of the period. It was different to that of the Mongol empire of the thirteenth century, as even the most far-flung empire in Eurasia, that of the Ottomans, did not equal it, while the possibilities offered by the trans-oceanic span of the Habsburgs and Portuguese could not readily be brought to effect in Eurasia. Nevertheless, decisions to fight were understood to have a wide-reaching impact, one, moreover, that could be followed by Europeans in the newly more accurate world maps they used. The Ottomans also had the capacity for a far-ranging strategic vision, and one that had a maritime as well as a land dimension.

China

China, again, was not the centre of military activity, despite being the world's most populous state. Unlike its Manchu successor in the eighteenth century, the Ming empire neither sought to expand to the west, into Tibet and Xinjiang, let alone Central Asia, nor, again unlike the Manchu, did it intervene to try to direct affairs in Indo-China or Burma. Nor did China pursue a maritime course, challenging, for example, the establishment of Spanish power in the Philippines. Instead, having attempted to restrict coastal trade, the Chinese were put under considerable pressure by *wako* (Japanese and Chinese pirates and smugglers) who attacked coastal regions of China, establishing bases there, especially on the Shandong peninsula. Although better firearms and fortifications helped, in the 1550s the Ming used large numbers of men armed with traditional weapons – bows, lances and swords – to capture the pirate bases. Cannon were felt to be unreliable and/or inaccurate. The first success over a large *wako* force occurred in 1555, the key campaigns were mounted in 1556–8, and by 1567 piracy was no longer a serious issue, but the need to fight on two fronts at once – against the pirates and the Mongols, had greatly exacerbated the strategic problems facing the Ming, as well as underlining the plentiful resources they could draw on.[1]

The pressure on China from pirates and smugglers, like that from the Mongols, reflected the appeal of a wealthy society to outsiders and their determination to gain benefits by trade or force. The Western and Arab slave trade with Africa was a variant on this process of gaining benefits by trade or force. Given the difficulty of establishing terms of trade, and the extent to which trade itself compromised Chinese views on the outside world, it was not surprising that the relationship involved much violence.

Having lost their early lead in firearms, the Chinese had been introduced to matchlocks by the Ottomans via the Muslims of Xinjiang, and from Portuguese merchant adventurers, either directly, notably through the enclave at Macao, or via Japanese pirates. These European-style muskets and, later, European-style iron guns mounted on carriages, impressed the Chinese, who copied them.

In contrast to the early fifteenth century, there was not only no outward-looking maritime policy, but also no Chinese expansion into the steppe. Instead, China was under Mongol pressure. Moreover, there was to be no Chinese victory ending the Mongol threat. A bold plan to do so was advanced by Zeng Xian, governor of the northern province of Shanxi, who, in 1547, proposed detailed schemes to drive the Mongols from the Ordos, the arid region within the big bend of the Yellow River that was a base for Mongol pressure on China, not least Shanxi, which had been devastated in 1542. The scale of what he proposed indicated the boldness of planning made possible by Chinese resources, and also contrasted greatly with the more modest scale of Western expansionism. Zeng's initial proposal was for an attack by 300,000 troops, but the costs, which Zeng greatly underestimated, were of major concern to the ministry of war. Moreover, despite the possibility also of using water routes, the Supreme Commander, Weng Wanda, correctly argued that the problem of operating in the arid Ordos would require an enormous logistical effort that would be difficult to support. Zeng, however, began preparations, conscripting local people, while he and Weng lobbied for their respective case at court. The emperor was persuaded by those lobbying against Zeng and he was executed in 1548, which brought the idea of the conquest of the Ordos to an end.[2]

Altan khan (1507–82), who revived Mongol assertiveness after the weakness stemming from the disunity between the nine sons of Dayan khan (r. 1479–1517), rode beneath the walls of Beijing in 1550. The Mongol threat was lessened by disunity, notably between the eastern and western Mongols, but Altan khan defeated the Oirat confederation, capturing the capital, Karakorum, in 1552.[3] Instability on the steppe could make it difficult for the Ming to achieve stable relations with the steppe, but also provided possibilities for the Ming as they were able to play off rivals who wished to gain the support represented by Chinese legitimation of titles and trade with China.

However, in pursuit of booty and their unsuccessful demand for tribute trade, the Mongols, eventually both eastern and western Mongols, raided China every year from 1550 until 1566, and heavily defeated a Chinese army which they ambushed on the steppe in April 1552. There had been earlier Mongol victories in the field in June 1548, March 1549, and October 1550.

As a result, the Chinese, whose annual military expenses rose rapidly, returned to the defensive, relying on garrisons at strategic passes and walls. Moreover, the Great Wall was adapted for musketeers. The Mongol attacks ensured considerable improvement in the wall, which became higher than its predecessors, as well as containing room for cannon, troops and munitions in the wall itself, and being strengthened with an impressive network of watchtowers, beacons and fortified camps. In addition, mobile artillery was to be developed in the 1570s.

Defensive strategy was matched to a political counterpart. Having initially refused to trade, owing to xenophobia and a determination to appear strong, the Chinese used trade and gifts to accommodate Altan khan, agreeing a treaty in 1571. He was invested as a prince and regular trade fairs were established.[4]

From the north-east, China was also under pressure from Jurchen raids, but the Chinese response was stronger than that against the more powerful Mongols. In 1574 and 1582, attacking Chinese forces defeated and killed Jurchen leaders. Yet, as so often when comparing capability, it is necessary to put this in a wider perspective, as a key element in these Ming victories was help from Jurchen allies, which provided a demonstration of China's sophisticated political approach to warfare on its borders, and its willingness to divide and rule its antagonistic neighbours.

South-East Asia

South-East Asia saw more territorial volatility, but the prime source of change there was not Western power other than in the Philippines. Attacks on Portuguese-ruled Malacca by regional principalities, Johor in 1551, Achin in 1553, 1568, 1570 and 1573, and Japara in 1574, were unsuccessful; but, however successful in defence, the Portuguese were in no condition to mount wars of conquest. The situation was less favourable for them than in Ceylon (Sri Lanka).

The most dynamic state in South-East Asia was the Burmese kingdom of Toungoo, which, under Tabinshwehti (r. 1531–50) and Bayinnaung (r. 1551–81), overran surrounding states: Pegu in 1535–41, territory around Pagan in 1542, and the rival kingdom of Ava in 1555. However, as a reminder of the need to focus on more than the high points, there were also failed invasions of the maritime state of Arakan to the west in 1546 and of Thailand in 1548. Further gains for the dynamic Burmese state included the Thai state of Lan Na/ Chiengmai in 1558, which had been conquered by the Lao state of Lan Chang a decade earlier, and the Thai capital of Ayuthia in 1564 and 1569: in 1564, the Burmese brought a number of large-calibre cannon with them, and this led to a rapid surrender. The Lao city of Vientiane fell in 1574, and Bayinnaung felt able to call himself the king of kings. A puppet ruler, installed in Ayuthia in 1569, remained in power until a Thai rebellion in 1584. Burma's rise also contrasted with Vietnam's weakness in this period.

Firearms only played a relatively minor role in South-East Asia and the East Indies, which reflected cultural assumptions. The emphasis was on the fighting qualities of individuals, and on warrior elites some of whom duelled on war elephants; and not on large numbers of troops. In general, handgunners, who were not members of these élites, were treated badly. Effectiveness in the use of handguns, which were low-precision weapons, required their use in a regular manner in order to provide concentrated fire. The necessary discipline and drill did not match social assumptions about warfare in the region, because they subordinated individual skill and social rank to the collective, the disciplined unit.

Firearms were expected to fit into existing tactics in South-East Asia, which was more generally the case across the world when new weapons were introduced. Rather than a transformation of tactics or operational assumptions, there was often an attempt to use new weapons to give added power to existing practices. Although this practice could lessen the impact of the weapons, it was also a response not only to cultural conservatism but also to the social norms influencing military service and warfare, as well as to the difficulty of training troops for new tactics.

Furthermore, cannon were employed as symbolic supports of authority, rather than as killing machines, although they could be both. As displays of power, cannon were adjuncts of courts, and there was an emphasis on their size, as with the large ones cast in Java, not their manoeuvrability.[5] Moreover, although Western-type matchlocks were manufactured in Burma and Vietnam, the provision of a large number of similar, let alone identical, weapons was beyond local metallurgical capability, while the need for cannon was reduced by the extent to which most cities were not walled. Although the important role of Ayuthia is noteworthy, the notion of fighting for a city was not well established culturally across the entire region. Instead, the local culture of war was generally that of the abandonment of cities in the face of stronger attackers who then pillaged before leaving. As in sub-Saharan Africa, captives, not territory, were the general objective of operations. Western interest in annexation and the consolidation of control by fortification, especially of coastal ports, reflected a different culture.

Japan

Firearms played a far more prominent role in Japan than in South-East Asia, although, in discussing firearms, it is important not to underrate the role of political developments and administrative changes in Japan.[6] From the late fifteenth century, repeating a tendency seen in the civil warfare of the fourteenth century, as the pace of warfare within Japan accelerated, there were a series of major changes in Japanese warfare including larger armies, a greater preponderance of infantry, sophisticated tactics and command structures, and changes in weaponry, especially the spear and armour. The combination of larger armies and an emphasis on infantry was linked to a move away from the largely individualistic style of fighting hitherto followed and, instead, toward a focus on massed formations with a corresponding increase in the importance of command skills.

Spears were the key infantry weapon, paralleling the role of the pike in Western Europe and underlining the extent to which mass formations, unit fighting and discipline were not necessarily linked to firepower, whether archery or handguns. In response to spears, as earlier to arrows, body armour sought to combine flexibility with protection, but the effectiveness of armour was affected by the introduction of firearms. From the first half of the sixteenth century, effective guns were introduced in Japan as a result of trade, with firearms of Western provenance coming into Japan with modifications that had been applied to them in South-East Asia. As an instance of the degree to which the diffusion of new technology was dependent on more than receptivity, these handguns were widely copied rapidly as Japan's metallurgical industry could produce them in large numbers.

Firearms certainly played an important role in war after the battle of Shinano Asahiyamajo (1555), although the extent to which they changed tactics has to be handled with care: in many respects, firearms mostly just replaced bows one-for-one. The guns were still very expensive and in relatively short supply, which would argue against wholesale changes to tactics. But the desirability of owning firearms probably accentuated the trend toward political consolidation into larger units, since smaller *daimyō* would have had difficulty affording firearms, and would not have been able to acquire them in sufficient numbers to make much use of them.

The use of firearms added a new element to combined arms operations as handgunners had to be protected when they reloaded. As a result, they were integrated with spearmen and archers, the former offering protection while the latter maintained firepower. Thus, combined arms had differing consequences in terms of weaponry to the situation in Western Europe. The importance of guns was shown operationally, as well as tactically, as Oda Nobunaga, a leading *daimyō* who rose to power in the 1560s, seized control of major gun foundries at Sakai and Kunitomo.

Nevertheless, increasing army size, as a result of better *daimyō* organisation and mastery of logistics, was probably more important than changes in weaponry. By the mid-seventeenth century, handgunners were being drilled and organised in ways that had never applied to archers, but the earlier extent of tactical change was limited. The most important consequence appears to have been from cannon, which, while in short supply and not all that heavily used, did result in fundamental changes to castle construction.

Alongside his drive, ambition and skill, Nobunaga benefited from the extent to which other leading *daimyō* had exhausted their forces to a considerable extent in campaigning in the 1550s and early 1560s. This was the case with the rivalry between Takeda Shingen and Uesugi Kenshin, a rivalry motivated by their struggle for dominance in the Kantō and more particularly over the province of Shinano. This rivalry was linked by alliances into a wider network of alignments and hostilities. Nobunaga's rise to prominence owed much to a victory over an ally of Shingen, Imagawa Yoshimoto, at the battle of Okehazama in 1560. Nobunaga was outnumbered by roughly 5000 to 20,000 troops, but, rather than respond defensively to the invasion of his territory, he took the initiative in a surprise attack, allegedly benefiting from a very heavy downpour of rain after which he launched the assault in which Yoshimoto was killed. This victory showed the value of command skills, fighting quality, and the tactical offensive; and also made Nobunaga's reputation. The value of surprise reflected the ability to take and exploit the initiative, which was an ability that owed much to tactical flexibility. Rigid formations and fighting methods were generally incapable of this flexibility. Nobunaga also facilitated the mobility of his forces by building pontoon bridges and improving the road system.

Like other commanders, Nobunaga used fighting as a key component of a politics of alliance and betrayal, and, partly as a result, was reluctant to engage in battles in which losses might be heavy. Instead, the taking of forts was a preferred way to display power and advance interests. However, as with the Italian Wars in Europe, a politics of changing sides frequently did not prevent hard-fought battles. Furthermore, a bitter struggle for control between rival *daimyō* encouraged the search for comparative advantage. In 1568, Nobunaga had entered Kyoto at the head of about 50,000 troops and had made his ally Yoshiaki shogun. In turn, Yoshiaki turned against him and created a league directed against Nobunaga, only for it to be destroyed in 1570–3.

The battle of Nagashino (1575), in which Nobunaga defeated the Takeda, provides a key instance of the role of revisionism in affecting our overall account of military history. Conventionally, the emphasis was on the role of 3000 musketeers in the army of Nobunaga, which used volley fire to smash the repeated charges of Takeda cavalry, winning a decisive victory.[7] Placing musketeers in the front of an army meant giving them the position traditionally occupied by the bravest, often mounted, samurai. Now, however, the account of Nobunaga lining gunners up in ranks and having them shoot in volleys is queried. That idea was originally based on a screen painting produced more than a century after the fact, and there is good physical evidence to indicate that the conventional account would have been impossible under the conditions on the battlefield at the time. Instead, it is pointed out that the Takeda had almost as many gunners at Nagashino as Nobunaga did, and that victory for the latter was obtained by outnumbering the Takeda almost two to one and by fighting from behind pretty elaborate field fortifications that the Takeda could not see, because of heavy rain, until they were too deeply committed to the battle and almost on top of them. Moreover, Nobunaga tricked his opponent into letting one wing of his forces become encircled by a Nobunaga ally who pretended to be willing to defect.[8]

In 1577, Nobunaga deposed the shogun, becoming the leading ruler in the country. However, he faced serious opposition from other *daimyō*, as well as from the followers of the Honganjī branch of the True Pure Land Buddhism, the central temple of which defied attempts to subjugate it until 1580. These followers formed armies known as *ikkō-ikki*, who fought to assure their rebirth.[9]

The Mughals

Mughal success appeared short-lived under Babur's opium-addicted successor, Humāyūn (r. 1530–56). His problems indicated the limitations of Babur's success and, more generally, the difficulties of grounding a new regime and, related to that, the need for historians to move beyond headline battles, in this case (First) Panipat in 1526. Humāyūn was challenged by Sher Khān Sūr, an able Afghan who had served first Ibrahim Lodi and then Babur only to leave the service of the latter in 1529 because he saw few hopes of advancement. Based in Bihar, and installing discipline by paying his Afghan troops, Sher Khān Sūr conquered most of Bengal between 1534 and 1538, bringing to an end the independent state there ruled by the Husain Shāhīs. Their capital, Gaur, fell in 1538, and this challenge led Humāyūn to march east, only for Sher Khān to cut off his line of retreat. Outmanoeuvred, Humāyūn was defeated at Chausa in a surprise attack in June 1539, while Sher Khān declared himself an independent king, Sher Shār.

In May 1540, a decisive victory over a demoralised Mughal army closer to Delhi at Kanauj led to a transformation of the situation in north India, a transformation that tends to be ignored in works on global military history which smooth out the pattern of Mughal history. The defeated Humāyūn fled India, and Sher Shār captured the centres of power, Delhi and Agra, as well as the breadbasket of northern India, the Punjab. He revived the Delhi sultanate in 1540 and founded the Sūr dynasty. Before a fatal explosion during the siege of Kalinjar in 1545 ended his life, Sher Shār had overrun much of northern India, conquering more than either the Lodis or, at that stage, the Mughals. Malwa was conquered in 1542–3, while Mewar submitted in 1544. Moreover, Sher Shār revitalised the government by asserting central control, reviving earlier administrative practices, but adding the vital ingredient of personal commitment. He also used Ottoman artillery specialists to help manufacture a large number of cannon, while he had a substantial force of handgunners.[10]

As a reminder of the extent to which victory in battle required the death of opposing leaders to help make it decisive, as at Mohacs, Humāyūn, who had not been killed in 1539–40, still challenged Sher Shār's position. However, he failed to establish himself in the region of Sind outside Sher Shār's dominions and subsequently to win the support of the Rajputs, a key force in northern India. As a result, Humāyūn left India in 1543, seeking exile in the Safavid empire. Past good relations between Babur and the Safavid rulers led to a friendly reception which, however, entailed Humāyūn becoming in effect a client, converting to Shi'ism and being given an army of 12,000 men with which he conquered Kandahar in southern Afghanistan from his brother Kamran. Shāh Tahmāsp had insisted that Kandahar be handed over to the Safavids, but, when most of the Safavid troops returned home, Humāyūn took control, pressing on, after repeated campaigns until 1550, to recapture Ghazi and Kabul from his brother, who, once defeated, was blinded so that he could not lead fresh rebellions. Blindings and killings were important to the dynastic politics of Islamic states, notably the Ottoman empire, in the period covered by this book.

Humāyūn remained eager to invade northern India anew, and, meanwhile, campaigned extensively, underlining the links between politics in India and Central Asia. His conquests in northern Afghanistan, where, in 1546, he took over Balakhshān and in 1549 attacked Balkh, showed that the mountains of central Afghanistan were not a bar to campaigning.

Meanwhile, in a dramatic display of the extent to which Indian empires and dynasties rested on individual ability, the Sūr sultanate declined under

Sher Shār's successors. His son, Islām Shār (r. 1545–52), resisted a number of revolts, but his death was followed by divisions between the Sūrs, the break-up of the empire between relatives in 1553, and a combination of civil war and revolts. As his father had done in 1526, Humāyūn grasped his opportunity in 1555, advancing from Afghanistan into the Punjab, where he won battles at Dipālpur and Machhiwāra, following up with capturing Delhi and Agra.

Humāyūn died in an accident in Delhi on 27 January 1556, but, although he was succeeded by his young son, Akbar (r. 1556–1605), who was only 14, this did not lead to a fresh Mughal collapse. Bairam Khān, the Iranian-born regent for Akbar, proved effective, decisively defeating the Sūr governor of Delhi, and would-be ruler, Hīmū at Second Panipat on 5 November 1556, after Hīmū had captured Delhi and Agra the previous month. The battle brought the Mughals control of Delhi and Agra anew, again demonstrating the extent to which victory in battle was generally followed by the fall of cities, both because they were vulnerable militarily to whoever controlled the surrounding countryside and could blockade them, and because there was no political logic to supporting the defeated.

At Second Panipat, the Mughal army defeated its much larger foe without the use of a *tābūr cengī* or, apparently, artillery. Hīmū relied on an elephant charge, but the Mughal centre redeployed behind a ravine and eventually prevailed thanks to their mounted archers, but with the wounding of Hīmū by an arrow proving a key element. The fate of commanders was very important to the course of battles, not only because of the significance of their professionalism in the shape of choosing the terrain and force deployment, and deciding when to launch attacks and deploy reserves, but also because this professionalism extended to heroic elements such as leading attacks and stiffening the defence. These tactical factors were not ones that could be readily dispensed with, but they also exposed commanders to the risk of death, capture or injury; and those could greatly sap morale. The captured Hīmū was killed by Bairam.

Second Panipat proved an instance of a clash between Indian and Central Asian means of warfare. The Mughal ability to control the supply of war horses in India ensured that they dominated mounted archery in the subcontinent, and this archery played a major role in a relative decline in the importance of elephants, which had hitherto been much more significant in north India. In contrast, in Kerala in southern India, a forested region that was unsuitable for mounted archers, elephants continued to play a role as they also did in the similar environment of South-East Asia. Elephants did not play a comparable role in Africa, primarily because the African elephants proved much more difficult to train.

During his four-year regency, Bairam Khān pressed on to defeat the Sūr princes, restoring Mughal control over much of northern India, including the territories of Oudh, Gwalior, Ajmer and Mewat. Sikandar Sūr, who had ruled Punjab from 1553, capitulated to Akbar at Mankot in 1557, bringing the Sūr dynasty to an end. Control over force was also important to the political situation within the Mughal regime. Winning control from Bairam Khān in 1560–1, in part due to Sunni objections to him as a Shi'ite, Akbar also had to displace hostile relatives, notably his foster brother Adham khan, whom he threw to his death from the harem balcony.

Once in complete control, Akbar pressed on to expand the area of northern India that he ruled or over which he had influence, although the divisive nature of his family ensured that, in 1566, he had to repel an attack by his half-brother, Muhammad Hakim, the ruler of Kabul, who had allied with the Uzbeks, who were bitter enemies of Akbar. Thus, as with other dynasties, such as the Ottomans, disputes within the ruling house were closely linked to international rivalries. Swift moves were crucial to Akbar's success, with his ability to act with alacrity important in gaining the initiative, in overcoming distances, and in asserting his interests and will in the complex political environment.

Akbar, in turn, devoted particular effort to trying to ease relations with the Rajput states. As Hindus, they were a potential source of opposition to the Muslim Mughals, but Akbar used the politics of dynasticism and patronage to settle the problem. From 1562, when the state of Amber submitted, he married a number of Rajput princesses, and he gave their kin positions in the empire, which helped to turn their alliance and acknowledgement of Akbar's suzerainty into co-operation. This process extended to appointing Rajputs to military positions. As such, it represented another aspect of the grounding of conquest and power seen, differently, with the Spaniards in the Americas and the Ottomans in the Balkans.

Co-operation, however, rested on strength and victory, while some states were not incorporated into the Mughal empire on the basis of co-operation. Thus, in 1567, Akbar declared a *jihad* against Udai Singh, rana of the Rajput principality of Mewar. Initial attacks on the Mewar fortified capital of Chittaurgarh (Chittor), which stood high on a rock outcrop above the Rajastan plain, were repulsed, and Akbar resorted to bombardment and the digging of mines: tunnels under the walls filled with explosives. The latter were particularly helpful in producing breaches in the walls, although the construction of a *sabat* (or covered way) to the walls to cover an attack was also very significant. After a night-time general attack, the city fell on 23 February 1568, with all the defenders and 20,000–25,000 civilians killed in hand-to-hand fighting. The fortress was then destroyed, while Mewar was annexed.

The following year, the major fortress of Ranthambor, held by a vassal of Udai Singh, surrendered after a bombardment by 15 enormous siege guns which had been dragged by elephants and bullocks to a commanding hill.

Many of the territories conquered by Akbar are scarcely known today, but mention of some of his campaigns provides an indication of the extent to which campaigning was a near-continual feature and not one that can be detached from an account of Mughal history. For example, Bhatta was conquered in 1563, becoming a vassal state, followed by Gondwana in 1564. The mid-1570s proved particularly important in Mughal expansion. To the west, north Sind was conquered and annexed in 1574, and Gujarat in 1572–5, giving the Mughals a coastline on the Indian Ocean and linking this coastline to the north Indian plain in a way that most rulers of either had failed to achieve. The Gujarati nobles, disappointed in the anticipated benefits of Mughal rule, swiftly rebelled, but Akbar responded speedily, taking the initiative with a rapidly advancing army. Cavalry conflict was crucial to the defeat of Gujarati forces in 1573. The conquest of Kāthiāwār began in 1572.

To the east, the region of Bihār had come under the Karranī Afghans in 1564, in which year they also replaced Sūr rule in Bengal, serving as a reminder of the number of expanding states. The Karranī Afghans offered nominal allegiance to Akbar, but they withdrew it in 1572, which led to a Mughal invasion of Bihār in 1574 followed by its annexation. The successful siege of Patna played a major role in this campaign. In 1575–6, Akbar pressed on to conquer and annex Bengal: at Rukaroi (1575), the Mughal army under Akbar's minister, Todar Mal, defeated sultan Daud Karranī by recovering from the initial shock of a successful elephant charge on the Mughal centre and wearing down their opponents in hard fighting in which archery played a major role.[11] Daud was killed, and victory was followed by the extension of Mughal control over Bengal, although resistance continued until 1587 while, moreover, a group of Mughal officers in Bengal rebelled in 1579.

The fighting effectiveness of Mughal forces was widely tested. In Mewar, despite the successes of 1568–9, resistance to Mughal control became serious from 1572. Four years later, at Haldighati, a Mughal force defeated a Rajput army, because only the Mughals had handgunners, and they and the Mughal archers killed the elephant drivers who were crucial to their opponent's army. Yet again, however, victory did not end resistance, which indeed continued until 1615.

In this struggle, like others, the Mughals were helped by the extension of their control over surrounding areas, not least isolating the Rajput opposition that existed, and also by weakening this opposition by demonstrating the appeal of co-operating with Akbar and winning benefits. Akbar also profited from the fact that Mewar was, unlike rebellious Yemen under the Ottoman sultan Selim II, within relatively easy distance of Mughal forces.

All comparisons face problems, but it is worth considering Mughal campaigns in the 1570s alongside those of Spain under Philip II. Akbar found it easier both to face a number of opponents and to reverse or limit the success of rebellions. In contrast, the difficulty of bringing Spanish power readily to bear in the distant Low Countries was an issue, notably because France, which very much separated them from Spain, was not part of the Spanish system and did not produce resources for it. Yet, as the Mughals showed in Mewar, failure, in the shape of continued resistance, did not necessarily mean long-term defeat, and, in that context, it is unclear that Philip II should be seen as having obviously failed yet in the Low Countries, especially if the point of reference is years of opportunity for the Spaniards there, such as 1579 or 1587.

In terms of contesting control over numbers of people, the campaigns in northern India were the most significant of the period 1535–75 across the world. The great extension of Mughal territory under Akbar reflected his energy and determination, the divisions among his opponents, the impressive demographic, economic and financial resources of Hindustan and the regions gained by conquest, and the strength of the Mughal military system. Firearms certainly played a role and Akbar took an interest in the improvement of his handguns, maintaining a special collection which he tested himself.[12] Much of his infantry was equipped with handguns and his artillery was superior to that of rival rulers. Akbar's siege artillery was instrumental in the capture of well-fortified positions, such as Ranthambor in 1569.

Like that of the Ottomans, Mughal military force, however, was not restricted to firearms. The Mughals also deployed mounted archers, heavy cavalry armed with swords and lances, and war elephants, and their cavalry was particularly important. Akbar's household cavalry was equipped with chain mail and armoured helmets, but few Indian cavalry forces wore anything heavier than that out in the field, as wearing plate and scale armour was difficult in the Indian climate. Nevertheless, the imperial or household cavalry of the Mughal emperor was a superior force, although it was small: Akbar had only 12,000 men. Instead, the bulk of the cavalry were light cavalry well equipped for long and arduous campaigning in the subcontinent.[13] Mounted archers were very important during Babur's reign but diminished in significance as the Mughal force became an Indian subcontinental army. The composite Central Asian bows that the Mughals used were more effective in range and penetration than those of many Indians, most of which were made of bamboo. The successful combination of a number of arms was important to Mughal success. In addition, Akbar anchored his position with a number of fortresses, especially Agra, Allahabad, Lahore, Ajmer, Rohtas and Attock. Furthermore, while gunpowder weaponry was important to Akbar, it also benefited his opponents, and his victories were not easy. The sieges of Chittaurgarh and Ranthambor were both lengthy and difficult, as, more generally, was the deployment of cannon.

Logistics played a major role in sieges, encouraging both sides to negotiate while they were in progress. Much of Akbar's success, indeed, was due to his political pull as well as his military skill and to the strong organisation of his state, notably the ability to produce resources that made co-operation attractive. The widespread dispersal of firearms ensured that the key to success, for both Mughals and others, was not the possession of such weapons, which was widespread, but rather organisation: among those who fought, as well as in terms of exploiting agricultural resources and sustaining effective alliances.[14]

Elsewhere in India

It is all too tempting, in the rush to focus on Europe, to discuss only the Mughals when considering India, not least because they were to subjugate the Deccan (south-central India) the following century. However, that is a mistaken approach as developments elsewhere in India were important in their own right and also indicative of more general trends. Firearms were readily adopted in the subcontinent. For example, the affluent maritime state of Gujarat in west India could afford the latest in military technology. In the 1530s, responding to pressure from Malwa and Mughal attack, which was part of the long-standing attempt of inland states to benefit from maritime trade, its ruler, Bahadur Shah, developed a large army equipped with new cannon manned by Portuguese gunners.

Further south, firearms were soon used in the struggle between Hindu and Muslim states. Under the dynamic Aliya Rāmarāj (r. 1542–65), the Hindu state of Vijayanagar maintained its position in the complex politics of the region and dominated southern India by deploying armies equipped with artillery manned by Portuguese or Muslim gunners. This policy reflected the same search for a response to Muslim expansion in India which had earlier led, in the fifteenth century, to the adoption of improved warhorses and archers. In addition, Muslim mercenaries were hired in the fifteenth century, and Portuguese in the sixteenth, providing expertise in firearms, while Vijayanagar also sought to buy all the imported horses and thus both to strengthen itself and to weaken its opponents. Expenditure on military modernisation, accompanied by monetarisation, helped to transform the economy of Vijayanagar, and Aliya Rāmarāj, in turn, benefited from the increasing customs revenue which this transformation generated.

This increased wealth encouraged three of the four Muslim sultans of the Deccan, Husain Nizam Shah of Ahmadnagar, Ibrahim Qutb Shah of Golconda, and Ali Adīl Shah of Bijapur, to put aside their rivalries and unite against Vijayanagar. At the battle of Talikota in January 1565, Aliya Rāmarāj was killed and his army was decisively defeated. The city of Vijayanagar was subsequently sacked, and Golconda made significant territorial gains from the defeated state, as did Bijapur.

Ibrahim of Golconda (r. 1530–80) then built a new capital at Hyderabad which was a clear demonstration of the new order and also an attempt to re-present sacred space as the new city was organised on the basis of Muslim power and sites. Similarly, Mexico City offered a Spanish Christian agenda very different to the razed Aztec capital of Tenochtitlán. Ibraham relied upon heavy cavalry, led by the Muslim nobility and supported by landholdings, and upon a Western artillery corps financed by the royal monopoly of diamonds, a newly discovered source of wealth. Golconda also provided arms and men to help Achin attack Malacca,[15] a commitment not seen with the Mughals, who did not use their position on the Indian Ocean and the Bay of Bengal to launch comparable maritime efforts, let alone to seek to match the Ottomans as a naval power.

The leaders of Vijayanagar meanwhile retreated to Vellore and Penugonda, more southern centres of authority that were both further from Deccani power and able to take advantage of the resources of the Tamil lands in southern India. Indeed, there was to be a reconquest of some of the lost lands north of the River Penner, with both Kandanavolu and Gandikotta regained. However, defeat had weakened Vijayanager because it helped lead local *nāyakas* (military leaders) to reach for independence.

Iran

To the west of India, the Safavids of Iran were less dynamic than earlier in the century. It is easy to focus on conflict with the Ottomans, but the Safavids also had to consider their eastern frontier. Rivalry with the Uzbeks diminished from the early 1540s, when the Uzbeks conquered Balkh from the Safavids, as Uzbek unity collapsed. Further south, Hūmayūn, the exiled Mughal leader, overran much of Afghanistan as a Safavid ally. However, once the Mughals were re-established in northern India, the province of Kandahar was seized by the Safavids in 1558, providing them with a strong position on their borderlands towards India. Mounted archers played a key role in these conflicts on the eastern frontiers of the Safavid empire.

Ottoman expansionism was the great threat on the western frontier. In 1534, learning from their defeat in 1514, the Safavids had preferred to avoid conflict, so that Süleyman the Magnificent abandoned operations in the harsh environment of the Iranian plateau and, instead, overran northern and central Iraq, capturing Baghdad. In 1535, the Safavids again avoided battle, and logistical problems helped ensure the failure of the Ottoman campaign so that only their earlier Iraqi gains were retained.

In 1538, however, in a classic instance of imperial power, and one that in this case reflected Ottoman success further north in 1534, the local ruler of Basra had himself recognised as an Ottoman governor-general, expanding Ottoman authority south-eastwards to the Persian Gulf, especially in 1546 when Ottoman power was established in Basra. In competition with the Portuguese in the Persian Gulf, and possibly largely as a defensive measure,[16] the Ottomans then extended their power along its western shores, occupying the port of Katif near Bahrain in 1550, but failing to capture the Portuguese base of Hormuz in 1552. The struggle between the Ottomans and Portuguese continued, with, in contrast, the limited Safavid role in the Persian Gulf most apparent. Moreover, the Safavids devoted only limited effort to southern Iraq,[17] which was less important to them than the more northern borderlands, notably of eastern Anatolia.

Conflict between the Ottomans and Safavids revived in 1548, with Süleyman capturing Tabriz and successfully besieging the city of Van. That year, the Safavid capital moved from Tabriz to Qazvin as the state became increasingly centred not on the heartland of Isma'il's initial operations but on the Iranian highlands. As such, the Safavids both posed less of a threat to the Ottomans but were also less easy to conquer. In 1549, the planned-for Ottoman conquest failed, in part because the plan to profit from the revolt of shah Tahmasp's brother, Alqass Mirza, miscarried when the latter was captured. Yet again, strategic planning focused on dynastic possibilities.

Safavid raids led Süleyman to advance into Azerbaijan again in 1554. He was successful at Nakhichevan (1554) and Tabriz (1555), but could not sustain a presence in the face of Safavid scorched-earth tactics, and, instead, had to confirm the existing frontiers in 1555 by the Treaty of Amaysa. The war had shown that the region of Azerbaijan, which repeatedly posed a problem for the slow-moving Ottoman infantry and artillery forces, could be taken in summer advances, only to be retaken by the Safavids when the Ottomans retired during the harsh winter. In particular, the burden of supporting large forces made it difficult to sustain the Ottoman presence. Similarly, Charles V's invasion of Provence in 1536 failed because the French, instead of fighting (other than from ambushes), fortified cities that could be held while denying food to the Imperialists who were reduced to foraging and also suffered from dysentery. After the invasion collapsed, Charles retreated.[18]

Thereafter, peace between the Ottomans and the Safavids continued during the reign of shah Tahmasp I (1524–76), not least because, in 1562, he allowed an Ottoman executioner to kill Süleyman's son Bayezid who had rebelled against his father in 1558 and, after defeat near Konya in 1559, fled to the Safavids. Philip II of Spain faced opposition from his son Charles (Don Carlos), but the latter was not able to mount a rebellion.

The Ottomans

Demonstrating the diversity of the opposition confronted, the range of Ottoman military activities continued to be impressive. While not as far-flung as those of Portugal or Spain, the range of large-scale Ottoman campaigning on land was not matched by any other power. The principal opponents were the Safavids and Habsburgs, and Süleyman, who personally led his army on thirteen campaigns, responded pragmatically to the challenges they posed; but the list of opponents also included Venice, Moldavia, Malta and Portugal, as well as rebellions in the Ottoman lands.

Ottoman strength was based upon the resources of a far-flung empire, especially of Egypt and the Middle East, on an ideology which saw war against the non-believer as a duty, and on a society structured for the effective prosecution of a war; and troops were deployed in accordance with a grand strategy based on a considered analysis of intelligence and policy options[19] and drawing on a formidable and well-articulated logistical system.[20] The most valuable of the regular troops were the *janissaries*, recruited from the *devshirme*, a tribute of children levied in the Balkans. Converts to Islam, they were a trained élite corps, paid from central funds and partly armed with firearms, and their availability lessened the potential independence of the Türkmen cavalry.[21] The *janissaries* achieved levels of military professionalism unmatched in Europe or elsewhere in the Islamic world.

The true value of the *janissaries* lay in the fact that they were a full-time, regular professional force who owed their allegiance solely to the Sultan, as opposed to the traditional feudal and regional troops which made up the bulk of the Ottoman armies. Their discipline, especially when on the march and when in camp, was commented on by numerous Christian observers who witnessed their operations. They were also quick to adopt handheld firearms, and during the siege of Malta (1565) their accuracy with them was considered by the Knights to be superior to those of the Christian troops. In Christian Europe, the cost of maintaining a full-time body of soldiers proved onerous, although the French monarchy tried to establish and maintain the *compagnies d'ordonnance* from the middle of the fifteenth to the middle of the sixteenth centuries. The *janissaries* never wore armour, and this meant they suffered heavy casualties during major siege operations, such as Rhodes (1522), Malta (1565) and Famagusta (1570). However, their administration and organisation of the *devshirme* was such that a steady stream of new recruits was always available in the cadet schools to replenish the combat units, and this ensured that they remained at the core of all Ottoman armies, and to a lesser extent their navies when on campaign.

Süleyman the Magnificent

Having consolidated his eastern frontier in 1534–6, Süleyman responded to Charles V's expedition against Tunis in 1535 and to the outbreak of Ottoman war with Venice in 1536, by planning a joint attack with Francis I of France on Italy in 1537, part of a pattern of attempted co-operation.[22] However, Francis did not act, and Süleyman unsuccessfully besieged the Venetian fortress of Corfu. This campaign showed the value of fortresses and also the vulnerability of Italy, which is close to Corfu. This vulnerability helped focus attention on the Ottoman threat. Failure in the siege led the Ottomans to evacuate the island of Corfu, but, in 1538, the Venetian islands in the Aegean were captured, and the fleet of the Holy League defeated at Prevesa on Greece's west coast. Suffering economically and seeing no prospect of regaining their territories, the Venetians accepted their losses as part of the peace with the Ottomans in 1540. The 1538 campaign was conducted by Hayreddin, 'Barbarossa', whereas Süleyman, that year, invaded Moldavia (modern eastern Romania), annexing the region of Jedisan, including the Black Sea port of Bendery. This conquest created a land route under Ottoman control from Constantinople to the Crimea while driving home the need for obedience to his Moldavian vassal.

In turn, the ambition of Ferdinand of Austria led to war in Hungary, where Ferdinand's effort to become king after the death of Szapolyai in 1540 was opposed by Ottoman forces who supported the appointment of an Ottoman governor-general to central Hungary. Unsuccessful sieges of Buda by Ferdinand's army in 1540, 1541 and 1542 were followed by Süleyman leading his army into Hungary in 1543, capturing a string of fortresses.

Peace between Charles V and Francis I in 1544 ended the co-operation that Süleyman had sought with the latter in mounting a joint attack on Charles. Such an attack was seen as the way to exploit Charles's vulnerability in Italy, and thus to weaken the support his territories there provided for resisting the Ottomans in Hungary and the French both there and in the Low

Countries. However, despite the end of co-operation, the Ottomans were still a formidable challenge on their own, and fresh Ottoman successes against Habsburg fortresses in 1544 underlined the vulnerability of the border, while the scarcity of Hungarian aristocratic support for the Habsburgs also put pressure on Ferdinand who reached an accommodation with Süleyman in 1547, agreeing to pay an annual tribute for the Hungarian territory he continued to rule.

This treaty enabled Süleyman to turn against the Safavids, campaigning in person in 1548 and 1549, but tensions in Europe rose again in 1550, leading to another failed attempt to secure Franco-Ottoman co-operation, as well as to an Ottoman invasion in 1551 of Transylvania (north-west Romania), part of the Hungarian kingdom, that had mixed success. In North Africa, the Ottoman fleet did, however, capture Tripoli, the base of the Knights of St John, that year, which further increased tension in the Mediterranean. Malta, which Charles had also given the Knights in 1530 was, thereafter, their base. Moreover, in 1552, when Charles V faced rebellion in Germany and war with France, the Ottomans made gains in Transylvania and Hungary. This success enabled Süleyman to turn with confidence to war against the Safavids. In turn, the negotiation of peace with the Safavids in 1555 combined with pressure in Hungary, forced Austria to focus on the defence of the eastern frontier at a time when imperial authority was being seriously challenged in Germany.

Süleyman had a number of strategic advantages that assisted his impressive military performance. The central position of Constantinople in the Ottoman empire allowed the maximum use to be made of the extensive road and route system that the Romans and Byzantines had developed. His interior lines of communication along these routes in a geographically homogeneous empire allowed him to switch his point of attack while using the well-established military machinery to mobilise his forces rapidly and efficiently. In contrast, the empire of Charles V was extensive, but had France as a major obstacle in the centre of his dominions, the Alps as a major physical barrier separating its northern from its southern halves, and vital overseas territories in the Americas that could not be ignored as they were critical to the financing of his operations. Like Süleyman, Charles had strong ideological motivations that affected his operational decision making, and he fought against non-believers, heretics and internal rebels and pirates, as did Süleyman. However, Charles lacked the administrative, organisational and military infrastructure to respond rapidly to the widespread threats that he confronted, although these were similar in nature to those confronted by Süleyman. Unlike the Ottoman state, the Habsburg empire was not structured for the successful prosecution of expansionist war, while the culture of international relations within Christendom ensured that Charles's measures were less generally expansionist than those of Süleyman. Given the disparity in capability, it is perhaps surprising that Charles managed to achieve as much as he did.

Meanwhile, rivalry with the Portuguese and a wish to exploit the opportunities created by the replacement of the Mamluk empire led to the occupation of Yemen from 1538, with the acquisition of Aden that year followed by the Yemeni centres of Ta'izz in 1547 and San'a in 1552. The Ottomans also developed their position on the western shore of the Red Sea, supporting garrisons at Suakin and Massawa and intervening in the struggle between Adal and Ethiopia. In 1541, the Portuguese dispatched 400 musketeers to the aid of Ethiopia and, with their aid, the Ethiopians defeated Ahmäd in 1541. He then turned to the Ottomans, who provided him with 900 musketeers and ten cannon with which he defeated his opponents in 1542, killing 200 Portuguese, including their commander, Christopher da Gama. Thus, the conflict in Ethiopia – hitherto, for Europeans, the land of the mythical Prester John – had been integrated with global military relations.

Ahmäd was defeated and killed in 1543 at the battle of Soina-Dega on the shores of Lake Tana. Lebna-Dengel's son and successor, Galawdewos, then reconquered Ethiopia. The Ethiopians rewarded Portuguese musketeers with land in order to retain their services, a variant on the idea of military colonies; and these musketeers and their descendants continued to play an important role into the following century.

The struggle, however, continued. A new Ottoman territorial unit on the Red Sea, the *eyelet* of Habes, established in 1555, was designed to focus resources for the conquest of Ethiopia. Massawa was captured in 1557. An Ottoman invasion of Ethiopia in 1557 was driven back to the coast, but in 1559 Ahmad's nephew, Nūr, led the forces of Adal on a fresh invasion in which the Ethiopians were beaten and Galawdewos killed. External pressure exacerbated divisions within the Ethiopian royal family and élite, and these divisions further encouraged intervention with Bahr Nagash Ishaq, a leading Tigrean noble, proving a key Ottoman ally. In 1562, Ottoman cannon fire helped decide the battle that temporarily determined the conflict over the Ethiopian throne. A renewed Ottoman attempt to dominate northern Ethiopia was defeated in 1579. This southward direction of Ottoman interest tends to be underplayed and, despite concerns with protecting Egypt and the Hejaz, was certainly not central to Ottoman activity. Nevertheless, action around the Red Sea was an important indication of the Ottoman ability to operate in several directions simultaneously.

As a far more minor sphere for operations, the Ottomans also advanced up the Nile valley, although there is relatively little information on the struggle with the Funj kingdom to the south, the rulers of which converted to Islam. The Ottoman frontier moved to the First Cataract on the Nile near Aswan around 1555, and, by the early 1580s, to the Third Cataract. A number of fortresses garrisoned by Bosniak troops marked the advance of Ottoman power, notably Qal'at Sai.

In 1565, the Ottomans, in a major amphibious offensive, failed to conquer Malta, but in 1566 Süleyman, on his last campaign, besieged Szigetvār in southern Transdanubia which had been unsuccessfully besieged a decade earlier. It surrendered two days after he died.[23] The vitality of his military system at the close of his life contrasted both with Charles V's enforced flight from Germany in 1552, and with the difficulties faced by his son Philip II in the Low Countries in 1566 as the Dutch Revolt began.

Selim II, 1566–74

Süleyman's only surviving son, Selim II (r. 1566–74), confronted revolts in Iraq and Yemen and war in Hungary at his accession. His Grand Vezir, and son-in-law, Sokollu Mehmed Pasha, was the key figure and he responded firmly, ending the rebellion by the Marsh Arabs in Iraq, both by displaying force with a river-borne expedition and yet also making the revolt's leader, Ibn 'layyan, governor. Moreover, Yemen was reconquered, although this took a major effort. The rebellion by the Shi'a Zaydis of Yemen was encouraged by oppressive government. The capital, San'a, fell to the rebels in 1566 and was only recaptured in 1568. As with the Duke of Alba in the Low Countries, an outside force in the shape of an army under Koca Sinan Pasha was necessary to restore control, although this took until 1571. In 1569, Aden had sought Portuguese aid against Ottoman reconquest, but the Ottomans acted first and, once they had regained Yemen, made a greater effort on the Ethiopian side of the Red Sea.[24] Meanwhile, in 1568, Sokollu had made peace with Ferdinand of Austria's son, the Emperor Maximilian II.

The following year, an army was sent to dig a canal between the Don and Volga rivers, in order to enable the Ottomans to develop their alliance with the Uzbeks against the Safavids and, more specifically, to counter the Russian annexation of Astrakhan by sending their own fleet there from the Black Sea, and then on to the Caspian Sea in order to act against Iran. The intractability of the task led to the abandonment of the scheme, but an Ottoman–Tatar force reached Astrakhan. However, short of artillery, the siege was soon abandoned, and food and water shortages claimed much of the army on its return journey to Azov. Despite local interest in resuming the canal scheme the following year, it was abandoned, but the scheme indicated the extent to which the Ottoman strategic imagination was not limited by existing constraints.[25] A lack of support from the Crimean Tatars, which had also been a factor in 1569, hit plans for a joint Uzbek–Ottoman attack on Astrakhan in 1587–8, and in 1590 the Ottomans refused to send troops to help in such an attack.[26]

Instead of such operations on the margins of Ottoman power, Venetian-ruled Cyprus was attacked by a large-scale amphibious force in 1570. The conflict there became a campaign of sieges, not battles, with Nicosia captured in 1570 and Famagusta in 1571. In response to the invasion, a league of Venice, Spain and the Papacy defeated the Ottoman fleet at Lepanto in 1571, although this defeat did not prevent the Ottomans from consolidating their position, with Venice accepting the loss of Cyprus as the price of peace in 1573. Moreover, the Ottomans regained Tunis the following year.

The effort devoted to Cyprus contrasted with the Ottoman failure to provide significant support to the unsuccessful *morisco* rising of 1568–71 in the Alpujarras mountains of Granada in southern Spain. After failure at Malta in 1565, the western Mediterranean seemed too remote and difficult to allow a large commitment, and, prior to Cyprus, Selim's forces were busy in Aden and southern Russia. Moreover, Ottoman attempts to intervene in Morocco failed.[27] Yet, too much should not be made of physical distance. Aside from both Aden and southern Russia, the Ottomans had sent a fleet to Indian waters and, in 1577, were to overrun the Fezzan region in inland modern Libya. Distance was most important when it was also an expression of mental horizons. In the Mediterranean, these had expanded in the early decades of the sixteenth century, but closed from the 1570s as the Ottomans turned mostly to concerns close to home. Moreover, the Indian Ocean proved an 'afterthought' and the end of the line for the Ottomans, rather than a new horizon.

The weight to be placed on the military dimension when explaining imperial strength and expansion clearly varied with reference to the strategic situation, notably the need to respond to a number of challenges. For example, Rhoads Murphey has argued that 'it was in the optimisation of available resources rather than in their development of either superior technology or sophisticated battlefield tactics that the Ottomans most distinguished themselves in comparison with their sixteenth-century military rivals'. This is linked by Murphey to a realism in the assessment of what was achievable, such that real limits were understood.[28] At the same time, such assessment was mediated through personal and factional rivalries, as with the assassination in 1579 of Sokollu, who was not enthusiastic about war with the Safavids, and in 1567 of Mahmūd Pasha, the governor of Egypt, allegedly because he had planned to send troops to Yemen to suppress the rebellion, a course opposed by both the military in Egypt and the governor of Yemen.[29]

Charles V

For long, Ottoman expansion had been mirrored by that of the Habsburgs and, indeed, this perception seemed particularly appropriate in the 1540s. The Emperor played a direct role in command. In 1540, he supervised the successful siege of Ghent, while in 1543 he led an army down the Rhine, defeating Duke William of Cleves, a Protestant allied to France, and made him cede sovereignty over the Duchy of Gelderland, thus strengthening the Habsburg position in the Low Countries. In 1544, with a new shake of the kaleidoscopic relationship of the three kings, Charles V and his ally, Henry VIII of England, invaded France, forcing Francis I to accept terms with the Treaty of Crépy; while, in 1546, Habsburg forces were directed against the Schmalkaldic League of German Protestants.

At Mühlberg aside the River Elbe, far distant from Spain and Italy, the following year, Charles V in person at the head of 51,000 troops defeated and captured John Frederick, Elector of Saxony, the leading German Protestant prince. The League forces had destroyed the bridge across the Elbe, but the Imperialists both built a temporary bridge and found a ford. Crossing the river, they launched a surprise attack on the unprepared League forces.

This victory, and the campaign as a whole, were greatly helped by rivalries within the Protestant camp, notably between John Frederick, the head of the Ernestine branch of the Wettin family, and Landgrave Philip of Hesse, who was also the father-in-law of Charles's ally, Duke Maurice of Saxony, the representative of the Albertine branch of the Wettin family which was a rival of John Frederick's Ernestine branch. As a result of Mühlberg, Charles transferred the electorate from John Frederick to Maurice, who was called the 'Judas of Meissen' by fellow-Protestants. Despite the efforts of France, the Ottomans, and the German Protestants, Christian Europe was dominated by the Habsburgs.

Yet, Charles continued to face major challenges. In the face of his military successes in Germany, the princes of the Holy Roman Empire, led by the Catholic dukes of Bavaria, in 1547 threw out Charles's proposal for a league of all the states within the Empire, a measure that would have underlined the Imperial position and provided support against foreign opponents. Moreover, the Augsburg Interim of 1548, a measure proposed to the Imperial Diet by Charles for a temporary settlement of religious differences in the Empire that would safeguard the Catholic position, was widely ignored. In addition, in 1552, Charles was successfully challenged by a new rebellion by Protestant princes, including now Maurice of Saxony, a rebellion backed by a French invasion. Charles was driven from Germany and Henry II of France left with territorial gains, in the shape of the prince bishoprics of

Metz, Toul and Verdun to the east of France. Charles's unsuccessful siege of Metz with an army of 48,000 troops was a key episode in the conflict. His artillery, about fifty siege cannon, breached the city's walls, but the French had constructed new defences within them, and the harsh winter proved deadly for Charles's army, leading him to abandon the siege, not least when his main mine had been countermined by the French.

The crisis was resolved in 1555 when the Peace of Augsburg recognised Lutheranism, the leading German Protestant faith, as a confession, allowing Lutheran territorial rulers within the Empire to make Lutheranism the religion of their territories. Moreover, the nature of the settlement was important for, far from the terms of the settlement being a privilege and the Emperor granting a religious peace that re-created harmony, this settlement was the product of hard bargaining at a Diet, and set the basis for decades of contention that would challenge Imperial authority and political cohesion.

Compromise was the tone in Charles's last years in Germany, but in Italy and the Low Countries his heir there, his son Philip II of Spain, faced a revival in conflict in 1557–8. The Italian Wars were resumed when the French, backed by the anti-Habsburg Pope Paul IV, invaded Naples. However, that year, Spanish forces under Ferdinand, 3rd Duke of Alba defeated the Papal army, forcing Paul IV to terms; while the French in the Low Countries were defeated at St Quentin (10 August 1557) and Gravelines (13 July 1558), the Spaniards making effective use of mounted pistoleers in both battles, although in 1558 the French captured Calais, the last English position in mainland France. On 2 April of the following year, at Cateau-Cambrésis, Henry II of France accepted terms that confirmed Spanish dominance of Italy. He died in a jousting accident soon after, leaving France without a strong ruler. At the same time, the cost of the wide-ranging war with France had placed a major financial strain on the dominions of Philip II, a strain that was to contribute to political breakdown in the Low Countries in the 1560s.

Christendom

More generally, there was a contrast between the caution and respect for traditions and established political structures displayed by Charles even when most successful, and the processes of expansion characteristic of the contemporary Ottomans, Safavids and Mughals. In practice, they co-operated with some existing interests, the Mughals, for example, with the Rajputs. Nevertheless, the Ottomans, Safavids and Mughals were also more able than Charles to push through change in their core areas of control, not least because they were less constrained by law. In addition, the monarchs of these dynasties were able to benefit from rulership cults that gave them semi-sacral authority alongside an imperial pomp linked to the obedience of those who benefited from a practice of hereditary imperial service.

In contrast, the rulers of Christian Europe compromised far more with existing interests and ruled by virtue of, and through, systems of privilege, rights and law that protected others as well as themselves. The nature of political culture was clearly important to this situation, but so also were the circumstances of power and the legacy of war, notably the extent to which authority did not generally rest on a process of conquest in which the existing order was swept away. Authority and power, moreover, were gravely limited in Christian Europe by religious differences stemming from the Protestant Reformation as the apparently crucial character of these differences made it difficult to compromise, and, in particular, introduced a major ideological barrier to the renewal of Papal and Imperial authority. This barrier undermined the prospects for the strengthening of power flowing from contingent events, most prominently, first, the discovery of large quantities of exploitable silver in the New World territories of Spain; and, secondly, the Ottoman advance which offered the possibility of rallying support around the Emperor as well as providing the Habsburgs with the opportunity to grasp the crowns of Bohemia and Hungary.

Wars of Religion

There were also more specific crises in Western Christendom after the Peace of Augsburg in 1555 and the end of the Italian Wars with the Peace of Cateau-Cambrésis in 1559, especially the Wars of Religion that affected much of Europe, most notably France, the Low Countries and the British Isles. In France, the Low Countries, England, Ireland and Scotland, rebellion was linked to religious disaffection, although other factors also played a role, particularly tensions within the élite. Charles V's inheritance in the Low Countries, Spain, Italy and the New World, descended to his son, Philip II of Spain, and he was affected by religious disaffection most clearly in Spain and the Low Countries. In the former, an Islamic rising in Granada in 1568 was brutally suppressed, with large numbers of the *moriscos* slaughtered. This suppression was an instance of brutal counter-insurgency conflict,[30] a form of warfare that does not tend to attract much attention for this period. It was also waged, over a longer period, by the English in Ireland.

In the Low Countries, Philip's unpopular religious and fiscal policies and his neglect of the Dutch nobility led to riots in 1566–7, to an enforced change in Spanish policy, in August 1567, and then to the arrival of a powerful Spanish army, 10,000-strong, under the Duke of Alba. This Army of

Flanders imposed control and defeated attempts to challenge the new order from abroad, notably with Alba's crushing victory at Jemmingen on 21 July 1568 of an army under Louis of Nassau that was foolishly deployed with its back to the River Ems. On 20 October 1568, Alba went on the defeat Louis's elder brother, William, Prince of Orange, known as William the Silent. The Spanish Army of Flanders had an effective organisational structure and was a professional force, well disciplined on the battlefield, and characterised by a meritocratic ethos in which aristocratic background was no substitute for expertise.[31]

The control that was reimposed, in the face of continuing guerrilla-style opposition from the 'Wood Beggars', was authoritarian and fairly brutal, with over 1000 people executed and about 60,000 going into exile. Such conduct certainly made scant concession to the local political culture and, in particular, to the role of consent in the shape of consulting local Estates (parliaments). Moreover, the arrival of the army created problems. On the one hand, the army promised order and control, as it seemed able to suppress local opposition and outside attack, but, on the other hand, the need to support it financially posed a serious fiscal strain on the local government and population and weakened political backing for Philip's rule.

It was in this context, that, in 1572, Alba had to turn to the French border to deal with a threatened French attack and an actual invasion under Louis of Nassau, who seized the fortress of Mons in May. This focus for Alba, who regained Mons in September, provided a window of opportunity in which the 'Sea Beggars', a rebel fleet of Dutch privateers, seized the Zeeland towns of Brill and Flushing in April. In turn, the threat of French attack was ended by the killing of the Huguenot (Protestant) leaders in France in the St Bartholomew's Day Massacre on the night of 23–24 August as King Charles IX turned against them. This event provided an instance of the relationship of developments in different countries, as, freed from the risk of French intervention, Alba was able to re-establish Spanish power over most of the Low Countries. He did so in a brutal fashion. The slaughter of civilians, for example cutting the throats of the population of the town of Zutphen, led many other towns to surrender. However, Alba was delayed by a siege of the fortified city of Haarlem from December 1572 to July 1573 (after the surrender of which about 2000 troops had their throats cut in cold blood) and, short of money and ships, he was unable successfully to contest coastal waters or to regain Zeeland.

Alba was recalled in 1573, and under his replacement, Luis de Requeséns, the Army of Flanders reached a peak strength of over 80,000 men in 1574. The Army retained its battlefield superiority, destroying, under Sancho d'Avila, Louis of Nassau's army at Mookerheyde on 14 April, and killing both him and his brother Henry. However, the coastal regions proved far harder to control. Indeed, the Dutch starved the Spanish garrison in the Zeeland town of Middleburg into surrender in February 1574, while the siege of the town of Leiden in the province of Holland from May to October ended when the Dutch breached the dykes, flooding the region and forcing the Spaniards to retreat. Unable to suppress the rebellion and close to bankruptcy (which occurred in September 1575), Philip II moved to negotiate. In turn, the crisis in finances and army support led in November 1576 to a mutiny in which Antwerp, the entrepôt of the Low Countries, was sacked, with the killing of many civilians, a step that discredited Spanish rule.

Spanish failure serves as a reminder of the interrelationship of conflict and politics, the need to move from outputs, in the shape of military achievements, to outcomes, in the form of political settlement. If Philip II found this move very difficult in the Low Countries, he was scarcely alone among rulers, and this element needs to be integrated more consistently into military history. Ideas of ensuring peace through limited religious toleration, as advocated by the *politiques* in France, in England under Elizabeth I, and by the Warsaw Confederation of 1573 in Poland, were unacceptable to Philip, a ruler who saw his orthodoxy as simultaneously a providential, dynastic, political and personal necessity. In 1577, Philip, nevertheless, eventually accepted the compromise terms of the Pacification of Ghent of 1576, but in 1577 this compromise broke down, with Don John, the victor of Lepanto, now Governor General from November 1576, capturing the town of Namur and the Estates General turning to the rebel leader, William, Prince of Orange.

Spain was more successful in the New World, with the initial conquest stage followed by widespread expansion in Central and South America, alongside resistance that limited this expansion, notably in Chile and northern Mexico. The two factors are discussed in Chapter 7, but mention here serves to underline the variety of military environments confronted by the major powers. The same was true of the Portuguese in Morocco, sub-Saharan Africa and around the Indian Ocean, and of the Russians, who, under Ivan IV, Ivan the Terrible (r. 1533–84), fought Swedes, Poles and Crimean Tatars, and were far more successful at the expense of Kazan and Astrakhan, which again is considered in Chapter 7. In conquering Kazan, firepower, in the shape of Russian cannon, was crucial, but so also was an appropriate strategy as well as the adroit exploitation of divisions among the Muslims.

Yet, on the world scale, it was also divisions among the Christians that became much more apparent in this period; inviting the counterfactual question of what would have happened but for the Protestant Reformation. The Hispanic world would have been more powerful both had there been no Dutch Revolt and had Philip II's alignment with England under his wife, the Catholic Mary Tudor (r. 1553–8), been maintained under her Protestant successor, Elizabeth I (r. 1558–1603). Instead, she settled for spinsterhood after rejecting a proposal from Philip II and consideration of marriage with, among others, a French prince.

The scholarly focus in military history for the late sixteenth century is on the Dutch Revolt, with valuable discussion both of the proficiency of the Spanish army and military system,[32] and of the Dutch role in the early stages of the military changes subsequently referred to as the Military Revolution. As with the Christian conflict with the Ottomans, however, this approach can lead to an underplaying of 'war' in the largest sense, including the battlefields of religious activity, education, publications, censorship, marriage, the household and poor relief. To use a modern distinction, the conflict was as much about soft power as hard power, and it is no accident that the Society of Jesus, or Jesuits, was established by Ignatius Loyola in 1534 as a quasi-military Catholic order. Nor is it surprising that clerics were slaughtered by both sides in the Low Countries and France, and that worshippers were intimidated, if not killed. Image-breaking was important to the process of gaining control over churches which Protestants used to establish their position as in the Dutch cities of Utrecht and Nijmegen in 1578 and 1579, respectively. In this respect, the Wars of Religion may look like a prefiguration of the ideological struggles of the twentieth century, for example between Fascism and both liberalism and Communism, or between Communism and liberalism; although the Wars of Religion also sat in a tradition of the violent extirpation of Christian heresy seen, for example, in the crusade against the Albigensians in southern France in the early thirteenth century and the Hussite wars in Bohemia in the early fifteenth.

Crucial to all religious conflict, as, to a different extent, with that between Safavids and Ottomans, was a degree of popular engagement which is not captured by the customary emphasis on conventional warfare by regular forces. This problem is more pronounced if the emphasis is on the Military Revolution, which, like so many accounts of military developments, is top-down, focusing on the governmental role in tactics, force structure, fortification and policy. Instead, of this account, a narrative of much of the French Wars of Religion from 1562 to 1598, or the Dutch Revolt, or the successful opposition to Mary, Queen of Scots, or the unsuccessful Northern Rising by Catholics against Elizabeth I of England in 1569, captures a situation in which direct popular action played a prominent role, including in the form of riots and massacres, while military forces were created by churches and aristocrats able to elicit popular support, which was true, in France and the Low Countries, of both Protestants and Catholics.[33]

More generally, concern about popular action, and indeed of opposition as a whole, led governments to seek to destroy the fortifications of real or potential domestic opponents and to erect their own.[34] The capture of Granada in 1492 was followed by the establishment of a Spanish garrison and citadel. After Pope Paul III suppressed a revolt in the city of Perugia in the Papal States against the salt tax, he built a citadel there; while Pier Luigi, Duke of Parma (r. 1545–7) built a citadel at Piacenza as part of a campaign to establish his power that also saw moves against the castles of the aristocracy. This unwelcome campaign led to his assassination. Cosimo de'Medici, ruler of Tuscany from 1537 until 1574, built three citadels around Florence, each under the command of a non-Florentine. This overawing of the city was important to the consolidation of his power and, in 1569, Cosimo became the first Grand Duke of Tuscany. Moves against the fortifications and weapons stores of autonomous towns and nobles limited the military capability outside royal and princely hands, but, at the same time, rulers needed the military support of these bodies, both against foreign rulers and against domestic opposition.

Publications

Publications served to spread knowledge about religious warfare, and thus sustained a sense of crisis and division. For example, Frans Hogenberg's vivid engravings of the Dutch Revolt, depicting scenes such as the massacre by the Spaniards of nearly all the population, including women and children in the town of Naarden in December 1572, were swiftly published in Germany. Publications also recorded and encouraged the process by which a self-conscious method of rational analysis was applied in Western discussion of warfare and weaponry. Thus, Paolo Giovio combined narrative with comments about military matters, emphasising, in his discussion of the Schmalkaldic War (1546–7), the importance of drill and praising the *landsknechte* (German pikemen) for their discipline. His Italian original was translated into German as *Eine warhafftige Beschreyhung aller namhafftigen Geschichten* (Basle, 1560). When Thomas Morgan returned to England, having served with the ill-fated expedition to the Low Countries in 1572, he produced an illustrated account, which showed in considerable detail the tactics and difficulties of operating in such a water-girt landscape. Morgan was subsequently to serve for many years in the Low Countries, as well as fighting in Ireland.

The prevalence of conflict helps explain the cultural and intellectual significance of warfare. Subjects and themes from war played a central role in culture, from ballads to engravings, and were also crucial to the iconography of power, as rulers sought to establish their prestige through victory and to lay claim to the successes of their forbears. Victories were depicted in a heroic light, with the emphasis on leaders, as in Bassano's painting *Charles VIII recovers the Crown of Naples*, produced in 1585–90.

The intellectual significance of warfare reflected the attempt to apply knowledge in order to solve its problems. The best way to organise defences and to use cannon were clear instances. Thus, Girolamo Cattaneo (d. *c.* 1584), who settled in the Venetian city of Brescia in 1550, teaching military matters, and who was consulted by Vespasiano Gonzaga concerning the transformation of the fortress of Sabbioneta into a town, also wrote a number of works, published in Brescia, including *Opera Nuova di Fortificare, Offendere, et Difendere* (1564) and *Nuovo Ragionamento del fabricare le fortezze; si per prattica, come per theorica* (1571). Cattaneo's works were frequently reprinted.

The emphasis on novelty was important in his works and those of many others, as was the complementing of theory by practice. Thus, Girolamo Ruscelli's *Precetti della Militia Moderna*, a work dealing in large part with artillery, mines and rockets, was published in Venice in 1568, with another edition following in 1572. These emphases reflected particular characteristics of Western thought. The concern with fortifications could be seen in works such as *I Quattro Primi Libri di Architettura* (Venice, 1569) by the architect and mathematician Pietro Cataneo, who also wrote on firearms; *Discorsi di Fortificationi* by Carlo Teti (Rome, 1569); and *Delle Fortificationi* (Venice, 1575) by Galasso Alghisi, the architect to the Duke of Ferrara, a work dedicated to Emperor Maximilian II. Antonio Lupicini published his *Architettura Militare* in Florence in 1582, following with a *Discorsi Militari* in 1587.

The place and impact of such works were shown in their reprinting and the role of their authors in military activity. Teti, whose work was published in a greatly expanded form in 1575, had this expanded version republished, including in Venice in 1588 and 1589. Italian-born, he spent much of his career in Munich, a centre of Counter-Reformation activity, where he taught the art of war to the future Duke, then Elector, Maximilian of Bavaria (r. 1598–1651), a key figure in the Thirty Years War, not least as head of the Catholic League. Thus, Italian military influences accompanied the Counter-Reformation. Similarly, Lupicini, a military architect and engineer, also worked north of the Alps, in his case in Vienna.

Education was seen as an important product of the world of print. This education was designed both for established soldiers and for the 'young soldiers' who were the target of Thomas Styward's *The Pathway to Martial Discipline* (1581), a work copiously illustrated with battle plans. *A Brief Discourse of War, with his opinions concerning some part of Martial Discipline* (1590), by Sir Roger Williams, was based on his extensive service in the Low

Countries, which, from 1589, was followed by service in France. The book was dedicated to Robert, 2nd Earl of Essex, his patron in the early 1590s and commander of the English force besieging Rouen in 1590.

Entrepreneurial opportunities also emerged, as in Venice where the publisher Giolito and the entrepreneurial editor Tommaso Porcacchi produced a *collana* (necklace) or group of works on war, which included Domenico Mora's *Il Soldato* (1570), and three works by Bernardino Rocca: *Imprese, Stratagemi, et Errori Militari* (1566), *Governo Della Militia* (1570) and *Discorsi di Guerra* (1582). Widespread interest in such works was shown by the publication of two different French translations of the first of Rocca's works in Paris in 1571. War was very much part of the knowledge economy and system, yielding profit.[35]

Italy was the centre of publication on war, with the Venetian cities, such as Brescia, proving particularly active. Thus, 1568 saw the publication in Venice of Camillo Agrippa's *Trattato di Scienza d'Arme* and Achille Marozzo's *Arte dell' Armi*. Giulio Ferretti's *De Re et Disciplina Militari* followed in 1575, and Alessandro Capobianco's *Corona e Palma Militare di Artegliera* in 1598. *Della Fortificatione delle città* by Girolamo Maggi and Giacomo Castriotto was published in Venice in 1583, while Buonaiuto Lorino, a Florentine who designed fortifications for Venice, France and Spain, published *Le Fortificationi* in Venice in 1596.

The number of Italian authors is a reflection of the highly fortified nature of the Italian cities, and also the Venetian investment in fortifications in its Mediterranean colonies and outposts, notably Cyprus. In addition, Italian cities such as Ferrara and Milan were early leaders in gun founding and armaments production.

Italy, however, was not alone. Thus, the first book printed in Chaumont in France was Joseph Boillot's *Modèles artifices du jeu et divers instruments de guerre avec les moyés de s'en prevaloir* (1598). Boillot, who served in the army of Henry IV, was responsible for its supply of saltpetre, a vital ingredient in gunpowder. Leonhard Fronsperger's *Kriegsbuch* was published in Frankfurt in 1573. Works on fortification and artillery involved a commitment to mathematics, as firing lines and ballistics became central issues, which led to interest in employing theorems in practical works, as in Thomas Digges's *Stratioticos* (1579). Print permitted the ready transmission of images as well as text, while translations and the use of parallel texts also spread knowledge. Thus, the Italian Agostino Ramelli, who moved to France in 1551 and worked for Henry, Duke of Anjou, later Henry III, published his designs for warfare and hydraulics in *Le Diverse et Artificiose Machine* (Paris, 1588), a work with a parallel text in French and Italian. A German translation followed in 1620.

Conclusions

With the exception of China, reference to contemporary debate about war in this period tends to focus on Western Europe. Yet, there is also instructive evidence of discussion elsewhere. Thus, in 1547, Sahib Giray, the khan of the Crimean Tatars, advised his ally and overlord, Süleyman the Magnificent, that the large armies used by the latter against the Safavids were less useful than a reliance on smaller, more mobile, forces. Such forces were easier to support logistically, and thus less of a pressure on local resources, as well as less expensive, and also better able to fix and fight the Safavids who used similar forces. This advice, however, was not followed, and, although the high-cost methods of the Ottomans helped lead to territorial gains, there was no commensurate ability to support and sustain them.[36]

From the perspective of the time, it is unclear that the advice was flawed even though it clashed with the focus in the modern scholarly literature on the development of large professional infantry forces. Looked at differently, professionalism had very different meaning in particular contexts. A parallel argument to that of Sahib Giray was provided by those Western commanders who sought to use tactics of mobility and surprise in order to break free from protracted and expensive siege-centred warfare.[37]

The counterpart to the argument that large infantry forces backed by artillery posed serious operational problems because of the burden of support,[38] thus limiting, for example, the effectiveness of Ottoman campaigning against the Safavids, was provided by the problems created by the deployment of cannon at sea. What appears again to be a clear instance of enhanced effectiveness can be seen as more complex, not least because, to carry cannon, and then to increase the number of cannon carried, galleys had to become bigger and stronger, which meant larger crew and therefore the need to carry more provisions at a time of rising food prices. The resulting increase in both the construction and running cost and the logistical burden of galley warfare challenged its viability.[39] A larger number of cannon on sailing ships entailed requirements for shot, gunpowder and crew able to act as gunners, but, conversely, reduced the requirement for soldiers. The development of the galeass by the Venetians can be seen as a way of compensating for a lack of manpower by increasing firepower.

Moreover, the non-linear character of military activity, the succession of different challenges, was to be demonstrated in the closing decades of the century, as Spain turned from conflict with the Ottomans to take the leading role in the Wars of Religion within Western Europe, while China, with its relations with the Mongols settled, became newly active in support of Korea as an opponent of a united Japan. There was also a large-scale war between Ottomans and Safavids that took the Ottoman empire to its greatest extent. These conflicts in part drew on the developments of the period 1535–75, but, in each case, the tempo of politics and international conflict also differed greatly from the earlier situation.

5 Conflict, 1575–1600

The closing quarter-century saw both conflict between empires, and warfare at a smaller scale. Some of the conflict took familiar form, notably that between the Ottomans and the Safavids, the Ottomans and Austria, and the Safavids and the Uzbeks; but there was also the unexpected in the shape of a large-scale Japanese invasion of Korea that led to Chinese intervention and to conflict between Chinese and Japanese forces. As far as the other major populated areas were concerned, Mughal consolidation and expansion in northern India continued, while the Deccan sultanates in central India were unable to sustain their success of the 1560s against the rival Hindu state of Vijayanagar to the south. In Africa, a Portuguese invasion was crushed in Morocco which subsequently sent an expeditionary force across the Sahara that defeated the Songhai empire, greatly altering the politics of the western *sahel*. Christian Europe was increasingly divided as the Wars of Religion spread, while a new focus of international conflict came to be more significant as warfare involving Denmark, Sweden, Russia and Poland became both larger in scale and more important for European trade patterns. Although far from a complete list, this introduction gives some indication of the continued primacy of conflict, as well as of the impossibility of reducing it to any pattern.

Ottoman–Safavid Conflict

The reign of Murad III (1574–95) saw a revival of Ottoman bellicosity which had been relatively subdued under his father, Selim II, in part because the Grand Vezir, Sokollu Mehmed Pasha, had favoured caution, negotiating peace with Emperor Maximilian II, the ruler of Austria, in 1568 and opposing the invasion of Cyprus in 1570. In turn, Sokollu did not support Murad's attempt to exploit Safavid instability following both the deaths of shahs Tahmasb and Isma'il II, in 1576 and 1577, respectively, and, in 1578, renewed attacks from the Uzbeks on Iran.

In 1578, however, claiming that the Safavids had broken the Treaty of Amasya of 1555, Murad ordered the conquest of the province of Shirvan on the Caspian Sea, a long-standing region in dispute. That year, his general, Lala Mustafa Pasha, achieved impressive successes, despite the logistical strains of supplying the invading army. The Safavids were defeated at Cildir, the submission of local rulers in the Caucasus was obtained, the city of Tbilisi was captured, and Shirvan was conquered.

Sokollu was assassinated in 1579, reprising a pattern frequently seen with Ottoman ministers and commanders, and the Ottoman war party came to the fore. Nevertheless, the year also saw a Safavid counter-attack which was helped by the extent to which Ottoman intervention in the complex politics of the Caucasus had resulted both in winning allies and in making enemies of their rivals. The Safavids besieged both Derbend and Tbilisi. However, the sieges failed, with both positions relieved, the first after the khan of the Crimea had marched from the Kuban along the north side of the Caucasus mountain chain, a dramatic episode of power-projection. Yet, Safavid pressure was maintained and, although the Ottomans held their strongholds of Derbend and Tbilisi, lesser positions were taken by the Safavids in 1581–2. Moreover, the Ottomans lost local support, which compounded the problem of holding the strongholds.

Nevertheless, in 1583, in a four-day battle at Meshale on the River Sana, the Ottomans defeated the Safavid–Daghestani attempt to drive them from Shirvan. Victory, in turn, led to a shift in the fortune of war, encouraging local rulers to transfer allegiance, with the Georgian prince, Simon Khan, turning to the Ottomans in 1583. Furthermore, the Ottomans occupied the city of Erivan in 1583, and Tabriz in 1585 after a victory at Sufian. The Ottomans built a large fortress in Tabriz, but the difficulty of fixing victory was shown by the need of its garrison to resist an 11-month Safavid siege, followed by further Safavid attacks. Defections by the rulers of Meskhetian and Georgia were overcome by the Ottomans in 1587, and Georgia was brought under greater Ottoman control. Moreover, Uzbek pressure on the new shah of Iran, Abbas I (r. 1587–1629), enabled the Ottomans to make major gains in 1588, gains that reflected the range of their operations. Thus, their commander in the north, Ferhad Pasha, seized Gänjä, an important Safavid position in Shirvan, while, from Baghdad further south, an expedition captured Nihavend.

Under this pressure, in 1590, Abbas felt obliged to negotiate a peace, which gave the Ottomans what they had conquered in Azerbaijan, the Caucasus, and western Iran. As a result, the Ottoman empire reached its greatest extent territorially, at the same time that Spain's reconquest of much of the Low Countries, initially successful intervention in the French Wars of Religion, ability to thwart the English attacks on Portugal and the Spanish New World, and dominance of Italy, all suggested that it was also approaching an apex of power.

Iran

Abbas was not to resume hostilities with the Ottomans until 1603, when he began a series of victorious campaigns that had led him, by 1606, to regain all the territory lost in 1578–90. In the meanwhile, Abbas was focused on the Uzbeks. Abd Allah Sultan, the Uzbek leader, an ally of the Ottomans, made the last real attempt to unite Transoxiana and conquer a wider area, seizing Balkh, Samarqand and Badakhshan, the last conquered in 1585. In 1589, moreover, the Uzbeks captured Herat and advanced on the city of Meshed in north-east Iran. Six years later, under Uzbek pressure, the Safavid governor of Kandahar turned the province over to the Mughal ruler, Akbar, which was an aspect of the latter's consolidation of his vulnerable Afghan frontier, a consolidation that included a settlement with the Uzbeks. There was no sense that any Uzbek advance into Iran would stop, indeed there was no physical border to limit this advance, and this concern led Abbas to end the war with the Ottomans in 1590, which offers an instructive prioritisation for military historians who tend to underplay the Uzbeks and to focus on powers that fought the Christian Europeans, notably the Ottomans.

Abbas devoted considerable attention to improving his army, an attempt that focused more on organisation than technology, although the latter played a role. He transformed a largely tribal military into an army, and did so in order to increase both success in war and political stability. The late 1570s and 1580s saw acute instability in the Safavid empire as the Qizilbash tribal confederation, on which Safavid power rested, was affected by a civil war that was related to disputes in the ruling dynasty. Tahmasp's death in May 1576 had been followed by civil strife, including the murder of Prince Haidar, and the slaughter by Isma'il II of his brothers. Isma'il's successor, Muhammad Khudabanda (r. 1578–87), had only limited interest in ruling and was weak, and in the 1580s conflict among the tribes again became serious.

Once he had seized power in a coup in 1587, overthrowing the shah, Abbas removed the most troublesome tribal amirs, before changing the confederation by bringing in non-Qizilbash tribal elements, including for example Kurds. This policy, which Abbas did not begin, had an impact comparable to the Mughal recruitment of Rajput support and was important in strengthening the Safavid state so that it was better able to fight lengthy wars.

Abbas also sought to develop a strong, centrally controlled force based on Caucasian military slaves (*ghulams*). This force included, by the end of the century, a 12,000-strong corps of artillerymen with about 500 cannon, as well as a corps of 12,000 musketeers, but, rather than solely mentioning these and thus focusing on firepower, it is important to note that there was also a corps of 13,000 royal squires, mostly Muslim converts, who fought as cavalry, and that many of the *ghulams* used traditional weapons. In 1598,

when Abbas defeated the probably slightly larger army of the Uzbeks at
Rabát-i Pariyán, the battle was decided by an old-fashioned charge by
Abbas's mounted bodyguard, led by the shah himself. This victory gave
Abbas control of the city of Herat. The previous year, he had retaken
Meshed further west.

Abbas's victory in 1598, which regained the key region of Khurāsān for
the Safavids, was important to Uzbek failure, although the Uzbeks were
also affected by pressure from the north-west by the Kazaks, another
steppe people, including an advance on Tashkent in 1586, as well as the
death of Abd Allah, which led to Uzbek divisions. Operational factors were
also significant to Abbas's effectiveness. Mobility was seen in successful
forced marches, while he proved better able than the Ottomans to maintain
troops in the field during the winter.

At the same time, the matrix of constraints produced by distance,
terrain, logistics and costs affected Abbas, as in 1602 when he marched on
Balkh with 40,000 troops, including 10,000 musketeers and about 300
cannon, a larger field force than those in Western Europe at that period. In
the event, a lack of provisions and water caused problems that led Abbas
to a humiliating retreat,[1] with most of his cannon lost. Aside from being
outmanoeuvred in 1602 by the Uzbek leader, Baqi Muhammad khan, Abbas
suffered from the lack of any equivalent to the logistical support system
enjoyed by the Chinese military, although, alongside resources, communication and administrative skill and experience, the effectiveness of the latter
owed much to the Chinese focus on the defensive. Thus, the Ming lacked
the capability for power projection onto the steppe that was to be shown
from the 1690s by their Manchu successors. The size of the Safavid military, and the inclusion by the 1600s of a significant infantry and artillery,
increased the operational strain posed by its campaigning, making it more
similar to the Ottoman army.

India

Abbas was initially less successful in regaining Kandahar than Khurāsān,
and did not do so until 1618, which reflected the greater strength of Mughal
India under Akbar compared to the Uzbek state. Mughal expansion
continued under Akbar, notably, after an abortive revolt in 1581 by his half-
brother, Muhammad Hakim, who invaded north-west India only to retreat
in the face of Akbar's large army. Akbar defeated Hakim outside Kabul,
but allowed him to retain his throne. Hakim's death in 1585 and the Uzbek
conquest of Badakshan led Akbar to occupy Kabul in 1585. The region of
Kashmir was conquered in 1585–9, Sind in 1574–93, Kāthāwār in 1572–92
and Orissa in 1590–2. The process was frequently difficult for the Mughals,

with allegiance obtained and provinces annexed, only for uprisings to follow. Once suppressed, these rebellions led to pacification, as in Orissa, in Bengal, where uprisings and pacification continued until 1587, and in Khandesh, where submission in 1577 was followed by rebellion in 1599, and then by conquest and annexation in 1600–1.

To the south, Mughal rivalry with the sultanate of Ahmadnagar focused on the sultanate of Barar, conquered and annexed by Ahmadnagar in 1572–4. This rivalry led to a Mughal intervention that included an invasion of Ahmadnagar in 1596, ending in the cession of Barar to Akbar that year. Akbar, however, felt it necessary to command in person against Ahmadnagar and Khandesh in 1599–1601. Despite the opposition to Akbar, Mughal ability, supported by the effective use of cannon and handguns, to operate successfully across a range of frontier zones was impressive, while there were no serious rebellions in the central area of control. Other rulers would have been very happy with Akbar's achievements.

South-East Asia

Akbar's achievement certainly surpassed that of Burma which, having put a puppet king on the throne of the Thai kingdom of Aynuthia, faced a Thai rebellion from 1584. In 1593, a Burmese attempt to reimpose control failed. Moreover, it proved impossible to sustain the Burmese war effort. The demands of the Burmese army had placed too great a burden on economy and society, leading villagers to flee and hitting the ability to recruit. Burmese failure was followed by a successful Thai invasion of Burma. The Thais made major territorial gains and, in 1599, the Burmese government collapsed. In practice, distance, logistics, and resilient political cultures combined to ensure that it was difficult for states based in Burma or Thailand to subjugate the other for any length of time, which matched the experience of rival states based in Iran and the Near East. Meanwhile, in Dai Viet (northern Vietnam), the ruling house was overthrown in 1592 and the previous house restored.

War in the Far East

The situation in the Far East was also suggestive, as neither Japan nor China were able to impose a military solution on the other. Their respective political position, however, changed greatly in the 1580s and 1590s, as a result of the unification of Japan. Oda Nobunaga, who had achieved much in this direction in the key political and economic region, central Japan, was forced by Akechi Mitsuhide, a rival general, to commit suicide in 1582, and the succession to his position was disputed. One of Nobunaga's protégés, Toyotomi Hideyoshi, rapidly defeated Mitsuhide before fighting another major commander, Shibata Katsuie, the following year. As with Nobunaga, Hideyoshi's mobility was a key feature in these campaigns, which led in 1583 to the suicide of Katsuie during the battle of Shizugatake. In 1584, Hideyoshi fought another major commander, Tokugawa Ieyasu, but he was unable to out-general him or to win the battles of Komaki or Nagakute. Instead, peace was agreed, with Ieyasu responding to the larger size of Hideyoshi's army. Ieyasu became a vassal.

In 1585, Hideyoshi pressed on to conquer the areas of Kishu, Shikoku and Hokuriku, while, in 1587, a successful amphibious invasion was mounted of the island of Kyushu, the southern one of the main islands of Japan. There, as at Shizugatake, firepower led to a stress on defensive tactics: in Kyushu, Hideyoshi's forces were deployed behind entrenchments. Finally, in 1590, Hideyoshi, with 15,000 troops, attacked the Hojo who controlled the eastern part of the main island, Honshu. Hideyoshi's long-standing success in siegecraft was seen with the fall of Odawara and the other Hojo fortresses, and the Hojo surrendered. Cannon became more important from the 1580s, but Hideyoshi's success in sieges owed much also to other factors, notably the use of entrenchments to divert the water defences offered by lakes and rivers, these entrenchments threatening fortresses with flooding by rising waters, or with the loss of the protection by water features on which many in part relied.

Japan was now largely united, with a successful campaign in 1591 bringing the north-east under control. Already, in 1588, after the Shimazu clan had been defeated in southern Kyushu, Hideyoshi had demanded the surrender of all weapons held by farmers. This monopolisation of the means of violence was matched by the policy of systematically destroying the fortifications of defeated rivals.

Hideyoshi then decided to conquer China, an invasion that would provide new lands and tasks for his warriors and enable him to keep his control over them. Continual success had led Hideyoshi to lose a sense of limits while the cult of the warrior, anyway, discouraged an interest in limits. He planned to advance via Korea, a Chinese client state, and to rule the world from the Chinese city of Ningbo. From there, Hideyoshi intended to conquer India. He also demanded that Taiwan and the Philippines submit to him, an ambition that reflected his maritime hopes. In 1593, Hideyoshi was to press for equal status with the Wanli emperor of China (r. 1573–1620), which was a major challenge to Chinese views of the world. He wished to be invested with the title of King of the Ming as a way to legitimate his seizure of power in Japan, as well as to receive the privileges of tribute trade.[2]

Hideyoshi, however, had exceeded his grasp. Korea refused to transfer its allegiance to Japan, while the Wanli emperor had no intention of heeding his demands. A Japanese invasion of Korea, with about 168,000 men, mounted on 23 May 1592, was initially successful, helped by a weak resistance. Having taken the fortress city of Pushan on the south coast, defeating its large garrison, the Japanese rapidly won victory at Ch'ungju, using their handguns and bows to great effect. They then captured the abandoned capital, Seoul, and advanced north to the Yalu river. King Sŏnjo had already fled towards China.

Korean naval resistance helped alter the situation. The Japanese fleet had been initially successful, but was defeated in a number of battles by Yi Sun-Shin, more particularly the battle of Sachun on 30 May 1592. The Korean fleet included some of the more impressive warships of the age: 'turtle ships', oar-driven boats, equipped with cannon, and possibly covered by hexagonal metal plates in order to prevent grappling and boarding. They may also have been equipped with rams. Yi Sun-Shin, who had a good understanding of the coast and its tides and straits, won a series of further victories in June, July and August. In addition, Korean guerrilla tactics on land undermined Japanese control, and, like other invading powers, the Japanese were also seriously affected by logistical problems.

Although already challenged by a rebellion at Ningxia (see p. 198), Wanli, concerned about the situation in Korea, his tributary, sent a 3000-strong cavalry force into Korea in late July. This force was ambushed in the city of P'yongyang on 23 August and mostly killed, a failure that caused consternation in China which was exacerbated by the continued Japanese advance. Worried about its frontier, in a way that prefigured its position in 1950 when American forces advanced north toward the River Yalu during the Korean War, the Chinese committed large forces to Korea in January 1593. Without this Ming aid, Korea would have fallen to Japan, at least for the short term. Instead, coordination by the Chinese and Korean allies proved effective, the Japanese were driven back, and P'yongyang was recaptured by storming on 8 February 1593.[3] The Chinese force that took the city numbered about 44,500 men.

Japanese sources emphasised the size of the Chinese army in explaining their defeat, although its technology was also important, notably the use of cannon in the field. This use was significant because the effectiveness of the Chinese was affected by the extent to which their northern forces, configured to fight the threat of attacking cavalry from the steppe, were confronted in Korea by the Japanese, who had themselves developed infantry, equipped with spears and firearms, who had driven cavalry from the field. Although the use of firearms in their army had spread, the Chinese also deployed large numbers armed with traditional weapons: bows, lances and swords. They also deployed troops from the southern provinces who had been trained in the 1560s to fight the *wako*.

The Sino-Korean allies benefited from having stable land and sea lines of support from China. The Japanese, while being able to get some supplies from the homeland, were stymied by guerrilla efforts on land and by the Chinese and Koreans at sea from supplying their armies on the western side of the peninsula. They also failed to extract the expected resources from the Korean countryside, mirroring their supply woes in China during the Second World War. The Chinese and Koreans made use of Buddhist priests, peasant conscripts and soldiers to transport supplies and enjoyed the fact that they moved through friendly terrain, unlike the Japanese. As with the South Koreans in 1950, the Japanese, who evacuated Seoul on 9 May 1593, were pushed back to a bridgehead on the southern coast around Pushan, but the Chinese were unable to destroy the bridgehead. The numbers put into the field on both sides were considerable. In 1593, there were about 45,000 Chinese troops in Korea and perhaps 25,000 Korean regulars, although some experts think the latter figure is inflated. There were also the Korean guerrilla units, although it is difficult to get any real sense of their numbers. Of the 168,000 or so Japanese who had landed in 1592, about 100,000 remained alive by the spring of 1593, although that number was greater than their opponents. Until the large-scale demobilisation by the Japanese in late 1593, they had numerical superiority. The Korean fleet was victorious anew off Tanghangpo in March 1594.

In 1596, Hideyoshi rejected the Chinese attempt to get him to accept a more subordinate status, for example equivalent to that of Altan khan, the Mongol ruler,[4] and in early 1597, the year of a Spanish invasion scheme against England, a fresh invasion of Korea was mounted by 140,000 Japanese troops. However, the Chinese, and the Koreans in particular, although affected by factional strife, were now better prepared for resisting attack. Despite initial successes, the Japanese were unable to repeat their success of 1592, even though the Chinese were affected by grave logistical problems. Superior Chinese firearms again played a role while the Chinese also increasingly used mercenaries rather than hereditary soldiers. By the end of 1597, there were probably about 75,000 Chinese troops in Korea. The Japanese advance was stopped south of Seoul and the Japanese moved onto the defensive. The Korean admiral, Yi Sun-Shin, had been dismissed for refusing to obey a royal order to attack, but his successor, Won Kyun, was defeated and killed in July. Recalled to command, Yi defeated the Japanese at Myungyang on 16 September 1597.

In 1598, the Koreans were supported by a Chinese fleet under an artillery expert, Ch'en Lin. The Japanese had rapidly deployed cannon on their warships, but their tactics remained focused on boarding and their fleet was defeated between 15 and 18 December 1598 by Yi Sun-Shin at the battle of the Noryang Straits. In this battle, the Koreans and Chinese navies made more extensive use of cannon and firearms and sunk over 200 Japanese ships, although Yi was killed in the battle.[5]

Hideyoshi had died of illness on 18 September 1598, having already decided to withdraw from Korea. The Chinese and Koreans probably achieved numerical superiority in the summer of 1598, but contemporary Japanese sources were wont to exaggerate the numbers of their foes so as to accentuate their own prowess. The Japanese forces withdrew in the spring of 1599, and Hideyoshi's plans against China were not pursued by his successors, which was an important moment in East Asian and, thus, world history.

Far from invulnerable, China was to fall to Manchu attack in the 1640s, which raises the question whether the Japanese could have succeeded earlier. Despite the problems the Japanese faced in securing their sea lines of communications, and the resource and logistical strains of invasions of East Asia (a strain also seen during the Russo-Japanese War of 1904–5, and then again when the Japanese invaded, first, Manchuria and, then, all of China between 1931 and 1945), the Japanese had the manpower and agricultural resource base necessary for operations in the 1590s and, had they continued, the 1600s. This capability was especially the case if the Japanese were not diverted into internal conflict, a factor contributing to international power in this period that was more generally important than administrative development. However, the Japanese did not have the comparative advantage over the Chinese provided by the mobility, flexibility and firepower of the Manchu mounted archers, a force the Chinese could not match as they lacked a comparable supply of horses.

Hideyoshi's position in Japan was taken by Tokugawa Ieyasu, a *daimyō* whom Hideyoshi had never trusted. His rise to power was resisted by a rival league of *daimyō*, but Ieyasu had undermined his opponents by secretly winning several of them over, and this led to victory at the battle of Sekigahara on 21 October 1600. As with many battles, betrayal proved a key element, with Ieyasu benefiting from bringing over about 15,000 troops from the 82,000-strong opposing army.[6] Ieyasu then established the Tokugawa shōgunate, which lasted until 1868. Hideyoshi's son, Hideyori, and his supporters were defeated when Osaka castle was successfully besieged in 1614–15 by Ieyasu's 200,000-strong army.

China did not face comparable pressures on its other frontiers, which, indeed, was a reason why it was able to mount a major effort in Korea, offering a comparison with Philip II's ability to focus on the Low Countries in the mid-1580s. The Chinese benefited greatly because Mongol power had declined after the death of Altan khan in 1582. Indeed, the defeat of the Japanese and the end of the Mongol threat were aspects of the late Ming vitality seen under the Wanli emperor. As yet, the Manchu were not a major threat to China. Partly as a result, the sixteenth century closed for China with an impressive display of force in a way that failed to indicate the military challenges of the following century, challenges that focused on Manchu attack and major domestic rebellions.

Africa

Korea's success in resisting Japan owed much to China, which proved an obvious contrast with the overthrow of another state by invasion, that of the Songhai empire by Morocco; Songhai, unlike Korea, did not have an existing overlord to offer protection. First, however, the Moroccans had crushed a Portuguese invasion. On 4 August 1578, King Sebastian of Portugal was heavily defeated at the battle of al-Qasr-al-Kabir/Alcazarquivir. This battle scarcely fits into the general narrative of military history and, indeed, is difficult to place: it is an episode in the expansion of Europe considered in Chapter 7, but did not lead to such expansion, and is more part of the story of Moroccan capability. Whereas Western pressure in sub-Saharan Africa was an important factor in Angola and Mozambique, equivalent pressure on Western interests occurred in North Africa, and was part of the Islamic assault on Christian Europe as much as an episode in African history. Study of the military struggle between Christendom and Islam focuses on the Ottoman–Habsburg conflict, however, to the detriment of other conflicts, notably in Morocco, Russia, the Horn of Africa and South-East Asia. Furthermore, Morocco has never received much attention from military historians, or indeed most other ones, and, if Alcazarquivir is considered, it is dismissed with reference to Sebastian's fatal folly. This dismissal, however, is unhelpful both for what it shows about warfare in the period, and with reference to the history of North Africa.

Sebastian's tactics provided an instance of what can be seen as crusading warfare, but also showed how this was different to the policy and tactics on display earlier at Nicopolis (1396), Varna (1444) and Mohacs (1526). Yet, the fate of his campaign also threw light on the need for caution when the Habsburgs fought the Ottomans, and indeed, in December 1576, Philip II had unsuccessfully tried to deter his nephew from an invasion. In the end, with Philip offering only token help, Sebastian, who in 1574 had strengthened the Portuguese hold on the town of Tangier by successfully taking an army into that area, in 1578 led a poorly prepared army of 18,000–20,000 men, crucially short of cavalry, further into the interior of Morocco, in order to challenge the sharif, Abd al-Malik, and his force of about 70,000. Sebastian sought to benefit from division within Morocco by helping Muhammad al-Mutawakhil, the former sharif, who had appealed for Sebastian's assistance, having been deposed by his uncle, Abd al-Malik. Sebastian wished to displace the latter as he had been supported in his seizure of power by both Ottomans and Habsburgs. Instead, Sebastian hoped to establish a client ruler, on the pattern seen with Portuguese expansionism in the Indian Ocean.

Sebastian sought battle on 4 August 1578, believing that his infantry would successfully resist the Moroccan cavalry. He deployed his infantry units in a deep phalanx, with cavalry on the flanks and artillery in the front, whereas the Moroccan army consisted of lines of arquebusiers, with cavalry, including mounted arquebusiers, in the rear and on the flanks. The Moroccans opened the battle with harrying attacks by horse arquebusiers and the unsupported Portuguese artillery was overrun. As so often, an effective combined arms defence required mutual protection and an inability to offer that led to vulnerability. However, the Portuguese infantry, which included a large contingent of German *landsknechts*, fought well and pressed hard on the Moroccan infantry. A second Moroccan cavalry attack pushed back the Portuguese cavalry on both flanks, but the Moroccans again lost impetus. Nevertheless, a renewed attack by the Portuguese infantry allowed a gap to open in their left flank, which the Moroccans exploited with great effect. The Moroccan horse arquebusiers then succeeded in destroying the cohesion of the Portuguese rear right flank, and Sebastian's army disintegrated. He was killed and his entire army either killed or captured, although legends about his survival in secret circulated for long. The skilful, well-disciplined Moroccan force had won a crushing victory thanks to superior leadership and discipline, more flexible units and tactics, and the events of the battle;[7] factors usually cited when discussing Western success.

In contrast, only about half of the 4000 men sent in 1590 across the vast dry expanse of the Sahara Desert by sultan Mūlāy Ahmad al Mansūr of Morocco survived the crossing, but their victory, under Judar Pasha, at Tondibi on the River Niger on 13 March 1591, made a decisive difference to the politics of the middle Niger valley, as it led to the collapse of the Songhai empire. In this battle, Moroccan musketry defeated the 12,500-strong Songhai cavalry and about 30,000 infantry, an army equipped with spears and bows; and lacking firearms. The sultan wanted to secure gold, as well as recognition for his claim to be caliph, the Muslim chief civil and spiritual ruler. As an instance of the porosity of barriers between military cultures, many of the troops sent were renegades: Christians who had become Muslim, notably

2000 musketeers. Such porosity was widespread and a means for obtaining military skills and also for the transmission of military methods. Moreover, the Moroccans benefited from the Portuguese arms seized in 1578. They also bought cast-iron artillery from English traders to whom they supplied salt-petre. The English defeat of the Spanish Armada in 1588 lessened the chance of Spanish intervention in Morocco, which, in turn, encouraged the expedition across the Sahara. As an example, however, in 1591 of the different styles and very varied success of attacking Islamic armies, the Moroccan expedition proved a marked contrast to the defeat outside Moscow that year of an invasion by Crimean Tatars.

At Tondibi, the Moroccans benefited from the poor leadership of their opponents. The flight of the Songhai emperor, Ishāq II, helped lead to a collapse of his army. The emperor also abandoned the city of Gao without fighting. Timbuktu fell without resistance soon after, while many of the royal dynasty who had suffered under Ishāq turned to the Moroccans. More Moroccan troops were sent in 1591, but opposition increased, particularly under Muhammad-Gao, who deposed and replaced his brother Ishāq. The harshness of Moroccan rule led to rebellions in Timbuktu (1591) and Jenne (1591–2): they failed but indicated the strength of the opposition.

The Moroccans, however, used the pretext of peace talks to capture Muhammad-Gao, and thereafter the Songhai world was divided between an occupied north, and south Songhai where strong resistance prevented further Moroccan expansion. Campaigning there in swampy terrain in 1593–4, the Moroccans suffered the effects of guerrilla resistance, disease and humidity, while, in January 1594, the (Moroccan) *pasha* (governor) of Timbuktu was killed in battle by the animists of the region of Hombori, who were effective despite their not having firearms. Songhai resistance gathered pace and from 1604 to 1617 Songhai took the offensive and regained much of the Niger river valley. Songhai archers and spearmen proved effective, not least as the terrain did not favour the Moroccan musketeers.[8]

Songhai, indeed, continued to be a fairly extensive state down the Niger from Timbuktu. Moreover, Mali remained a powerful state upriver until around 1660. Thus, the arrival of Moroccan power did not lead to a long-term transformation in the regional system; the contrary, indeed, as the trans-Saharan Moroccan empire could not be expanded, nor, in the end, sustained.

Thus, as an instance of the difficulties of assessing relative military capability, the Moroccans under Abd al-Malik had crushed the Portuguese invasion at the battle of Alcazarquivir in 1578, and this military verdict against European invasion lasted until 1844, but there was no comparable Moroccan success across the Sahara. In contrast, European powers using maritime links, notably Portugal, were able to sustain distant presences, including in West and East Africa, but not, to any extent, in North Africa.

It is necessary to emphasise the obscure clashes in the Niger region after 1591 because, all too often, warfare there is discussed solely in terms of the battle of Tondibi, which is then employed to provide an instance of the effectiveness of gunpowder technology and the diffusion of the Military Revolution. This method is a parallel to the unhelpful treatment of eighteenth-century warfare in India largely in terms of the victory of the forces of the English East India Company over those of Siraj-ud-daula, the nawab of Bengal, at Plassey in 1757, or the focus, in the discussion of Charles VIII of France's campaigning in Italy, on initial success supposedly due to cannon, rather than on a more complex account both of the initial invasion and of its overall failure (see pp. 45–6). The emphasis on Tondibi also reflects a frequently misleading preference for supposedly decisive battles that underrates the often lengthy and difficult process of conquest, while pressures of space in books moreover lead to a focus on particular battles, but these can provide a misleading impression of weak societies that apparently succumbed readily.

Further east in the *sahel* belt, firepower helped Idris Aloma, *mai* (ruler) of Bornu (1569–*c*.1600), an Islamic state based in the region of Lake Chad. He probably obtained his musketeers from Ottoman-held Tripoli on the Mediterranean, but Ibn Fartuwa's contemporary account of his wars with the neighbouring principality of Kanem makes no mention of guns playing a crucial role. Instead, Fartuwa concentrated on other units of Aloma's army, which included archers, shield-bearers, cavalry and camel-borne troops, and on non-firearm tactics. In his campaigns, Aloma made careful use of economic measures, attacking crops or keeping nomads from their grazing areas in order to make them submit, both longstanding practices in such campaigns.

Similarly, in Ethiopia, the use of firearms was restricted by the limited availability of shot and powder, a frequent problem affecting their use. Both Ethiopia and its rival Adal were put under pressure by the expansion northwards of the Oromo peoples, nomadic pastoralists who made effective use of horses, which increased their mobility. This mobility helped the Oromo raiding parties invade territory and live off the land, outmanoeuvring the more cumbersome Ethiopian forces,[9] which also suffered because war with Adal had hit the system of frontier defence.[10]

In facing this problem which added another key front of conflict to those with Adal and the Ottomans, Ethiopia benefited from vigorous leadership by Serse-Dingil, the emperor from 1562 to 1597, who commanded in person.

Adal was defeated in 1576, as, three years later, was an alliance of Ottoman forces with Bahr Nagash Ishaq of Tigre and the ruler of Harar, which ended Ottoman attempts to overrun Ethiopia from the Red Sea. Ottoman forts were shown to be vulnerable, Debarwa falling to the emperor. Serse-Dingil then also expanded Ethiopia to the west, while he defeated the Oromo in 1572 and 1586.

Serse-Dingil also changed Ethiopia's military system, in a fashion similar to shah Abbas in Safavid Iran, complementing the traditional reliance on the private forces of provincial governors and other regional potentates by an extension of the troops directly under imperial control, both the imperial bodyguard and the militia. As with other similar developments, this change can be seen in terms of centralisation, but that analysis over- looks the extent to which such an imperial policy was a traditional means of wielding patronage and maintaining control in face of the factors that limited it.

Further south in Africa, especially in West Africa, rule was segmented and most polities were not far-flung. This segmentation helped encour- age widespread conflict, conflict that was to feed the slave trade both within the continent and also to the Islamic and Atlantic worlds. Nomadic warrior tribes posed a particular problem in some areas, the Faga bringing devastation to East Africa in mid-century, and the Zimba from the 1580s, including to Mombasa in 1589.

Austro-Ottoman Conflict

Defeat at Alcazarquivir led to the end of Portuguese independence, with Philip II of Spain able to enforce his claim on the succession with a decisive invasion in 1580 by an army of 47,000 troops supported by a fleet, and also helped explain Habsburg caution in conflict with the Ottomans. Indeed, in 1596, the main battle in the next war, at Mezö-Kerésstés, between the two helped indicate why the Christian powers preferred to rely on fortifications. Yet, the Habsburgs did better than the Portuguese, not least in 1593 when an Ottoman force, seeking to relieve the besieged fortress of Székesfehérvár, was routed, an episode repeated outside Hatvan in 1594. Moreover, the Austrian offensive that year put pressure on the Ottomans before the arrival of a larger Ottoman force led the Austrians to withdraw and was followed by the Ottoman capture of the fortress of Györ (Raab). However, the fall of Györ was not seen by the Ottoman commentator Ibrahim Peçevi as a step that the state of the garrison made likely.

In 1595, the situation markedly deteriorated for the Ottomans, with the loss of the fortress of Esztergom (Gran) in Hungary to the Austrians after failed relief attempts, and, more seriously, a collapse of their alliance system as the rulers of Moldavia, Wallachia and Transylvania all came out in support of the Habsburgs. Wallachia (southern Romania) was strategically the most important territory as, from it, Bulgaria could be attacked, putting greater pressure on the heartland of Ottoman power in the Balkans, and also cutting the crucial Danube route for supplies to Hungary. Moreover, the Ottoman attempt to regain Wallachia was defeated by Prince Michael of Wallachia supported by the Transylvanians.

The presence of the new sultan, Mehmed III, with the army in Hungary in 1596 testified to the sense of crisis. Ottoman victory at Mezö-Kerésstés, however, was hard-won, with the Ottoman cavalry proving unable to hold the field against the firepower of the combined-arms Austrians, as the latters' musketeers were protected by pikemen and supported by cannon. Having repelled the Ottoman advance, the Austrian infantry formations advanced on the Ottomans, employing their firepower and causing much of the Ottoman army to flee, only for the Austrians to break formation in order to plunder the Ottoman camp. This provided the Ottomans with an opportunity to counter-attack and drive the unprepared Austrians back. However, the victory brought the Ottomans no gain of particular value to add to the fortress of Eger, which had repelled siege in 1552, only to be successfully besieged earlier in the campaign. In 1597, there was no battle of note when the Ottomans advanced anew, while the Austrians regained Györ; and renewed Ottoman advances in 1598 and 1599 led to sieges but no decisive developments. That indeed was the pattern for the rest of the war, which ended in 1606 with a peace that essentially returned the situation to the pre-war position.

The Thirteen Years War (1593–1606) is interesting for the light it throws on the problems of assessing and using capability advantages. The Ottomans were able to capture many of the fortresses recently modified by the Austrians using the cutting-edge Italian expertise of the period, including Györ in 1594, Eger in 1596, Kanissa in 1600 and Esztergom in 1605. Thus, rather than providing a paradigm leap (or revolution) forward in the defensiveness of Christendom, it is necessary to consider the advances in fortification, like other developments, in terms of particular circumstances,[11] and not least to remember that defences were only as good as their defenders and logistical support. Moreover, although the Ottomans had no equivalent to the *trace italienne*, nor to the extensive fortifications built in the Austrian-ruled section of Hungary, as well as along the coasts of Naples and Sicily against Barbary raids, they did not require any such development as they had not been under equivalent attack. Thus, yet again, capability should be related to tasking, and means to gaols, and this in a context in which both Westerners and Ottomans had a realistic perception of the potential and might of the adversary.[12]

Nevertheless, it would be mistaken to suggest that there was not a change in the balance of advantage in some respects. The Austrian combination of firepower and battlefield fortifications proved particularly effective. Ottoman reports admiring Austrian cannon captured in the Thirteen Years War suggest that a technological gap in cannon-casting had begun to open by then, although recent work has corrected the earlier view that the Ottomans concentrated on large cannon, rather than larger numbers of more manoeu-vrable smaller cannon, and has instead emphasised that their ordnance was dominated by small and medium-sized cannon. It has also been shown that they were able to manufacture an adequate supply of gunpowder.[13]

Yet, no clear superiority on land was to be demonstrated until the defeat of the Ottomans by the Austrians and their allies in the 1680s. It is far from obvious that a comparable Western superiority existed in India until the 1750s, and more clearly 1790s and 1800s, and in China until the 1830s and, more clearly, 1860. Prior to that, rather than assuming any Western supe-riority, whether or not based on (or amounting to) a military revolution, it is more appropriate to note the more complex, contingent and varied nature of relative military capability, and also to give due weight to the non-military factors that help account for differences between success in particular regions. Indeed, the Thirteen Years War repeatedly indicated the significance of a form of coalition warfare, in the shape of the importance, yet unpredictability, of subordinate parts of imperial systems, notably Wallachia, Transylvania and Moldavia. Thus, Transylvania changed sides to back the Ottomans in 1599, only to be defeated by the Wallachians.

At the same time, the Austrians had improved their military response to the Ottomans, not least by regularising the transfer of funds from the Empire (Germany) and the Habsburg dominions and by establishing a new administrative system for the frontier. For example, armouries were transformed into arsenals, the activities of military architects were coor-dinated in the Border Fortress Captain Generalcies by a Superintendent of Construction, and, after 1569, by the Fortress Construction Commissioner, a new post, the Chief Provisions Supply Officer for Hungary, was estab-lished, and in 1577 a military conference in Vienna produced an informed plan for the administration and improvement of frontier fortresses.[14]

At the same time, the improvements in the Austrian military did not match Ottoman capability: there was a lack of standing forces, and the central administration and logistical underpinning of war were overly dependent on the support of the local Estates (Parliaments). On both heads, the Ottomans were far stronger, which helps explain their earlier conquest of Hungary. The Austrians, indeed, required a formidable effort in order to stem the Ottoman attacks that followed this conquest.

Russia and the Baltic

The difficulties of moving from success in individual campaigns to a more decisive outcome was also seen in north-eastern Europe where the long-standing attempt by Russia, Poland, Denmark and Sweden to profit from the volatility caused by the demise of weaker polities in the eastern Baltic, the Teutonic Knights and the Livonian Knights, ended with no one power in a dominant position. Ivan IV, the Terrible, of Russia, who had played a key role in sustaining international rivalry, and who was determined to annex Livonia (much of modern Latvia) and thus gain a position on the Baltic, found success eluded him in large part because Poland acquired a new dynamic ruler in Stephan Bathory who became king in 1576. Emphasis on the role of individuals may appear outdated in a discussion of states and war, but leadership was important, not least to the contrast between Ivan's success against Kazan and Astrakhan and his failure against Poland.

Co-operating with the Swedes, Bathory defeated the Russians at Wenden in 1578 as part of the reconquest of Livonia, while, in 1579, he recaptured the Polish town of Polotsk, moving on to seize the Russian town of Velikii Luki the following year. In 1581, Bathory besieged Pskov, cutting off the Russian forces in Livonia from those in Russia; while the Swedes conquered Estonia. Ivan had to accept a peace with Bathory in 1582 in which he agreed to cede Livonia, and, in 1583, he followed with a three-year truce with Sweden. Over-extension in a lengthy war had brought Russia nothing, and Ivan died in 1584 with Russia in crisis.

When war with Sweden was resumed in 1590, the Russians regained the fortress of Ivangorod (lost in 1581), but then found it prudent to accept a peace treaty in 1595 that left Sweden with Estonia, Narva and Kexholm (eastern Karelia), so that Russia's presence on the Gulf of Finland was only a foothold. In negotiating a settlement with the Swedes, the Russians were concerned by the possible implications of the 1590 peace between the Ottomans and the Safavids, notably the danger that the Ottomans would support an attack by the Crimean Tatars.

Land warfare in the Baltic area involved relatively few battles, and sieges were more significant. Devastation was used to reduce opponents' fighting capability. The tactics employed were less formalistic than those developed in Western Europe, and the troops sometimes less specialised in weaponry, but the warfare was well suited to the Eastern European military circumstances of great distances and small populations. The continued usefulness of cavalry helps counter claims that Eastern European states were backward because their interest in infantry firepower was less than that in Western Europe.[15] As a reminder of the range of military activity involving Russia, an invasion by the Crimean Tatars in 1591 was less successful than in 1571, as Moscow did not fall, but, on the other hand, the Tatars got as far as its southern outskirts. There, the Russians successfully used *guliai-gorod* (rolling fortresses), as well as field artillery and musketeers, to repel the Tatars, inflicting considerable losses on the latter. This Russian success led to a peace that reduced pressure on Muscovy's borders.

In considering such episodes, there is the question of whether to emphasise the threat in 1591 or its failure. There is also the issue of how best to compare the Russian defence with the earlier response of the Chinese to Mongol attack. The Russians did not have a wall system to compare with that of the Chinese, and, in 1591, engaged, instead, in the field. In doing so, their defensive field fortifications and firepower provided valuable force multipliers, offering an effective response to the Tatar cavalry.

Wars of Religion

Like Ivan IV of Russia, Philip II of Spain found it impossible to fulfil his goals, although, again like Ivan, Philip had achieved much in his early years. Ivan's success in conquering Kazan and Astrakhan was matched by Philip's in holding the Ottoman advance and conquering Portugal, the latter uniting Iberia for the first time since Classical Rome and also joining the two trans-oceanic Western empires. However, just as Ivan's reign came to be defined by the Livonian War, so Philip's failures in the Low Countries, France and the British Isles came to the fore.

In the Low Countries, the Dutch Revolt led, in the long term, to the overthrow of Philip II's rule in the northern provinces, but, in the more populous and economically advanced south, it was possible for him to regain control. This success owed much to the achievements of the Army of Flanders from 1579, especially under its brilliant commander, Alexander Farnese, Duke of Parma, a veteran of Lepanto and a key figure in the diaspora of Italian military talent. However, it was also necessary for Philip's representatives to make concessions. A series of agreements, such as the Perpetual Edict of 1577, marked the attempts to devise a settlement acceptable to both Spanish Captains-General and the influential Walloon nobility, those of the southern provinces in the Low Countries. In a parallel fashion, the opposing States General of the newly-independent Dutch Republic had to negotiate for support rather than command it. The Dutch state was dominated economically by the towns of the province of Holland, especially Amsterdam, and this dominance led to a different social politics to that in the southern provinces, and thus to contrasting issues of political incorporation.

Spanish superiority in battle was repeatedly demonstrated during the Dutch Revolt between 1568 and 1578 while, thereafter, when sieges came to the fore, the success of Parma was impressive. The list of towns captured included Maastricht and 's-Hertogenbosch in 1579, Courtrai in 1580, Breda and Tournai in 1581, Oudenaarde and Steenwijk in 1582, Dunkirk, Eindhoven, Nieuwport and Zutphen in 1583, Bruges, Ghent and Ypres in 1584, Antwerp, Brussels, Geertruidenberg and Mechelen in 1585, Deventer, Sluys and Zutphen in 1587, and Geertruidenberg in 1589, and this list was far from exhaustive. Successes were followed by the end of Protestant activity in these towns.

The pace of Spanish advance was greatly helped by the extent to which the superiority of the Army of Flanders prevented any real chance of the relief of fortified positions, and thus encouraged their garrisons to take the better terms that a swift surrender ensured, so that Parma's reputation as a diplomat was enhanced. This synergy was linked to Parma's ability to achieve predictable results with an effective army. By securing his border with France, his lines of communication along the Rhine, and the coastal ports, Parma created a solid base area. The size of his army also increased, from 45,000 men in 1580 to 61,000 by October 1582. Parma's steady, remorseless, systematic advance enabled him to bring considerable pressure to bear on the Dutch Republic, inducing a sense of acute crisis both there and in sympathetic Protestant territories.

As a result, England entered the war in 1585, sending an expeditionary force under Robert, Earl of Leicester. The effectiveness of this force was limited, not least because of the competence of the Army of Flanders, but English participation in the war helped both in its internationalisation and in the spread of military knowledge. Deventer and Zutphen were betrayed to Parma in 1587 by their English commanders, both of whom were Catholics. Sluys, which was also captured that year, was a major siege that was part of Parma's strategic preparation for the link up with the Armada, and thus shows the extent and ambition of Spanish planning for the latter. In 1588, however, Parma failed to capture Bergen-op-Zoom, despite a considerable military effort and a determined attempt to suborn elements within the largely English garrison.

As a further reminder of the need not to consider countries in isolation, the run of Spanish military success in the Low Countries came to an end in large part because of the commitment of effort in intervention elsewhere, first, in support of a planned invasion of England in 1588, the Spanish Armada, and then, more seriously, in the French Wars of Religion. These wars were marked by a series of truces and peace treaties and, although some of the subsequent periods of peace lasted only a few months, this was not true of all of them. Nevertheless, the root causes of dissension in France remained, notably religious division, aristocratic factionalism and royal weakness; and, whatever their length, periods of peace were characterised by a degree of mutual suspicion that helped fan the flames when conflict resumed.

There was a genuine popular dimension to the wars: they were not simply a matter of the struggles of king, nobles and their affinities. However, the Crown, both then and earlier in the century, also sought to elicit popular support for war, and by both traditional forms, for example royal entries into towns, and more recent ones, notably printed works such as edicts, books, pamphlets, engravings and maps.[16] During the French Wars of Religion, particularly in the towns but not only there, there was a high level of engagement with the confessional struggle. This engagement led to outbursts of mass violence, as well as to a degree of independence from aristocratic leadership among both the Catholic League and the Protestant towns. Royal power and authority collapsed during the crisis, reaching its nadir in 1589 when Henry III of France, the Catholic king, was assassinated by a Catholic zealot while unsuccessfully besieging Paris, from which he had been driven by the more radical urban elements of the Catholic League.

Thereafter, with the royal succession contested, much of the Army of Flanders under Parma was committed by Philip II in support of the Catholic League, in an eventually unsuccessful attempt to prevent the Protestant Henry of Navarre, Henry IV, from gaining effective control of the country: Henry III had no children and Henry of Navarre had the next best claim. The Spaniards relieved Paris from siege in 1590 and Rouen in 1592. The Army of Flanders also operated into neighbouring German territories of the Holy Roman Empire: in 1581, Parma sent troops to overawe the Imperial Free City of Aachen, while a contest over the Electorate of Cologne led Parma to capture the towns of Neuss (1587), Bonn (1588) and Rheinberg (1589). Moreover, in pursuit of its interests in the strategic Jülich–Cleves area in the lower Rhineland, the Spaniards seized the fortress of Wesel in 1598. Parma, meanwhile, had died in December 1592 of wounds received during the siege of Rouen.

Similarly, the English, with troops in the Low Countries from 1585, also intervened in France. The English sent forces to Brittany, Normandy and Picardy in 1591–2 to oppose the Catholic League as they feared that its alliance with Philip II would provide Spain with invasion ports, as had already happened with Calais in 1588.

Henry IV's eventual success in France owed much to success on campaign and his own inspirational military leadership, but the political element was also crucial. In particular, Henry proved willing to make concessions to key groups, which was the real aspect of his apparent restoration of strong monarchy. The context was different from that in the Holy Roman Empire in 1555, but the reality of compromise was similarly apparent. The Pope, the major aristocrats of the Catholic League, led by the Duke of Mayenne, the last survivor of the powerful Guise family, and the Huguenots, each accepted Henry on terms. His famous renunciation of Protestantism in order to gain the throne – 'Paris is worth a mass' – was a testimony to the importance of affirming the attributes of Catholic kingship in order to secure his position. Although it is disputed by modern scholars whether he actually used the phrase, the sentiment it expressed was a reflection of his political pragmatism.

The major Catholic aristocrats were bought off with a recognition of their provincial power-bases, which was necessary in order to ensure their renunciation of alliance with Philip II as well as their abandonment of the more radical urban elements of the Catholic League, notably those in Paris and Marseilles. The resulting compromise both reflected the realities of power and laid out the prospectus of French monarchy until the French Revolution began in 1789. Moreover, in 1598, by the Edict of Nantes, the Huguenots were granted liberty of conscience, a measure of public worship, and the right to retain garrisons in about 200 towns, with the Crown agreeing to pay the garrisons of about half the towns. The parallel with Charles V's concessions to Lutheranism by the Peace of Augsburg of 1555 was readily apparent, not in the terms, but because the ruler had been forced to concede religious liberties that challenged his authority.

After Henry was crowned in 1594, Spanish forces continued to intervene, especially in north-eastern France, where they seized Calais and Amiens. There were also Spanish expeditions to Brittany, aimed against England, and to eastern France, designed to strengthen the Spanish position on the overland route to the Low Countries, the 'Spanish Road'. Classically, these efforts were seen as failures, but the demonstration of Spanish power helped force Henry to compromise with domestic opponents, which thus assisted Spain by keeping the French crown weak. In 1598, it was unclear whether the compromises of authority and power that had characterised the establishment of Bourbon rule would not leave France lastingly weak. Indeed, the problems that faced France in the 1610s during the minority of Louis XIII after the assassination of his father, Henry IV, by a Catholic zealot in 1610, indicated that there was reason to believe that the developments of the 1560s–1590s had left France very weak.[17]

Moreover, by the Treaty of Vervins of 1598, Henry had to accept Spanish hegemony in Western Europe, with the highpoint of Spanish success, registered in the 1559 Peace of Cateau-Cambrécis, confirmed. Spain remained in control of the southern provinces of the Low Countries, as well as dominant in Italy where Philip II ruled Sicily, Sardinia, Naples and Milan. Spanish hopes of putting a client on the throne of France had failed, but, as also for England, there had been no good candidate and, without one, the basis for any lasting success was limited.

Spain's commitment in France and against England lessened the Spanish resources available for conflict in the Low Countries, which allowed Maurice, Count of Nassau, commander of the Dutch army, and his cousin, William, the Captain-General of the troops of the north-eastern provinces, to drive back Spanish forces and to experiment with new tactical formations. An increase in the size of the Dutch army, from 20,000 men in 1588 to 32,000 in 1595, was also significant, while the availability of resources was important, not least in order to ensure pay, and thus maintain cohesion and prevent mutinies. Resources were linked to an effective supply system in order to deliver tactical and operational effectiveness. Thus, 10,000 cannonballs were fired by the Dutch in their successful two-month siege of Groningen in 1594. Maurice made much use of cannon in his sieges. Breda was regained in 1590, Delfzijl, Deventer, Hulst and Zutphen following in 1591, Coevorden and Steenwijk in 1592 and Groningen in 1594. Countering the Spaniards, these operations spread into neighbouring German principalities, as with the successful siege of Lingen in 1597.

Tactical experimentation was the centrepiece in the efforts by military reformers linked to the House of Nassau in the United Provinces, and in the German Protestant principalities of Nassau, the Palatinate, Baden, Hesse-Cassel and Brandenburg. The reformers consciously used Classical Greek and Roman models for their efforts to improve military organisations, and their limited sense of changing conditions was matched by the contemporary theoretical work of Justus Lipsius, François de la Noue and Francesco Patrizi on the army of Classical Rome. In preparing for the siege of Steenwijk, Lipsius, who emphasised the value of Roman stoic philosophy to help professionalise troops,[18] was consulted by his former pupil Maurice on Roman siegecraft.

The use of Classical models and the sway of the ideal model in discussion of tactics and discipline encouraged an emphasis on standardisation and on the need for effective training. Alongside the increased use of firearms, the greater size of the Dutch army, and Dutch economic growth, the standardisation of weaponry furthered rationalisation and concentration among arms producers, which, in turn, facilitated standardisation.[19]

The developments of the 1590s, notably the introduction of volley fire by the Dutch, had a major impact.[20] Prior to the Nassau reforms, firearms could be important but did not tend to play more than a supporting role in many battles. Instead, pikemen, swordsmen and cavalry took a central part. Soldiers with handguns often operated in loose formations and had to retreat quickly when the armies closed. Hand-to-hand combat frequently decided the outcome of the battle. In contrast, the drill and tactics developed and introduced by the Nassau reformers helped the handgunners to operate successfully in close formations in the open field.

However, the general significance of the changes introduced by the Oranien [house of Orange] reformers, both for the putative Military Revolution and for long-term military history, is a matter of debate. At any rate, these changes were less significant for conflict in the Low Countries in the 1590s when sieges still predominated, than for subsequent conflicts in Western Europe, notably in the Thirty Years War of 1618–48. Indeed, the difficulties encountered by Spain in the 1590s can better be explained in terms of the competing commitments of the Spanish government and military. Like the Ottoman empire and China, Spain was capable of military effort on more than one front at a time. However, the key force in the north, the Army of Flanders, did not have that capability as far as large-scale offensive operations were concerned, and suffered from vulnerable lines of communication with Spain, both by sea and land. As a result, the commitment against France proved a serious bar to the continued pursuit of successful operations against the Dutch.

Royal authority was more successfully challenged in Sweden than in France, but in part that was because Catholicism was far weaker in Sweden. The Catholicism of the king, Sigismund Vasa, who was also Sigismund III of Poland, helped lead to civil war in 1597–8. Indecisive campaigning was followed in 1599 by the *Riksdag* deposing the king. In contrast, authority was imposed in Portugal and Ireland, their very different circumstances indicating the range of relevant political context.

In Portugal, Philip II of Spain used both widespread bribery and a successful invasion by land and sea in 1580, the process eased by the willingness to maintain distinct institutions and separate practices and privileges: Philip II became Philip I of Portugal, and, although Iberia, divided among four rulers in 1470, was united under one in 1580, no new state was created. This was not simply a prudential choice on the part of Philip, but also a reflection of the deep sense of legitimism that affected both rulers and élites and helped bind them together. Religious division, the factor that most challenged legitimism, was not at issue in Portugal, which was also Catholic, while there was no good rival candidate for the throne: Sebastian had left no children, while Philip's mother was a Portuguese princess. The calibre and rights of claimants were key issues. In Poland, where the elective throne was contested in 1575 between the Emperor, Maximilian II, and Stephan Bathory, Prince of Transylvania, the speedy death of the former brought the conflict to a close in favour of the latter.

In Ireland, unlike Portugal where it was not a factor, the Protestant Reformation encouraged attempts to impose royal authority. The English crown had had a claim to Ireland since the twelfth century, as well as a political and military presence there, but, anxious about the risk of Papal or Spanish intervention, Henry VIII of England had himself proclaimed king of Ireland in 1541, while, with the Catholics increasingly treated under Elizabeth I (r. 1558–1603) as a potentially rebellious threat, there was pressure for the 'plantation' of areas with English settlers, a process that further exacerbated relations. From the late 1560s, in a process of government different to that across most of Europe, rulership in Ireland became increasingly military in character and intention, leading to fresh attempts to extend and enforce control.[21]

Rebellions led the English to resort to the routine use of force and ensured that Catholic landowners increasingly lost their land. In turn, religious joined with political considerations to encourage international Catholic interest in Ireland, notably by Spain and culminating with the dispatch of an expeditionary force that was defeated on land at Kinsale in 1601. Ireland showed that conquest as a basis for rule was possible, but also indicated its heavy cost to conquerors and conquered alike. In general, the greater the degree of rapid political incorporation and accommodation, the more readily conquest could be grounded. Equally, the path to political incorporation was paved by military activity. Thus, victory in the Italian Wars had left Spain dominant in Italy.

Intellectual links

This dominance helped ensure intellectual links between Italy and the Spanish world that were important to the dissemination of ideas on conflict. For example, Luis Collado, an engineer in the Spanish army in Italy, published in Italian in 1586 a manual covering all aspects of artillery and, in 1592, a reworked Spanish version was published in Milan. Spanish rule also provided a link with the Low Countries, so that Bernardino de Escalante's *Diálogos del arte militar*, published in Seville in 1583, also appeared, in Spanish, in Brussels in 1588.

Similarly, there were rival political alignments and intellectual currents, and these also were reflected in publications. A key rival to that of Spain was provided by the Protestant British–French–Dutch–German alignment that mounted a vigorous resistance in the Low Countries. Veterans of this struggle became important thinkers, writers, and teachers on military matters. Thus, Paul Ive, an Englishman who served in the Low Countries, published a translation of Fourquevaux's *Instructions sur le fait de la guerre* in 1589 and, with it, his own *The Practise of Fortification*, which devoted particular attention to Dutch-style fortifications. Other works by Huguenots translated into English included François de La Noue's *Discours politiques et militaires*, the translation of which was published in London in 1587. A central part of this alignment was provided by Maurice and William of Nassau and their connections. The theories and practices of Maurice and William, on which the later idea of the Military Revolution was first centred, were thus part of a wider intellectual current and can be profitably considered in this context.

The world of print contributed to these and other currents, speeding up the dissemination of ideas. Views on tactics, fortifications and weaponry could be readily spread. These views included both calls for change (however much often framed in terms of revival and defended by frequent backward-looking reference to the Classics), and also pressure for continuity. An instance of the latter was provided by Sir John Smythe's *Certain Discourses … concerning the Forms and Effects of Divers Sorts of Weapons* (1590), which focused on the retention of the longbow. Smythe's argument that the longbow was both useful militarily and associated with true manliness recalled wider currents of uneasiness with firearms, seen for example in parts of the Islamic world, especially earlier in the century. Smythe's book failed to take proper account of the social changes that had reduced the protracted practice with the longbow, which was essential to its successful employment.

Conclusions

The ability of force to combine with political factors in order to deliver a verdict was important. This ability characterised some militaries regarded, both generally and in their regional context, as at the cutting edge, as well as others that were very different. To take the latter, most of the Spanish army that suppressed the 1591 Aragonese revolt was scarcely professional, instead being recruited by the Castilian nobility from their estates, but it was successful. Rather, therefore, than seeing the type of army as establishing capability in some overarching thesis of proficiency through change and of change in proficiency, it is more pertinent to focus on the concept of fitness for purpose in particular circumstances.

This fitness could be noted in tactical, operational, strategic and organisational terms. For example, the role played by cavalry was in part linked to the nature of the theatre of operations. Areas which were defended by lines of fortresses with strong garrisons required large forces made up of infantry to breach them, as well as numerous infantry for the garrisons. In contrast, areas defended by a small number of fortresses permitted the attacker to bypass the enemy strongholds and to live at the expense of the enemy, providing more opportunities for attacking cavalry, which, in turn, increased the value of cavalry to the defenders. As an instance of the organisational case, the Dutch rebellion against Spain had seen, in the 1560s and 1570s, military entrepreneurs raising armies of their own accord, but this practice worried the urban oligarchs because they feared that mercenaries would leave them to their fate when pay was in arrears or, even worse, betray their towns to the Spaniards. To ward of this danger, the oligarchs declared that supreme command over the troops lay with the provincial States [Parliaments] and the States General, and the right to appoint officers was assigned to the former. The army thus served as the military expression of the rebellion. Thus, yet again, the circumstances of the individual struggle were important to the development of particular forces.

6 Naval Capability and Warfare

Introduction

Reconceptualizing the world for land warfare in demographic terms, so as to focus on population distribution and thus on East and South Asia, can be matched at sea by considering not only the deep-draught naval capability that classically attracts attention, but also by emphasising shallow-water capability. The latter invites attention to rivers, lakes, deltas, estuaries, lagoons and inshore waters, alongside the oceans and seas that dominate Western attention and analysis. These rivers *et al.* were important because they saw much of the world's movement by sea, whether of goods or troops. In contrast, the oceans were largely empty of maritime activity, and this situation was particularly true of areas far from land. The significance of the land indeed for naval activity was such that oceanic waters should really be rethought in terms of routes that largely focused on particular areas of land, which might be the source of goods for trade, such as the East Indies, or the site of supplies for operations or replenishment, such as the Azores. There were also important choke points where maritime routes were vulnerable to attack such as the Straits of Malacca.

Returning to shallow waters leads to discussion of canoes that were shallow in draught, and therefore enjoyed an inshore range denied to most Western warships. Their crews fought both hand-to-hand and with missile weapons. Areas where canoes were particularly important included inland waterway systems, especially in Amazonia, the eastern half of North America as well as its Pacific coastal region, and the valleys of the Brahmaputra and Irrawaddy; coastal systems, particularly the lagoons of West Africa; and island systems, such as the Hawaiian archipelago; and this is a far from exhaustive list.

As yet, these and other forces are not only largely unstudied,[1] but also scarcely mentioned in general accounts of naval power and warfare. In practice, the key element in such warfare was not conflict between navies for 'control of the sea' but, rather, the use of amphibious operations in order to mount attacks and raids. Moreover, both in order to transport troops and to reduce exposure to bad weather, there was an emphasis on operations across narrow waters rather than seas.[2] Thus, much inshore use of ships was not too different from that of river navies, which were important in a number of areas including Africa (for example on the rivers Niger, Congo and Kwanza) and north India. Sonni Ali of Songhai captured the Niger river port of Jenne in 1471 despite its defenders using fire ships against his fleet. After the Moroccans captured the city of Timbuktu in 1591, they made the local population provide wood and build canoes for military operations on the Niger.

Despite the problems posed by winter ice, spring spate, and summer drought, transport of troops and supplies on rivers was important, for example on the Danube and Tizsa in Hungary. This transport was the case both along and across rivers. Thus, Mehmed II's army was able to invade Moldavia because he sent his fleet up the Danube and it transported the army to the northern bank,[3] whereas, in 1598, Ottoman campaigning in Transylvania was affected by attacks on supply ships on the Danube and Tizsa. The Ottomans had established their own flotillas on the Danube and its tributaries, in part by taking over the shipbuilders on the Sava and Drava rivers who had served the Hungarians.[4]

There was generally only limited specialisation in river vessels, which helped make them useful for military purposes. Moreover, river vessels were usually lightweight and therefore could be dismantled in order to carry them round areas of shallow or rocky water. This porterage, however, provided a series of choke points similar to those in coastal waters, and again ensured a degree of vulnerability.

Nevertheless, there were also parts of the world with an emphasis on a long-range power projection by sea. For the early fifteenth century, Chinese naval activity takes the limelight, but there were, and had been, other naval powers in medieval Asia, for example Srivijaya, centring on eastern Sumatra from the seventh to the eleventh century, and the Chola empire of southern India in the eleventh century. In so far as long-range activity takes attention, this sphere was to be dominated by Westerners once China ceased such power projection in the 1430s, essentially due to its cost but also because of a change in factional politics as well as rising concern about the Mongols. The contemporary Ottoman assault on Christian Europe did not have a comparable effect in lessening Western interest in trans-oceanic activity, in part because this assault did not challenge most of the centres of Western power, but also because the multipolar nature of the Western state system left Portugal, the leading trans-oceanic naval power, well able to take independent initiatives.

More generally, and significantly, the Western advantage in technique and infrastructure rested on the foundation of centuries of economic, technological, social and institutional change. Moreover, this Western naval power projection had an important consequence in demonstrating strength and affecting trade routes, creating profit and the prospect of gain that encouraged fresh activity. In a key instance, the Portuguese navigator Vasco da Gama arrived in Indian waters in 1498, dropping anchor near the port of Calicut on 20 May, with vessels carrying cannon that Asian warships could not resist successfully in battle.[5] However, a foretaste of the difficulties Portugal was later to face in the Indian Ocean was provided by the clashes that occurred en route between his expedition and the Muslims of East Africa and also, in December 1500, when the Portuguese factory (trading post) which he had established in Calicut was destroyed after fighting broke out there. More generally, the Portuguese were seeking trade, but their arrival disrupted established trading relationships, leading to conflict. Yet, the technological gap in their favour helped give the Portuguese victory over the Calicut fleet in 1502, despite the latter being supported by Arab vessels. In the battle, Portuguese gunfire, especially the heavy guns carried close to the waterline in their smaller caravels (rather than the lighter guns in the larger Portuguese carracks), saw off boarding attempts and thus countered their opponents' numerical advantage.

Dramatic moments tend to rest on longer-term developments, not least because naval strength entailed a commitment of resources which was often greater than that required for warfare on land. Sailing warships were costly, but the great costs of naval operations were food and wages because fleets could not live on local resources as armies did, the latter, for example, relying on wayside grass for the draught animals. Instead, facing challenges even greater than those of armies crossing deserts, fleets had to be provisioned and watered, needs that made the size of the crew a particularly serious matter. Moreover, despite the possibilities offered by obtaining supplies from fish and rainwater, this issue was far more significant for long-range voyages, and led to the establishment, by the Portuguese in particular, of ports whose primary purpose was to replenish passing fleets.

Lethality as well as range was an issue, for warships equipped with cannon, whether driven by sails, muscle-power (for galleys), or both (for galleys were equipped with masts and sails), were the single most costly, powerful and technologically advanced weapons system of the period. Lethality, moreover, became a key contrast in specifications between warships, while the cannon carried on some Western warships from the middle of the fifteenth century were made with a particular concern for their use at sea in a fashion distinct from that of land-based weaponry.

This concern was an important aspect of specialisation although, despite different cannon mountings, cannon for siege warfare, fortifications and naval warfare were to a large extent interchangeable, unlike field artillery which, to be mobile, had to be as light as possible. Thanks to the introduction of efficient gunpowder weapons at sea, a process furthered by the introduction of the gun-port around 1500, capital, in the shape of what was required to provide such firepower, was in part substituted for manpower.

Galleys mounting a heavy gun in the bow were the first ships to use heavy cannon. This development ensured that convertible galleys, able to be used for both trade and war, were replaced by specialised purpose-built war galleys, and the latter were not only dominant in the Mediterranean but also newly important in north-west Europe and the Baltic, from the 1510s and 1540s, respectively.

Weaponry was not the sole factor, for the propulsive system was also important: the management of sails was difficult, but required less manpower than oars. The substitution of sails for oars increased dramatically the operational radius of seaborne fighting forces as only a limited number of men had to be fed and watered on long journeys. In contrast, the large crews required by galleys, and their limited storage space, ensured the need for frequent anchorages in order to take on food and water. This, however, was not a problem if relatively limited-range operations were planned, as by the Koreans in the 1590s. In resisting the sailing ships used by the Japanese to invade Korea in the 1590s, ships which were supplied by merchants and pirates, the Korean fleet included 'turtle ships' that were propelled by rows of oars on both sides, as well as carrying plentiful cannon (see p. 122). Many of the Chinese warships that took part in the Korean war used oars as well as sails. The metal plates supposedly covering the sides of these Korean ships were also seen in Japan under Nobunaga, for whom they had defeated the conventional wooden ships of the Mori at the time of the siege of Osaka. He apparently had seven ships of this type mounting cannon,[6] which serves as a reminder of the need to include Japanese naval conflict in the wider account.

In Atlantic Europe, as in Korea and Japan, the sixteenth century saw the rise of the large specialised warship, the ship of the line built and maintained just for war, rather than also acting as a peacetime trader. This trend was mirrored in the Mediterranean, where specialised war galleys had been developed into galleasses, which were heavily armed with artillery. These vessels could not be used for trading, although there and in the Atlantic, the wartime conversion of merchantmen into warships remained important. Specialised warships, able, with their strengthened hulls, to take part in sustained artillery duels at close range, were expensive to build and maintain, and could only be deployed by major states. As a consequence, the number of potential maritime powers came to be restricted, and, in the seventeenth century, the naval state was no longer coterminous with the commercial territory or port.

Portugal, the First Global Naval Power

Concern with artillery was much less significant in the fifteenth than the sixteenth century, and Portuguese naval capability in the fifteenth was not simply a matter of firepower. Instead, drawing on recent developments in ship construction and navigation, specifically the fusion of Atlantic and Mediterranean techniques of hull construction and lateen and square-rigging, as well as on advances in location-finding at sea, the Portuguese enjoyed advantages over other vessels, whether the latter carried cannon or not. Developments in rigging permitted the Portuguese greater speed, improved manoeuvrability, and a better ability to sail close to the wind, although the wind dropping was a major problem in conflict against galleys, as in the early stages of a battle off Hormuz with Ottoman galleys in July 1553.

Information also played a major role in Portuguese effectiveness. Thanks to the use of the compass and other developments in navigation, such as the solution in 1484 to the problem of measuring latitude south of the Equator, it was possible to chart the sea and to assemble knowledge about it, and therefore to have greater control over the relationship between the enormity of the ocean and the transience of man than ever before. The Portuguese made a major effort to accumulate information that would aid navigation, and also to keep it secret from rivals. They had also built up a pool of experienced seamen during the fifteenth century, who were able to exploit the technological advances to maximum effect.

The Egyptian (Mamluk) and, later, Ottoman vessels that sailed to the west coast of India, or between the Red Sea and the Persian Gulf, were different to the Portuguese ships in their long-distance capability, and were also less heavily gunned. Indeed, as early as 1518, the standard armament of a Portuguese galleon was 35 guns. Therefore, there was a technological dimension to the geopolitical competition that became acute in the Indian Ocean from the 1500s. Portuguese warships became the single most powerful naval force in Indian waters, defeating the navies of Calicut, Japara and Gujarat in 1502, 1513 and 1528, respectively.

Portugal's successes challenged the Mamluk rulers of Egypt, threatening the profitable trade route from India to Suez, leading to the dispatch of a fleet, partly of galleys, from Suez in 1507. Supported by Gujarati vessels, this fleet, under Hussein al-Kurdi, defeated a greatly outnumbered Portuguese squadron at Chaul on the west coast of India. However, in 1509, the Egyptian fleet was largely destroyed off Diu, also on the west coast by Francisco de Almeida, the first Viceroy of Portuguese India. This defeat owed much to a withdrawal of Gujarati support which reflected suspicion of Mamluk intentions.

Another key element in Portuguese expansion was their string of forti-fied naval bases which replicated the role of the ports that were so indispen-sable to Mediterranean galley operations, but over a vastly greater distance. Portuguese sailors knew that they could replenish in safety at a series of 'way stations', such as Luanda and Mozambique, on their long voyages to and from Asia. Naval power thus provided a cover for the spread of Portuguese bases which, in turn, supported the Portuguese military and commercial systems.[7]

Portugal had begun to establish bases on the west coast of Africa during the fifteenth century, at Arquim (in Senegal), El Mina (in Ghana) and Luanda (in Angola). Portugal expanded these along the east coast after 1500, notably at Zanzibar (established in 1503), Kilwa (1505), Mombasa (1505), Sofala (1505), Mozambique (1507), Malindi (1520) and Pemba (1520). These were followed by bases on the west coast of India, including Cochin (1503), Cannanore (1505), Anjediva (1505), Chaul (1509), Calicut (1510), Goa (1510), Quilon (1512), Bombay (1530), Diu (1535), Surat (1540) and Daman (1558). These bases provided the Portuguese with a powerful presence on the eastern side of the Arabian Sea, but there were also bases closer to the heartlands of Islamic power. One was established on the island of Socotra near the approach to the Gulf of Aden in 1506, only to be abandoned in 1511 because of a lack of water. The Portuguese were more persistent in the Persian Gulf, establishing bases at Bandar Abbas (1507), Bahrain (1515), Hormuz (1515) and Muscat (1550), the latter two providing a strong position at the mouth of the Gulf. The Portuguese discovery of Brazil also enabled the establishment of replenishment facilities for fleets returning to Portugal from India, although Brazil was not actively developed by them until 1530, and then in response to incursions by French seamen.

The establishment of a far-flung Portuguese presence marked a major change in the frontier or fault-line between Christendom and Islam. As a result of the Portuguese arrival in the Indian Ocean, suddenly there were many more contact zones between Islam and Christendom, while the already existing contact zone in the Horn of Africa became more violent.

Not all the Portuguese targets, however, fell. In particular, the Portuguese attempt to advance into the Red Sea failed, which was important as the Red Sea was the primary route for Islamic naval counter-attack, as well as

a major route for trade from the Indian Ocean to the Mediterranean. Had
the Portuguese been successful in seizing Mecca and Medina, it would have
demonstrated Portuguese support for Christendom, winning great prestige, and helped to advance the cause of the recapture of Jerusalem. Having
succeeded at Goa and Malacca, Afonso de Albuquerque, the Viceroy of the
Indies, however failed at Aden in 1513, and the clash indicated the extent to
which the technological gradient was not necessarily in favour of the West,
while, in the absence of such a capability gap, fortifications posed a serious
challenge to them, as to other attackers: the Portuguese sought to assault
the walls of Aden, using scaling ladders, not to breach them with prelimi-
nary cannon fire. Instead, cannon, firing stones rather than iron balls,
were employed by the defenders. A second Portuguese attempt, made in
1517, also failed. This was not just a case of Portuguese failure as Aden also
proved strong enough to repel Mamluk attack in 1516.

Thereafter, the Ottoman conquest of Egypt in 1517 meant that the
Portuguese faced a more potent opponent, although, under Bayezid II's
naval alliance of 1510 with the Mamluks, Ottoman ships had already been
sent into the Red Sea. The Yemeni port cities were brought briefly under
Mamluk/Ottoman control, with the Mamluks, who sent many handgunners to the Red Sea in 1513, attacking the Tahirid sultanate on the western
and southern coasts of Yemen in 1514.[8] Moreover, fortifications along
the Red Sea were greatly improved by Mamluk forces sent to provide
assistance against the Portuguese. Fortifications were particularly strengthened at Jeddah where, in 1517, an Ottoman galley fleet checked a Portuguese
attempt, under Albuquerque's replacement, Lopo Soares, to sail up the Red
Sea by taking up a defensive position in the reef-bound harbour under the
cover of coastal artillery. The Ottoman position was enhanced because they
were the only power in the Red Sea or Persian Gulf with the artillery and
naval resources to resist the Portuguese. Nevertheless, the Portuguese were
able to send fleets into the Red Sea in 1528 and 1529. On the later occasion,
the ruler of the port of Shihir, a strategic port city on the Hadrami coast
of Arabia, yielded trading privileges, the Ottomans were driven from their
base of Kamaran, and the emir of Aden agreed to become a Portuguese
vassal, to pay tribute, and to accept a small Portuguese garrison which took
control of the citadel.

Portuguese–Ottoman Rivalry

It was not only a question of the Ottomans resisting Portuguese attack.
Instead, Ottoman expansion into Egypt and, later, Iraq gave the Ottomans
a direct interest in both the Red Sea and the Persian Gulf, a policy

particularly associated with Ibrahim Pasha, Grand Vezir from 1523 until his execution for alleged disloyalty in 1536. Nevertheless, as a reminder of the problem of failing to place developments in context, in the 1520s and early 1530s Süleyman the Magnificent devoted relatively little attention to the area. Indeed, in 1532, he transferred cannon and munitions from the Red Sea base at Suez to the Mediterranean, which was of greater concern to him.

In 1538, however, a major effort was made in the Indian Ocean, with the Ottomans sending nearly 70 vessels and a total crew of close to 10,000, the largest fleet they ever sent there. Dispatched against Diu in western India, the fleet failed to win promised Gujarati support and, without the vital element of local backing, was repulsed by the Portuguese. The balance of local enmities proved crucial to the fate of external intervention. Bahadur Shah of Gujarat, whose navy had been defeated by the Portuguese in 1528, had been attacked by the Mughals in 1535, which had led him to make a defensive treaty with the Portuguese, who established a base at Diu and built a fleet there. Bahadur's son and successor, Mahmud, favoured courtiers critical of those linked to the Ottomans.

Although unsuccessful in their siege of Diu, the Ottomans, en route in 1538, had treacherously seized Aden, capturing and hanging the emir, helping create the basis for the Ottoman province of Yemen, and strengthening the Ottoman ability to defend the Red Sea and to intervene in the Horn of Africa. As a result of the Ottoman move, the Portuguese, who had had friendly relations with Aden, lacked both a base near the Red Sea and one able to challenge Ottoman naval moves from there towards the Persian Gulf, India, or the Swahili coast of East Africa. The Ottoman position was contested by the Portuguese, who sent an expedition into the Red Sea in 1541, which unsuccessfully tried to destroy the fleet at Suez, but the Red Sea essentially remained an Ottoman waterway.

From Aden, Basra and Suez, the Ottoman admirals Piri Reis and Seydi Ali Reis exerted much pressure on the Portuguese in mid-century, although this did not match the Ottoman efforts in Hungary, the Mediterranean and against the Safavids, and Aden and Basra were not developed as fully-fledged naval bases like Suez. In 1552, Piri Reis, with 30 warships and 850 soldiers, sailed from Suez, sacking the Portuguese base of Muscat and then besieging Hormuz. The latter, however, resisted successfully, leading Piri Reis, instead, to plunder the island of Qeshm. He was executed for his failure, a frequent occurrence for Ottoman commanders. Blockaded in the Persian Gulf, the Ottoman fleet, now under Seydi Ali Reis, broke through the Straits of Hormuz in 1554, but, with the loss of nine out of fifteen galleys, was then badly damaged by an ocean storm which forced the fleet to sail to

India, not the Red Sea. Firepower played a crucial role in the engagements, although the 1552 expedition was also compromised by the loss of a vital supply ship.[9]

After the failures at Diu (1538) and Hormuz (1552), no more full-scale official Ottoman campaigns were undertaken and Ottoman naval activity in the Indian Ocean declined, although, in 1608, artillerymen and gunsmiths were sent to help the Sumatran sultan of Achin against Malacca; earlier, dispatching an embassy to Süleyman, Achin had also requested specialists in shipbuilding and fortifications.[10] Relations with Portugal, furthermore, remained hostile, with the Ottomans in 1585 supporting opposition to Portugal at Surat in west India, while, in response, also in 1585, the Portuguese, with a fleet of 26 ships, tried to blockade the entrance to the Red Sea, only to be hit hard by logistical problems, notably a lack of water. This attempt made it possible for Hasan Pasha in Yemen to press the government in Constantinople to provide resources to back his plans for the Indian Ocean.

Accordingly, in July 1586, the construction of 20 galleys in the Suez arsenal was authorised. From the Red Sea, the Ottomans threatened the Portuguese position on the Swahili coast of East Africa in 1586 and 1589 as fleets under Mir Ali Bey were easily able to force most of the coastal cities between Mogadishu and Kilwa to accept Ottoman suzerainty. The 1586 expedition led to plans for a permanent occupation of the region, with envoys from Mombasa, Pate and Kilifi returning with Mir Ali to his home base of Mocha in Yemen.

In 1589, the Portuguese had to send a large force of 11 oared warships, 6 galleons and over 900 troops to the Swahili coast from India to check the advance of the Ottomans, and the Portuguese felt it necessary to begin new fortifications at Muscat in 1587 and at Mombasa in 1593. Mir Ali, who had 5 ships, 300 troops and some local support, was defeated at Mombasa in 1589 by the Portuguese fleet under Tomé de Sousa Coutinho, in part because the Ottoman defensive fire failed to prevent the Portuguese entering the harbour and seizing the beached galleys. Yet, the Ottoman defeat also owed much to Mir Ali's need to deploy most of his troops and cannon to protect Mombasa on the landward side from a force of Zimba warriors. The Portuguese subsequently allowed the Zimba to cross over to Mombasa island, and the defeated and fearful Mir Ali took refuge with the Portuguese, surrendering to them. Once the Zimba had left, Mombasa was handed over to its rival, the town of Malindi, which had provided the Portuguese with two ships and many troops for the expedition.[11]

The Portuguese were able to limit the Ottoman presence in the Persian Gulf, while Ottoman maritime power was essentially restricted to the Persian

Gulf[12] and the Red Sea, as well as to the Black Sea and the Mediterranean. This division was appropriate given the nature of the warships, but also the respective taskings of the navies. If Ottoman galleys were less suited to the Indian Ocean than Portuguese vessels, the Ottomans also preferred to attack Cyprus in 1570, rather than to send aid to distant Achin. Similarly, in 1588, Philip II of Spain (also Philip I of Portugal), turned down a request from the viceroy in Goa, the major Portuguese base in the Indian Ocean, for forces with which to attack Achin. War with England was a far higher priority for Philip, and the armada launched against it that year required Portuguese as well as Spanish warships, the Portuguese galleons proving to be particularly effective, rather as the Venetian galleasses had been at Lepanto in 1571.

By then, the Portuguese had better warships than a century earlier. They had initially relied on the caravel, a swift and seaworthy, but relatively small, ship, ideal for coastal exploration and navigation, as well as the *nau*, or 'great ship', a very large carrack-type vessel; but they then developed the galleon as a vessel able to sail great distances. It was longer and narrower than earlier carracks, with a reduced hull width-to-length ratio, and was faster, more manoeuvrable, and capable of carrying a heavier armament. The Portuguese brought galleons into the Indian Ocean from the mid-1510s, while continuing to use their large carracks to carry trade goods back to Portugal from the Indies. In so far as the spice trade returned to overland routes through the Near East, it did so because native shippers, mostly from the East Indies and Gujarat, learned to evade the Portuguese attempt at blockade.

The Mediterranean

More than the quality of warships was involved in success or failure at sea, as was also shown in the Mediterranean. The Ottomans had created a fleet to help prevent Constantinople from being relieved when they attacked it in 1453 and also moved ships overland to the Golden Horn, from which waterway they could bring further pressure on Constantinople's walls; an earlier Ottoman fleet had been destroyed by the Venetians in the nearby Dardanelles in 1416. Once the city fell to land attack in 1453, the Ottomans used it as their capital, and this move, to a port-capital whose support depended on maritime links, led to an increased role for naval concerns. Kritovoulos, the governor of the Aegean island of Imbros, noted of 1463 that Mehmed II decided to build up a fleet 'because he saw that sea-power was a great thing' and that the Venetians were a threat to the Ottomans.[13]

The Ottoman fleet was swiftly a major force in the Aegean Sea, and was employed to support amphibious attacks on Mitylene (1462) and

Negroponte (1470), deploying 280 galleys and other ships for the latter. The capture of Negroponte helped undermine the Western position in the Aegean as grain from the island of Euboea was used to supply the Knights of St John on Rhodes. The pattern of Ottoman amphibious attacks was also seen with the capture of several of the Ionian Islands to the west of Greece in 1479, notably Cephalonia, followed by that of the port of Otranto in southern Italy in 1480.

Under Bayezid II (r. 1481–1512), the Ottomans, in part by recruiting corsairs or naval frontiersmen,[14] subsequently developed their fleet for more distant operations beyond the Aegean and to carry cannon, which they used with effect to defeat a Venetian–French fleet at Zonchio near Modon in 1499; a reversal of a long run of Mediterranean naval history. Yet, as a reminder of the need for caution before focusing on cannon, or the swivel guns and other small-calibre weapons that had become common-place on Western ships by the end of the fifteenth century, contemporary images of Zonchio also show the hurling of spears and the firing of arrows, while rocks and barrels, probably of quicklime, are thrown from the fighting tops. The battle ended when the ships were burned, which was not caused by the cannon, which fired stone shot and with only limited effect. Galleys demonstrated their effectiveness in this battle.

By the time of their war with Venice of 1499–1503, the Ottoman fleet was more powerful than its opponent. In the pattern of navies of the period, the Ottoman fleet was intended to support amphibious operations, rather than to seek battle, and its operations combined with the heavy siege cannon moved by sea. As a result, they were able to drive the Venetians from bases in Greece: Lepanto (Návpaktos) fell in 1499, and Modon (Methón) and Coron, 'the eyes of Venice', in 1500. The fall of these bases threatened the articulation of the Venetian system as they were stopping points en route to the Venetian island colonies of Crete and Cyprus, as well as the advance-positions for the Venetian possessions in the Adriatic. The Venetian response was inadequate. A Venetian–French fleet sent in 1501 failed, as instructed, to reconquer Lepanto and Modon, instead, launching an unsuc-cessful amphibious attack on Mitylene (Mitilini) on the Aegean island of Lesbos, an attack beaten off on land. Fear of the Ottoman fleet became more potent in Venice.[15]

In the sixteenth century, the emphasis on firepower in galley warfare increased, with the Venetians redesigning galleys so as to carry large centreline cannon, an innovation rapidly adopted by Ferdinand of Aragon and Louis XII of France.[16] These cannon were carried forward and supple-mented the focus on forward axial attack already expressed by the presence of a metal spur in their bow. This spur might damage enemy oars and could be pressed into the hull of an enemy galley if a boarding was attempted. The strengthened and lengthened prow provided the access/boarding ramp onto an enemy ship. These spurs could not sink ships as the (underwater) ram was intended to do, but the latter was a weapon of the Classical period that had disappeared. Like spurs, cannon were intended to help to disable the opposing ship as a preparation for boarding.

Galley conflict was not unchanging and, although the exigencies of galley operations posed formidable constraints, it is a mistake to treat the galley simply as a conservative contrast to progressive developments of sailing ships. Aside from the introduction of cannon, galleys became easier to row in the mid-sixteenth century, as one-man oars (with the typical galley having three men on a bench with one oar each) gave way to rowing *a scaloccio*, in which there was one large oar for each bench, and this oar was handled by three to five men. This change, which reflected the shift from skilled volunteer oarsmen to convicts and slaves, led to an increase in the number of rowers, and also made it possible to mix inexperienced with trained rowers without compromising effectiveness. Experts were long divided about the respective success of the two systems, which is a reminder that it is difficult to assess alternative military methods.[17]

Naval conflict became more common in the Mediterranean because the Ottomans made a major effort in that direction, reviving the challenge mounted in the eighth to eleventh centuries to Christian Europe by Islamic naval powers based in North Africa. Aside from geopolitical considerations, competition for foodstuffs as well as the high price of grain supported the attempt to protect trade and to hinder that of opponents.[18] Assisted by the Ottoman fleet, the conquest of Egypt in 1517 facilitated and encouraged a major growth in Ottoman naval power and in the merchant marine, as links between Egypt and Constantinople were only really viable by sea. Whereas the Egyptian fleet had been defeated by Western pirates off Ayas in 1510, the Ottomans proved able to dominate the eastern Mediterranean. Selim I expanded the naval arsenal at Galata (on the other side of the Golden Horn to Constantinople), which became a major centre for shipbuilding. The conquest of Egypt also led to the end of the annual state convoys of Venetian ships for the Levant.

The Ottomans benefited from the decline of Genoese and Venetian naval power, neither of which were able on their own to mount a powerful resistance. This failure had implications for both Christendom and Islam. Christendom's naval capability was reconfigured away from the Mediterranean city-state maritime empires of the later Middle Ages towards states able to draw on large resource bases, with Spain becoming the leading Christian naval power in the Mediterranean. Spain benefited from the strong Catalan naval tradition and from the established port-city of Barcelona. The revival of a city-state maritime empire was to come from outside the Mediterranean in the shape of the Dutch Republic in the seventeenth century.

In turn, the weakness of Genoa and Venice enabled the Ottomans to dominate the Aegean and seize its islands. Karpathos and the northern Sporades (1538) and Naxos (1566) were captured from Venice, and Samos (1550) and Chios (1566) from the Genoese. Neither Venice nor Genoa had the capability to protect such exposed positions, which was a far cry from the naval reach enjoyed by both powers during the Middle Ages, a reach that had extended into the Black Sea.[19] Ottoman expansion was partly by conquest and partly by a coerced enhancement of control, as with Chios, where the Ottomans moved from tribute-takers to direct occupation; or Naxos which, in 1538, was allowed to recognise Ottoman sovereignty and pay an annual tribute. Subsequently, it was brought under direct rule.[20]

In response to the Ottoman advance, Charles V, Venice, and Pope Paul III deployed a combined fleet in 1538 against the Ottomans in the Adriatic, but the Ottomans were able to check them at Prevesa on 27 September. The battle demonstrated the importance of tactical problems in naval warfare and also the grave difficulties of arguing from them in order to assess general capability, as tactical issues played out in terms of the specific circumstances of particular engagements. Forcing battle is a key issue in naval warfare. Galley conflict in particular depended on fortified ports and anchorages, which often gave the advantage to the defenders.

This proved to be the case at Prevesa, where the Ottomans had withdrawn their galleys onto the beach under cover of their fortress guns, with their forward galley guns facing out to sea. This situation immediately robbed the Genoese admiral, Andrea Doria, of the initiative, as his crews were consuming their food and water as they tried to hold their station outside the port on the open sea. He had the choice of attacking the Ottomans in their fixed position, with the Ottomans able to fire from stable gun platforms with a secure retreat, or landing troops and attempting to storm the fort and its outer defence works with inadequate siege equipment. As neither option offered much prospect of success, his only realistic option was retreat. The moment he began to withdraw, however, Doria exposed his sailing vessels to the Ottoman galleys, whose fresh crews were able to overhaul and board them. Instructively, accounts of the battle vary, which is more generally true of naval (and land) battles in this period and thus make it difficult to judge the particular factors that led to successful capability. Recriminations among the mutually distrustful allies were linked to these different accounts.[21] However, one of the technological successes at Prevesa was the ability of a single, large Venetian galleass to hold off the sustained attacks of the

Ottoman galleys and to make good its escape. The Venetians built more galleasses as a result, and these were to prove crucial at Lepanto in 1571.

In 1541, Charles V led a crusade against Algiers, the key Muslim naval position in the western Mediterranean. This large-scale amphibious expedition was a considerable logistical achievement: 65 galleys, 450 support vessels, and 24,000 troops sailed from Majorca in mid-October. However, while landing the troops, the fleet was badly damaged by an autumnal storm and, with about 150 ships lost, the troops were soon re-embarked. Thus, the expedition failed, unlike that against Tunis six years earlier. In 1542–4, Hayreddin, known as Barbarossa, with 110 galleys co-operated with the French against Charles V, raiding Catalonia (1542), capturing Nice (1543) and harrying the Italian coast (1544). These successes were made possible by the use of Toulon as a base to 'winter' in. Tripoli (in modern Libya) fell to the Ottomans in 1551, and in 1552, when Henry II of France attacked Charles V, the Ottomans sent about 100 galleys to the western Mediterranean. Each year until 1556, and again in 1558, the Ottomans sent large fleets, although, for logistical reasons they returned every winter to Constantinople. The significant naval forces that operated from Algiers and the North African ports still remained in the western Mediterranean, but this return gave their opponents opportunities to contest the sea, so that in 1553 the Ottomans invaded the island of Corsica, only for Genoese control to be re-established when the fleet left. Corsica was at the limit of the Barbary vessels. Ottoman attacks still had a terrible impact. Thus, in 1554, the raiding of the Maltese island of Gozo, a possession of the Knights of St John, was accompanied by the seizure of much of the population as slaves, such that the island became largely depopulated.

Unlike their attacks on Rhodes (1522), Malta (1565) and Cyprus (1570), the Ottomans did not use these expeditions to seek to accumulate conquests that might establish a permanent position, but the expeditions created grave problems for the articulation of the Spanish empire as well as for the coastal communities in the region. During the period 1540–74, the number and scale of amphibious operations mounted in the Mediterranean by all of the major combatants was impressive. The size of armies that were transported, the distances they were moved, and the speed of transit, were all striking, and highlighted a degree of competence and capability that was largely due to the experience of the commanders and sailors involved.

In 1559, Charles V's son, Philip II of Spain (r. 1556–98), launched an expedition to regain Tripoli, but delays in assembling the forces meant that the expedition did not sail until late in the winter, and it became stormbound in Malta for ten weeks. When it eventually sailed for Tripoli in mid February 1560 it was driven back by bad weather, and, instead, occupied the low-lying island of Djerba, which lay to the west of Tripoli. Djerba had previously been used by Barbarossa as a base for his corsairs, and was flat and interspersed with sandy lagoons. The Spanish began to construct a fortress on the island, but chose to fortify the old town, rather than building a fortress next to the beach where the original landing was made. Dragut and Uluj Ali were well aware of the preparations and pleaded for immediate assistance from Constantinople. This was provided and a fleet left the city and arrived at Djerba twenty days later, on 11 May, an astonishing feat that took the Christian forces by surprise. As a result of the surprise attack, a large proportion of the galley fleet was destroyed or captured, although, thanks to the leadership of the younger Andrea Doria, a number of Genoese galleys extricated themselves from the unfolding disaster and reached safety. The fortress was blockaded, with all of the wells outside the fortress being captured. The water cistern within the fortress had run dry by July and the garrison was soon forced to surrender.

Malta

The Ottoman fleet was not deployed offensively between 1561 and 1564, despite the advantage that the victory at Djerba had brought. However, in 1565, Süleyman sent a powerful expedition of 140 galleys, 50 large transports and about 40,000 troops to capture Malta. The heavily-fortified harbour base of the Knights of St John at Valetta served as the centre for an unremitting campaign against Ottoman shipping as well as against Venetian shipping that was trading with the Ottomans. Malta was considered as a pirate base by both, and one of the contributory reasons for the attack was the seizure by the Knights of a large Ottoman carrack returning from Venice to Constantinople and belonging to Kustir Aga, the chief eunuch of the seraglio of the sultan. The Knights had made extensive preparations to receive an attack, and had been boosted by the gift by Cosimo I, Duke of Tuscany, of two hundred barrels of the finest corned gunpowder which proved a major advantage during the siege.

Naval power provided the power-projection capability, but the Ottoman forces were initially hampered by divided leadership, specifically the failure of the land and sea commanders to agree and implement a co-ordinated and effective command structure and plan. After an initial rebuff before the main defence lines at Birgu, the main Ottoman attack was focused on the small fort of St Elmo which commanded the entrance to the main harbour and to the important subsidiary harbour of Marsamuscetto, which Piali Pasha wanted to use as his fleet anchorage. The initial Ottoman attack on St Elmo was poorly co-ordinated, and it was not until the arrival of the experienced corsair, Dragut, that the attack made headway. Dragut had the reputation and ability to act as a successful intermediary between the land and sea commanders. For long, the Ottomans could not prevail over the determined defence. Positions and fighting were at close-quarters. Indeed, Francisco Balbi de Correggio, who was in the garrison, claimed: 'We were now so close to the enemy at every point, that we could have shaken hands with them.'[22]

The resistance, especially the extraordinary heroism of the defenders of the fort of St Elmo, which delayed the Ottomans for 31 days, was crucial as it exacerbated the logistical problems the attackers encountered, and also gave the Spaniards sufficient time to mount relief attempts. The Ottomans also lost a quarter of their force during the attacks on St Elmo, and Dragut was killed by a splinter of rock, thrown up by a cannonball. The ferocity of the fighting indicates the intensity of religious conflict. At the height of the fighting, the bodies of three dead knights were decapitated and disembowelled, then nailed to crosses that were floated across the harbour in order to discourage further reinforcements entering the fort. Most of the defenders of St Elmo died fighting. Only five badly wounded knights were captured, although none were ransomed and they probably died of their wounds. Five Maltese defenders leapt into the harbour and swam across to safety.

After the fall of St Elmo, the defenders of Birgu and Senglea could only try to repel attacks: they were not strong enough to mount a sortie, although they were aided by sorties from the small garrison at Mdina in the centre of the island. The garrison received and guided into the main defensive position at Valetta a small force of 700 reinforcements from the Spanish territory of Sicily, who arrived six days after the fall of St Elmo. A larger relief force, 11,000 strong, attempted to sail from Sicily, but was twice forced back by bad weather. It eventually managed to land unopposed on 7 September, 112 days after the initial landings by the Ottoman fleet.

Although the Ottomans attacked the relief force, they were demoralised and had been decimated by the severe fighting and disease. Problems with the supply of drinking water in the summer heat were considerable, and there was also a lack of siege artillery and ammunition. The Ottomans were routed by the fresh troops of the relief force, but, despite this, the discipline of the *janissaries* held, and they successfully covered the re-embarkation of the remnants of the Ottoman army in St Paul's Bay. As an instance of public interest, the first printed and illustrated accounts of the siege appeared in Italy and Germany within a month of the Ottoman withdrawal.

The attack marked the high water mark of westward Ottoman maritime expansion, and created a *de facto* maritime boundary that ran from Corfu, through Messina to Malta and Tunis. This boundary was consolidated when Cyprus was captured by the Ottomans in 1570, although Crete continued in Venetian hands for another century. The Ottomans never again attacked Malta.[23]

Effective resistance combined with relief by sea from a nearby base had saved Malta; not a naval battle. The strength of the Spanish response in 1565 reflected the major effort made by Philip II in the Mediterranean in the early 1560s. This effort included operations on the coast of North Africa. Aside from the Djerba expedition in 1560, the Spaniards broke the blockade of Spanish-held Oran in 1563 and sent an expedition to gain the Peñón de Vélez in 1564.

Cyprus

Cyprus was an easier target for Ottoman conquest than Malta. It was closer to the centres of Ottoman power and the Venetian rulers appeared less formidable. In 1570, Süleyman's successor, Selim II, sent 116 galleys and 50,000 troops, who, landing on 2–4 July, rapidly overran the island. The three leading Venetian towns on the island, Nicosia, Girne (Kyrenia) and Famagusta, had all had their fortifications expensively and comprehensively upgraded, especially Nicosia. However, Nicosia, which suffered from its position at the centre of the island without any hope of relief from the sea, fell on 9 September, largely due to poor leadership. The commander of Girne surrendered shortly afterwards, after he had been presented with the heads of the commanders of the Nicosia garrison as a warning to accompany the offer of a safe evacuation of himself and his garrison. They left safely for Crete, where, as a punishment for surrendering, the commander spent the rest of his life in prison.

A substantial garrison continued to hold Famagusta, despite the request for surrender being accompanied by the head of Niccolò Dando, the Lieutenant-General of Cyprus, who had been killed at Nicosia. Famagusta was an altogether tougher proposition than the other two fortresses. It was much larger than Girne and had sea access. Famagusta's defences, which the Venetians had spent much effort upgrading, were probably superior to those of Malta, and it contained one of the best ports in the eastern Mediterranean, as Richard I, the Lionheart, of England had been quick to spot in 1191 during the Third Crusade. Moreover, both its civil and military commanders were of exceptional courage and ability.

Although gunpowder stores ran down, Venetian relief vessels did break through with supplies during the siege, and in Venice it was felt that there was good reason to believe that the city would hold out. Ottoman cannon fire had failed to breach the land walls and the Ottomans had been forced to commence mining operations which took time. Had the garrison realised that the Ottomans would not honour the terms of their surrender, it is unlikely that they would have surrendered, although the garrison was starving and running critically short of gunpowder. A relief force was only days away and conceivably could have changed the outcome of the siege. The unusual refusal of the Ottoman commander to honour the terms of the surrender owed much to his anger with the success of the small garrison in inflicting such heavy casualties during a siege of 11 months.

Lepanto

In response to the Ottoman attack on Cyprus, a Holy League of Spain, Venice and the Papacy was organised by Pope Pius V in May 1571. The Christian fleet, under Philip II's illegitimate half-brother, Don John of Austria (1547–78), who had led the campaign against the *moriscos* in 1569–70, found the Ottoman fleet off the west coast of Greece, although, as with so many battles, not by the place from which it took its name: the battle took place forty nautical miles west of Lepanto near the mouth of the Gulf of Patras close to the Curzolaris islands. The Ottomans, under Müezzinzade Ali Pasha, had probably more ships, about 282 (although recent Turkish work has reduced that figure to about 230) to about 236, but fewer cannon, 750 to 1815. The Ottoman fleet was suffering from disease and lacked some of its usual complement of *janissaries*, while Don John had made modifications to his ships to widen their field of fire. More than 100,000 men took part in the battle on 7 October, a reminder of the major manpower requirements of naval power when strength was a function of a large number of ships, certainly in comparison to the situation for sail and steam warships. In the latter cases, numbers of ships and of men were both still important, but not to the same degree.

At Lepanto, Don John relied on battering his way to victory, although he also benefited from having a reserve squadron, which permitted a response to the success of the Ottoman offshore squadron. Superior Christian gunnery, both from cannon and handguns, the fighting qualities and fire-power of the Spanish infantry who served on both the Spanish and the Venetian ships, and the exhaustion of Ottoman gunpowder, all helped to bring a crushing victory in four hours' fighting. Moreover, the Ottoman fleet was exhausted because the campaign had begun in March, unusually early, while losses in the campaign and the departure already of many soldiers for the winter meant that there was undermanning. The effective cannon of six Venetian galleasses played a particularly important role in disrupting the Ottoman fleet. These galleasses were three-masted, lateen-rigged, converted merchant galleys which were longer and heavier-gunned than ordinary galleys, and they carried firing platforms at poop and prow and sometimes along their sides. Their height also gave them a powerful advantage as they could fire down on opponents. If they were able to crash into the side of, or sweep away the oars of, an enemy galley, the impact of their weight was much larger than that of a normal galley. The deployment of galleasses, to break the force of the Ottoman assault, represented a considerable tactical innovation, especially when it was combined with a reserve squadron.

The willingness of both sides to engage in an open sea battle was important and extremely unusual. The Ottomans could have pulled back under the guns of the fortress at Lepanto and forced the Christian forces into a risky amphibious assault. They were aware of the presence of the galleasses, but did not appreciate their potential and their use during the battle probably came as a tactical surprise to the Ottomans. Good morale and determined leadership characterised each of the sides, and this may have led to a riskier approach being taken by both commanders. The normal caution of the galley commanders was overridden on the Christian side by the charismatic and determined leadership of Don John, who brought a land perspective to the battle. On the Ottoman side, Müezzinzade Ali Pasha was initially reluctant to join battle, but was persuaded by the aggressive orders from the sultan, and by inaccurate intelligence reports.

Casualty figures vary greatly, and the limited extent of the Ottoman sources is a serious problem, but all agree that the Ottomans lost far more men, possibly 30,000 dead (including the admiral) to maybe 9000 Christians, while the freeing of maybe 15,000 Christian galley slaves accentuated the serious disruption to Ottoman naval manpower. The Ottomans lost about 113 galleys sunk and 130 captured, as well as their cannon and naval stores, whereas the victors lost only about 12 galleys.[24] The Ottomans also lost their pool of trained sailors and mariners, as the Spaniards had done at Djerba, and these were more difficult to replace than the galleys themselves.

The battle was applauded as a triumph throughout Christian Europe, a decisive victory over a feared foe, and was much celebrated in the arts, notably in paintings. However, it was also to serve as an important reminder of the complexities of naval power, particularly the extent to which, as on land, triumph in battle did not necessarily lead to success in war. Lepanto occurred late in the year, and could not be followed by the recapture of Cyprus, let alone, as Don John hoped, by the capture of Constantinople or the liberation of Palestine, the Crusader goal. More modestly, an attempt to retake the port of Modon in southern Greece failed in 1572, a major failure as this campaign represented much of the window of opportunity for the Holy League.

The ably commanded Ottomans carefully avoided battle in 1572–3, and rapidly constructed a new navy which included mahones, their impressive version of galleasses. As the result of a formidable effort, the Grand Vezir, Sokullu Mehmed, organised the building of about 150 new galleys, in just one season. By April 1572, about 250 galleys and 5 mahones were ready for action. In order to improve the firepower of the Ottoman fleet, there was a stress on an ability to use handguns among those called on to serve in the fleet, a recognition of the loss at Lepanto of the skilled marine archers who had predominated in 1571 over the Ottoman musketeers.

The role of alliance dynamics was also crucial, as so often in conflict. The outcome of Lepanto, although disappointing from the Christian viewpoint, was fatally undermined by the Venetian decision to sue for a unilateral peace with the Ottomans: in March 1573, Venice recognised the loss of Cyprus. Tunis, which had fallen to the Ottomans in 1570 and been regained by Spain in 1573, fell to the Ottomans the following year: they deployed 280 galleys and 15 mahones.[25] Under serious pressure, especially from the Dutch Revolt in the Low Countries, Philip II felt unable to respond, and, instead, Spain followed with a truce with the Ottomans.

Murad III's decision in 1577 for a full-scale invasion of the Safavid empire similarly led the Ottomans to other commitments. This shift in policy to a focus on the Safavids was also seen with an approach to Ethiopia for a truce, while Sokollu's plans for the Indian Ocean were shelved.

Lepanto was decisive more for what it prevented – a possible resumption of the Ottoman advance in the Mediterranean and Adriatic, than for pushing the balance of military advantage towards the Christians. The loss of skilled Ottoman manpower was also important. The end result was the *de facto* establishment of a maritime frontier between Spanish and Ottoman spheres of influence in their respective halves of the Mediterranean. Thus, there was a parallel to the Austrian success in stopping the Ottomans, albeit in less dramatic fashion, in Hungary, which similarly led to the establishment of a new boundary.

Large-scale naval warfare between Ottomans and the Mediterranean Christian powers did not revive until the mid-seventeenth century. Although the Ottomans and the Austrians were at war in 1593–1606, they did not fight at sea at any serious level, and Spain crucially did not use the opportunity to join Austria in attacking the Ottomans, although an unsuccessful Spanish assault on Algiers was launched in 1601. Nor was the Neapolitan system of coastal fortifications maintained sufficiently to prevent much of it falling into decay. This absence of conflict can be seen as a sign of a more widespread stagnation of Mediterranean galley warfare,[26] but, as always when discussing naval power, it is also necessary to give due weight to the other commitments of the combatants and the potential combatants.

In geopolitical terms, Ottoman naval power was confined, but, despite considerable Ottoman interest in the Indian Ocean, it is possibly more appropriate not to think primarily in later geopolitical terms of an attempt to break through to the oceans, as if the Ottomans were the Soviet Union. Instead, the geopolitics of galley warfare was very different. Carrying soldiers greatly increased galleys' consumption of food and water, and therefore affected their range, which also reflected the difficulties galleys faced in confronting rough winter seas. For example, unable to find water on the island of Djerba in 1510, the Spanish expedition lost over 3000 dead. Few harbours and anchorages were able to support and shelter large fleets transporting substantial numbers of troops, which affected operational methods and strategic goals, as access to, or the seizure of, these nodal points was crucial. This capability, in turn, provided a critical political dimension. For example, as long as Barbarossa had access to French ports through diplomatic efforts, his range was greatly enhanced.

South-East and East Asia

The trans-oceanic operational parameters of Portuguese warships were different, but the Portuguese also were concerned about nodal points, both in order to support their fleets and so as to control trade. Thus, in the Indian Ocean their route east from India's Malabar Coast was supported by bases in Ceylon (Sri Lanka), notably Colombo and Galle, both established in 1518, and then by bases in northern Sumatra en route for Malacca, in the strategic Straits of Malacca. Affonso de Albuquerque seized Malacca in 1511: with 1200 men and 17 or 18 ships, he outfought the sultan, but he also played on divisions among the large, multiethnic mercantile community in order to win support for Portugal. The following year, a Portuguese base was established at Bantam in the Sunda Strait between Sumatra and Java.

Particularly beyond Malacca, Portuguese bases were generally commercial centres, not major fortified positions like Goa and Malacca, although, in the East Indies, their base at Ternate, established in 1522, only fell after a five-month siege in 1575, and other fortified posts were built at Solor (1562) and Tidore (1578). The loss of Ternate reflected the deterioration of relations as Islamic identity in the Moluccas strengthened.

The Portuguese gained wealth from the trade routes they developed from Malacca to the Far East, with bases established at Macao in China (1557) and at Nagasaki in Japan in 1570. However, the Portuguese accommodated themselves to the regional powers and did not acquire any significant military capability in the region. In 1521, the Chinese clashed with Portuguese ships off T'un-men, near Macao, when they tried to enforce an expulsion of all foreigners after the death of the emperor, Cheng Te. The outnumbered Portuguese were put under heavy pressure with three Chinese attacks beaten off, but with difficulty and with one ship sunk. In 1522, knowing nothing about this clash, three more Portuguese ships arrived in order to negotiate a treaty and establish a garrison, but two were lost to attack by a Chinese naval squadron employing cannon. Thereafter, until 1528, Chinese fleets were deployed each year to prevent any Portuguese return.

Chinese junks were sturdier than Indian ships, and the Portuguese were fortunate that the Chinese did not contest their arrival in the Indian Ocean or, more plausibly, the Straits of Malacca and the South China Sea. Had there been such a war, the Chinese would have had large numbers of warships, but they would have been lightly gunned. However, although China had an inshore naval capability, it no longer deployed distant fleets, and its navy indeed faced difficulties in dealing with Japanese piracy. The quality of Portuguese cannon and ships were appreciated by the Chinese and, eventually, a process of mutual accommodation left the Portuguese able to trade at Macao. Nor did Japan or Korea, in spite of constructing plank-built warships from the fourteenth century, develop a long-distance naval capability for use against the Portuguese or Spaniards. Conversely, although the Portuguese obtained slaves from Japan as a result of its divided politics,[27] they did not intervene in the latter.

Despite their strengths, the Portuguese faced serious problems from a number of South-East Asian states, notably Achin, Johor and Brunei, which developed substantial fleets of war galleys. The heavily gunned Portuguese galleons, with their deep draught and reliance on sails, were vulnerable to shallower-draught oared boats. An Achin fleet of 300 ships with 15,000 troops attacked Malacca in 1553, and, following a turn in policy against Portugal in 1564, further attacks were launched in 1568, 1570 and 1573. Peace was not made with Achin until 1587, but there was a new attack on Malacca in 1595, while the north Javanese state of Japara mounted attacks on Malacca in 1513 and 1574. Johor (in southern Malaya), where the ruling family of Malacca had moved after its capture by Portugal, also launched attacks, including one in 1551. The network of fortified ports and well-found ships enabled Portugal to maintain its naval presence and trading capability despite the rise of local opposition.

Western Europe

During the period of the great Mediterranean galley wars, there was also a high level of conflict in the Atlantic area of operations. This conflict involved French Huguenot privateers and their Scots allies operating against Spanish and Portuguese interests in the West Indies and Brazil, where the ports and harbours were not fortified before 1556. The privateers attacked Cartegena, Santiago de Cuba and Nombre de Dios, and in 1555 captured Havana, which was looted and burned. These attacks prompted the Spaniards to implement a policy of fortifying these key ports which were crucial to the sailing of the annual treasure fleets to Spain. Spain removed the French Huguenots from Florida in 1565, and, until 1581, internal divisions within France reduced the threat that was posed to Spanish interests in the Atlantic.

There was also extensive Anglo-French naval warfare in the 1540s and 1550s, and English amphibious operations against Scotland and France. A major invasion of England was planned by the French in 1545, as part of their campaign to cut off Boulogne, which the English had captured in 1544, from supply by sea. The French also sent extensive aid to Scotland by sea, including a galley force that captured the castle of St Andrews from a Scottish Protestant force. English amphibious operations against Scotland had been carried out in the 1540s, to establish and support coastal fortresses. Under Elizabeth I (r. 1558–1603), in 1560, an English fleet under their admiral was decisive in leading to the defeat in Scotland of the French attempt to suppress the Protestant Lords of Congregation who had rebelled against Mary Queen of Scots, the wife of Francis II of France. The English under William Winter cut links across the Firth of Forth (leading the French to abandon operations in Fife), before successfully blockading Edinburgh's port, Leith. The English land assault against Leith failed, but the naval blockade was decisive and led the French to negotiate the withdrawal of their force. The English navy actually ferried the French force back to France as part of the agreement. Thus, sea power provided France and England with additional strategic options, as it had provided Spain and Portugal with strategic opportunities.

The potential of naval power was also shown during the Dutch Revolt. Philip II had sold his Dutch navy after peace with France in 1559, and was therefore unable to respond to the privateering attacks on the coastal waters off the Flanders coast and in the English Channel by the Protestant Sea Beggars that began in 1568. In some respects, this failure indicated a lack of responsiveness to the potential and threat of maritime power, but Philip had pressing problems in Spain (the *Moriscos* Revolt) and the Mediterranean (from the Ottomans), and the Duke of Alba, the Governor, appeared to have restored order in the Low Countries. The failure was highlighted in 1568 when ships carrying the pay for the Duke's army were attacked by Sea Beggars and driven into Plymouth harbour, where the money was impounded by the English. This created a crisis in the Low Countries and also in Anglo-Spanish relations.

The Dutch Revolt gathered pace anew from 1572, not least with a defeat of the local royalist fleet on the waters of the Zuider Zee on 11 October 1573. As a result, Philip was to change policy, building up a powerful Atlantic fleet, a choice that markedly contrasted with Chinese policy in response to the pirate/smuggler attacks. This choice, which owed much to the truce with the Ottomans, reflected the far-flung nature of Spanish power and commitments, although that range helped ensure a difficulty in focusing on any particular opponent. Thus, in the early 1580s, the fleet was required for the conquest of Portugal in 1580, and then, in 1582–3, of the Azores, a Portuguese island-group in the Atlantic that was a crucial staging post for the *flota*, the Spanish treasure fleet, on its return to Spain. In contrast, it proved difficult to apply Spanish naval power in the Low Countries. In 1574, Philip prepared a fleet in northern Spain for dispatch to the Low Countries, only for the scheme to be shelved when illness hit the sailors. In the absence of Spanish naval power, it required a huge military effort by the Duke of Parma to recapture Antwerp in 1585.[28]

Portugal and the Azores were more exposed to Spanish attack than the Low Countries. The Spanish fleets used a combination of galleons and galleys, while their expertise in amphibious warfare, built up during the galley wars in the Mediterranean, proved invaluable in capturing first Lisbon in 1580 and then Terceria in 1583. In 1582, in the battle of Punta Delgada, one of the major sea battles of the century, involving ninety sailing ships, the Spaniards intercepted and defeated a larger French fleet in open waters, most of the French ships being boarded. The tactics were essentially those used in the Mediterranean, with a reliance on troops to board, rather than cannon fire to sink opposing ships. The victor of the capture of Lisbon, Punta Delgada, and the successful amphibious assault on the Azores, was Don Alvaro de Bazan, Marquis of Santa Cruz (1526–88), the commander of the reserve at Lepanto.

The outbreak of war with England in 1585 ensured that now Spain had an enemy that could only be decisively attacked by sea. Philip decided to mount an invasion of England, although it had to be postponed because in 1587 the English under Sir Francis Drake successfully attacked the key naval base, Cadiz. The Spaniards were also delayed by the immensity of the necessary preparations. The Armada of 1588 was of a totally new order of magnitude for Spain and for Atlantic expeditions, and its scale and ambition helped mark a major extension in naval operations.

The plan required the fleet sailing from Spain through the English Channel to provide cover for an invasion of Parma's army from the Low Countries. The assumption that such co-operation could be obtained was overly optimistic, although Parma had systematically captured and occupied

Channel ports from which an invasion could be mounted. Moreover, the problems of mounting an expedition across part of the Atlantic Ocean were far greater than those posed by the Mediterranean, or indeed the narrow strait between Japan and Korea. Indeed, the majority of the Spanish losses in ships were due to the violent storms and jagged coast lines as the fleet sailed home around the north of Scotland and the west coast of Ireland, although the severe damage that many of the ships had received during the fighting undoubtedly contributed to the high number of ships that foundered.

Earlier, the English had harassed the Spanish fleet in the Channel, but had been unable to inflict any serious damage on the highly disciplined sailing formation that the Armada adopted. However, an attack by fire-ships on the fleet as it lay at anchor off Calais caused panic, and individual ships cut their anchor cables and were dispersed. When the Spanish fleet regrouped the following morning, they had lost their cohesion and formation which allowed the English fleet, in the battle of Gravelines, to engage in a mêlée at close range using their cannon and muskets. The English inflicted considerable damage off the Flemish coast, driving a number of Spanish ships onto the sandbanks, and the rest into the North Sea. At this point, their lack of anchors proved critical, and the Spanish ships were left with little option other than to sail home around Scotland. The English did not pursue them beyond Newcastle, as they were short of ammunition and food, and Elizabeth I was anxious to decommission the fleet to save money as soon as the invasion threat had passed.[29]

The war with Spain, which continued until a compromise peace in 1604 agreed by Philip III and James I, illustrated the limitations of naval power in this period, not least its vulnerability to storms, disease, the problems of combined operations, the heavy supply demands posed by large fleets, and the enormous cost of raising and sustaining a fleet. These factors adversely affected the Spaniards and the English in equal measure, and ensured that the English were unable to translate particular successes, such as the raid on Cadiz in 1596, into lasting benefit. Storms dispersed the two large-scale Armadas launched against England in 1596 and 1597. Failure helped ensure the exhaustion of both sides.

Strategic direction was also significant as Philip II's management of the war effort was affected by the absence of a coordinated strategy linking Spain's various commitments. Moreover, there was a lack of consistency in policy towards England – whether to overthrow the Tudor dynasty or to force England out of the war – and this problem was linked to a contrast between Spanish emphases on religious crusading and on pragmatic considerations. In addition, a lack of realistic strategic vision was linked to a reactive strategy of responding to English threats to the Spanish empire that gave the initiative to the English.[30] However, a programme of improved fortifications in the West Indies and Caribbean, for example to protect the trail across the Panama isthmus, and the use of fast *fregatas* (frigates, fast galleons), to carry gold and silver, rather than large, slow and vulnerable fleets, reduced the risk to the Spanish supply of silver from the Americas that sustained the Spanish empire. This supply was maintained throughout the war despite sustained English attacks.

More generally, despite an increase in Spanish naval strength as well as a standardisation of galleon construction, Philip II did not appreciate the constraints posed by the need to maintain naval capability.[31] This failure was related to the difficulty in Spain, despite having also taken over Portugal and being allied to Genoa, of creating political-mercantile alliances able to sustain naval power, which contrasted with the situation in England. That the capital, Madrid, was far from the coast, may have contributed to the situation. It made Spain more similar to Iran, China, Russia and Mughal India than to England or the Ottoman empire. Yet, this difficulty has to be set alongside the ability of Spanish private contractors and public officials to co-operate. In addition, England also suffered from over-stretch.

The defeat of the Armada demonstrated the growing technical skill of English seamanship and naval warfare, and underlined the importance of superior naval gunnery and appropriate related tactics and leadership. These skills were also developed in parallel by England's Dutch ally, and, by the end of the war in 1604, the Dutch were on a par with the English. This process was aided by the institutional separateness of the English and Dutch navies which, while similar to a European pattern including the Danish and Swedish navies and the Ottomans, contrasted with the situation in East Asia. Neither China, Korea nor Japan had a navy that was separate from the army, and, partly as a result, there were relatively few commanders and officers who specialised in naval operations.

Information

Skill was disseminated not only in the traditional way of learning on the job by personal instruction but also by means of print. Thus, cartographic information increased in the West and was disseminated. For example, the hydrographer Bartolomeo Crescenzi, who had travelled with the Papal fleet, produced a portolan map of the Mediterranean and Black Sea, dated 1596, which was printed as a map in 1602. Alongside the dissemination of skill and existing knowledge, there was also an attempt to gain additional information, although, in contrast to the situation in the West, no real Ottoman portolan chart school developed: Ottoman receptivity to

Western advances, which was considerable, was not the same as Ottoman creativity.[32]

At the forefront of trans-oceanic expansion, and thus of the need to fix, record and plan routes out of sight of land, the Hispanic world played a key role. De Navigatione, by the Portuguese Diogo de Sá, who had served in the Indian Ocean in the 1520s, was published in Paris in 1549. As an aspect of the advancement of opinion by debate, he challenged the theories of Pedro Nuñez, a fellow countryman. In his Breve Compendio de la Sphera y de la Arte de Navegar (Seville, 1551), Martín Cortés de Albacar, who taught cosmography and navigation in Cadiz, advanced the understanding of the compass, suggesting that the magnetic pole was different to the true pole, as well as discussing the construction of effective navigational instruments and thus of preparing accurate charts.

Translations and examples helped encourage the spread of such literature. The English navigator Stephen Borough, who visited the naval school in Seville in 1557, was instrumental in having Richard Eden translate Cortés's book into English, and The Art of Navigation was published in London in 1561. Ten editions in English appeared by 1630. The visit was one of the benefits of the marriage of Philip II to Queen Mary. Inspired by Cortés, William Bourne, a self-taught English mathematician, published, in 1574, A Regiment of the Sea, dedicated to the Lord High Admiral, Edward, Earl of Lincoln, which provided seamen with practical advice on how to plot coastal features, observe the sun and stars, and plot routes. This book, of which other editions appeared in 1580, 1584, 1587, 1592, 1596 and 1643, was followed by his Arte of Shooting in Great Ordnaunce (1578), which covered the assembling, loading and firing of weapons. The threat of Spanish attack was responsible for the publication of a new version of the latter in 1587, dedicated to the Master General of the Ordnance, Ambrose, Earl of Warwick. Rodrigo Zamorano's navigation manual Compendio del Arte de Navegar (1581) was published in English in 1610 and also translated into Dutch.[33]

In his De Havenvinding (Leiden, 1599), the Bruges-born mathematician Simon Stevin (also a key figure in the development of Dutch ideas on fortification), in pursuit of the quest of enabling ships to determine longitude, and thus to record their position, suggested a comprehensive worldwide survey of measurements of the deviation of the magnetic needle from the astronomical meridian during the course of a voyage where the latitude was known. This option was not pursued, but it testified to the global ambitions for the Western maritime world, as did the dissemination of Stevin's idea, with a French translation of the work also appearing in Leiden in 1599.

Navigational knowledge was also linked to naval activity. Thus, Edward Wright, a Cambridge mathematician, was sent by Elizabeth I in 1589 to join an attack on the Spanish-held Azores in order to make navigational observations. Wright applied Gerardus Mercator's ideas on cartographic projection, and published in 1599 *Certain Errors in Navigation ... corrected,* which was accompanied by a map including the Earl of Cumberland's route to and from the Azores. As an instance of the extent to which the European world of print permitted debate, the 1610 edition of Wright's work included his responses to Stevin's criticisms.

Conclusions

The period 1450–1600 is generally presented in terms of one central narrative, the rise of the West. This account apparently relates developments in Europe to those in the wider world, with the common theme proving that of the development and use of more effective naval capability. In this approach, technology is linked to geopolitics, with the former permitting the creation of the bifurcated modern world, one in which authoritarian, land-based, societies in Asia were challenged by the states of the Eurasian periphery, states that could draw on the economic opportunities of the New World. The latter, in turn, offered a developmental series in which Portugal and Spain were succeeded by the Dutch in the seventeenth century, the British in the eighteenth, and the Americans (after German failure) in the twentieth.

That, however, is not an account that makes much sense from the perspective of the eastern Mediterranean nor the Red Sea, let alone East Asia. In these areas, it is far less clear that Western shipping was particularly effective, and, instead, a naval history can be written, at least in part, around non-Western societies. Technological proficiency is readily apparent in the case of Korea, and organisational development and resilience, as well as the capacity to generate naval forces, with the Ottomans. The Chinese, although far from repeating the situation in the early fifteenth century, were able to mount a significant and successful effort against Japan in the 1590s. Moreover, as this study suggests, the value of oceanic economic and military systems was less apparent than was to be the case in the eighteenth century, and certainly paled in comparison with the resources deployed in the sixteenth century by China, the Mughals and the Ottomans.

The result, however, was not a clash between the oceanic and the Continental powers. Instead, the dominant theme was that of conflict between the latter, notably between Ottomans and Safavids, a conflict that was waged on land, as was that between China and the Mongols, or the wars of Mughal expansion. Compared to these struggles, the Western powers posed scant threat to the empires and states of East and South Asia.

The Western powers appear distinctive in this period in terms of voyages of exploration, an explosion of new cartographic and geographical description of the world, and a commercial and colonial transformation stemming from Portuguese entry in the Indian Ocean. These developments can be linked to forward-looking, even visionary, perspectives on the part of some Western rulers. Nevertheless, although there were now Portuguese ships in Chinese waters and bases in India, they, especially the former, were marginal to local politics. Moreover, Portuguese expertise could be bought in by alliances or by hiring mercenaries. The Portuguese challenge to the Ottomans involved an element of oceanic versus continental, but only on the fringes of the Ottoman empire, and only if the major efforts made by the Ottomans at developing naval capability are underplayed. Moreover, Portugal acted in Morocco as a would-be continental power, although this ambition was uncharacteristic and it came to grief as a result.

Thus, neither technological nor geopolitical explanations and characterisations of the rise of Western naval power can be accepted without significant qualifications. This discussion of the naval and maritime dimension is an important accompaniment to a consideration of the situation on land. The latter consideration often owes much not only to a misplaced notion of naval exceptionalism, but also to a view that this naval strength gave the Western effort a uniquely effective capability. While the latter was true in some areas, the ability to project power did not necessarily lead to any marked effectiveness on land. Thus, naval history should not be used to argue the case for a military revolution resting on Western overseas capability. Such a view might be valid for what was becoming Latin America and for the Caribbean basin, but it had scant basis in South, let alone East, Asia, regions containing much of the world's population.

7 The Expansion of the West, 1450–1600

At sea, it is readily possible to see Western expansion in the period 1450–1600, as well as impressive Ottoman expansion.[1] There were Portuguese ships in East Asian waters, not vice versa, and it was through the projection of Western power that the 'Old World' and the 'New World' were connected. Chinese colonies of traders settled at various places on the Malay peninsula, including Singapore, which was then known as Temarek; Japanese navigators and cartographers had a rather keen interest in the South Pacific, at the latest from the sixteenth century and probably earlier; and the Japanese took an active role along the coastlines of South-East Asia.[2] Nevertheless, neither China nor Japan, despite their long coastlines and maritime traditions, chose to establish settlement colonies across the Pacific.

The situation on land was very different and it is misleading to read between, and thus combine in the same analysis, wars with non-Westerners along Christendom's land frontiers in Europe and those waged across the oceans. The latter included a central role for expanding trade, ensuring that a set of values and relationships that did not focus on the control or defence of land came into play.

Russia

This situation was far less the case with land frontiers as defence played a leading role and did so even when expansion occurred. Thus, Ivan IV of Russia's conquest of the Islamic khanate of Kazan in 1552 can be seen as a defensive response to the khanate's alliance with the Crimean khanate.[3] In 1535, Djan Ali, the pro-Muscovite khan installed with the help of Vassily III in 1532, had been murdered and replaced by Safa Giray, a relative of the khan of the Crimean Tatars and, thereafter, relations deteriorated, with frequent raids on Russia by Tatar light cavalry.

In 1545, Ivan IV took the initiative against Kazan, helped by the divisions among the Tatars that were to be important to eventual Russian success.

He attempted two winter campaigns against Kazan in 1547–8 and 1549–50, but these failed because the Russian army had no fortified base in the region, had to leave its artillery behind as a result of heavy rains, and ended up campaigning with an exclusively cavalry army that was of no use in investing the city of Kazan. However, for the third campaign, a base was secured. In the winter and spring of 1551–2, the Russians prefabricated fortress towers and wall sections near Uglich and then floated them down the River Volga on barges with artillery and troops to its confluence with the River Sviiaga, 25 kilometres from Kazan; here the Russian fortress of Sviiazhsk was erected in just 28 days. Sviiazhsk not only provided a base of operations against Kazan, but also protected the upper Volga towns from raids by the Crimean Tatars. That summer, siege guns and stores were shipped down the Oka and Volga to Sviiazhsk and, a Crimean invasion of southern Muscovy, with artillery support probably from the Ottomans, was repulsed near Tula in mid-June. The Russian army then advanced on the city of Kazan, which it reached on 20 August. Including peasants levied as sappers and transport labour, the Russian army was allegedly 150,000 strong. It also had 150 siege guns, a capability far greater than that earlier in the century, and one on a par with Ottoman and Habsburg forces.

Kazan stood on a high bluff overlooking the Kazanka and Bulak rivers. It had double walls of oak logs covered over with clay and partially plated with stones. There were 14 stone towers with guns and a deep surrounding ditch. The Russians constructed siege lines from which cannon opened fire and also used wooden siege towers carrying cannon and mounted on rollers. The ditch surrounding the city was filled with fascines, and sappers tunnelled beneath the walls. The mines were blown up on 2 October, destroying the walls at two of the gates, upon which the Russian army, drawn up into seven columns, attacked all seven of the town gates simultaneously. They soon broke through and Kazan fell after a 28-day siege.

The campaign witnessed the first large-scale use of artillery and mining by Russians, and, in part, they owed their success to more advanced weaponry. Indeed, the war demonstrated the effectiveness of Ivan's new infantry and artillery units; but there were other important factors. The demographic balance favoured Russia, and there was a clear difference in consistency and quality of leadership, with repeated changes in leadership in Kazan providing numerous opportunities for Russian intervention.

Once the city of Kazan had fallen, there were several serious rebellions in the khanate – in 1553, 1554 and 1556. They were repressed with great brutality: towns were destroyed, men slaughtered, women and children taken prisoner, and the countryside devastated. Only in 1556 did organised resistance cease.[4]

After conquering Kazan, Russia was able to expand across the Urals into western Siberia, down the Volga to Astrakhan, which they conquered in 1556, and towards the Caucasus. This expansion owed much to non-state military entrepreneurs, largely Cossacks. Their motivation and success were strikingly similar to those of the Spanish *conquistadores*.[5] Russian success was highly significant for the reconfiguration of the geopolitics of Eurasia, both in the short and the long term. Moreover, although the Russians suffered setbacks, as in 1597 when they were defeated on the River Terek, this expansion was never reversed.

North Africa

The situation was very different in North Africa, where earlier European expansion was reversed. Just as Ivan IV's success reflected both the growing sophistication and capability of the Russian military, as well as political and regional divisions that the Russians could exploit, so Portuguese failure in Morocco was a product of growing Moroccan military quality and greater cohesion. In the fifteenth century, the Portuguese had displayed operational versatility, adaptability, tactical expertise, and superiority in guns.[6]

However, in the mid-sixteenth century, the situation changed radically. Having driven the Berber Wattasids, the emirs of Fez, from much of Morocco in mid-century, their more vigorous opponents, the Arab Sa'dis from Marrakech, built up forces equipped with firearms and artillery arsenals. The sharifs worked diligently to integrate arquebusiers and field artillery into their forces and developed combined infantry–cavalry tactics for their battles. As a reminder that firepower was not the sole issue, their light cavalry was more flexible than the heavier cavalry of Western European armies. Focusing on war with Christians, the Sa'dis captured the town of Agadir in 1541, and the Portuguese decided to abandon their bases of Safi (1542), Azamor (1542) and Arzila (1549). These coastal positions were not as important to the Portuguese once their oceanic reach had increased into the Indian Ocean. The financial benefits provided by the Moroccan ports were less than those from the latter, and the technical improvements in their ships made the Portuguese less dependent on nearby ports.

Meanwhile, Moroccan military capability improved as campaigns shifted from static sieges against Portuguese fortifications to the rapid manoeuvres of infantry–cavalry armies against Islamic foes, especially the advancing Ottomans in the 1550s. External success ensured that Morocco gained internal stability.

The Christians were not only in retreat in Morocco. Further east in North Africa, the Spaniards lost the town of Bougie in 1529, Charles V failed in an amphibious expedition against Algiers in 1541, the Knights of St John lost Tripoli in 1551, and a Spanish force sent to recapture it was defeated with heavy losses at Djerba in 1560. In October 1573, Don John of Austria, still in command of the reduced forces of the League, which Venice had left, led an expedition to the Spanish fortress of La Goletta at the mouth of the Bay of Tunis, and from there had recaptured the city of Tunis. A fortress was built at Tunis and it was garrisoned by 8000 troops, which were in addition to the 1000 in La Goletta. However, the cost and difficulties of maintaining the garrisons from Sicily and Italy proved to be logistically difficult and ruinously expensive. The following year, an Ottoman fleet under the command of Uluj Ali, and comprising 230 galleys, carrying 40,000 troops, arrived in July in the Gulf of Tunis, unopposed by any Christian galleys. To general astonishment, they had captured La Goletta, which Spain had fortified at vast expense, by 25 August, and the garrison of Tunis surrendered on 13 September. The two forts were too far apart to assist each other, and the Ottomans received a great deal of support from the local Arab population. Fundamentally, however, Philip II was facing bankruptcy and there was no prospect of any relief. By 1578, the Spaniards held nothing in North Africa east of Oran.

Fortifications

These repeated failures indicated that, whatever the apparent differences between the two sides in terms of technology, the reality on the ground was that there was no necessary advantage for the Christians, which helped explain the greater Western effort devoted to the Mediterranean compared with trans-oceanic expansion.[7] As so often when judging relative capability, the situation was complicated. For example, although the Ottomans were affected by improvements in Western fortifications, in 1570 they captured Nicosia in Cyprus, which was encircled with an extended *enceinte* constructed according to the most modern design. The Ottomans captured 160 good artillery pieces with the position. Yet, Nicosia in part fell because the command of the defence was poor.[8]

That the Ottomans did not have an equivalent fortification re-evaluation, in expenditure or style, was not so much due to a failure to match Western advances, as because the Ottomans scarcely required such a development as they were not under attack. Thus, an asymmetry in achievement reflected differing tasks. Moreover, the different nature of Ottoman attitudes toward territory and of fighting practice had an effect on their response to frontier positions. In particular, the Ottoman emphasis on field forces and mobility, as well as their interest in expansion, ensured that they were less concerned with protecting fixed positions. In contrast, Western losses of fortresses to the Ottomans early in the century, such as Modon and Rhodes, as well as a lack of confidence in mobile defence, encouraged the introduction of the new angle-bastioned military architecture, which the Venetians were very quick to use in their *Empire da Mar*.

When, however, the Ottomans needed fortresses they built them, as in Syria and Palestine where there were three lines of fortresses, one parallel to the coast from Beirut to El Arish, one along the Damascus–Cairo highway, and a third on the road from Damascus towards Mecca; in 1559, Süleyman ordered that four fortresses be added to the last. These fortresses were built to protect travellers and others from attacks by the Bedouin Arabs, and supplemented the allowances paid the Bedouin to protect the pilgrims en route to Mecca.[9] Later, in 1582, a chain of seven fortresses was built on the Red Sea coast from Suakin to Massawa in order to consolidate its recapture from Ethiopia.

Similarly, in Yemen, although it appears that much construction was to refurbish or expand earlier sites, a process that needs to be assessed through excavations, nevertheless the Ottomans built large fortresses between the mid-sixteenth and early seventeenth centuries, possibly on a scale that exceeded most regions of the empire. Whereas in the latter, the Ottomans probably felt that they had the resources and logistical capability to overwhelm their opponents, in distant Yemen they had to adopt a different strategy, perhaps more akin to what the Portuguese faced in the Indian Ocean.

Sub-Saharan Africa

Fortifications, like firearms, were very important to Western expansion, and each has therefore played a prominent role in the idea of a Western-focused military revolution. As the fortifications maximised the advantages of defensive firepower while lessening those of attackers, whether or not the latter used firearms, so the two were closely linked, which again contributes to the idea of a military revolution. The Portuguese certainly believed that their firearms were important. Armed with spears and daggers, the Jagas attacked and defeated the king of Kongo, a Portuguese ally, in the 1560s, leading the Portuguese to send 600 soldiers and a number of adventurers under Francisco de Gouveia Sottomaior. He reached Kongo in 1571, and Filippo Pigafetta reported: 'the king was restored to his throne, triumphing more by the noise and power of his guns, then by numbers, because the Jagas were greatly terrified by those engines'. In practice, it took a year and a half of fighting to win, and this success entailed fighting alongside the Kongolese.[10]

More generally, fortifications and firearms were important to Western success as part of a range of factors, with some of which they interacted, such as organisation, discipline and tactics, whereas, in other cases, notably disease, the links were tenuous or nonexistent. Impacting factors in a wider context in this fashion decreases the supposed revolutionary character of any individual factor.

In sub-Saharan Africa, the Portuguese explicitly sought to emulate the achievement of the Spaniards in the New World, only to reveal the ineffectiveness of the Western military system on land in the region. Both major Portuguese attempts – in Mozambique in 1569–75 and in Angola in 1575–90 – were unsuccessful. Disease was as devastating for the Europeans in Africa as it was for their opponents in the New World. About 60 per cent of the Portuguese soldiers who served in Angola in 1575–90 died of disease, and most of the rest were killed or deserted, while horses did not survive.

The operating environment was far more difficult for the Portuguese than the regions of the New World dominated by the Aztecs and Incas had been for the Spaniards. Whereas these regions were populous and had a well-developed agricultural system that could provide plenty of resources for an invader, including large numbers of human bearers for carrying supplies, Africa lacked comparable storehouses, food for plunder, and roads. The Aztec and Inca empires were also more centralised politically, and thus easier to take over once the ruler had been seized.

In contrast, Africa was more segmented politically, while the Portuguese also found the Africans armed with well-worked iron weapons as good in some ways as Portuguese steel weaponry, and certainly better than the wood and obsidian of the New World. Moreover, Portuguese cannon proved to have little impact on African earthwork fortifications,[11] while the slow rate of fire of muskets and the openness of African fighting formations reduced the effectiveness of firearms, and the Portuguese were successful only when supported by local troops.

In Angola, where, in 1575, the Portuguese established a base at Luanda, the only natural port on that part of the Atlantic coast, they entered an alliance with the inland kingdom of Ndongo and, when expelled from there with heavy losses in 1579, employed their existing alliance with the kingdom of Kongo to advance on Ndongo in 1580, only to be defeated. Thereafter, the Portuguese used their Kongo alliance and their naval power on the River Kwanza to persuade a number of local rulers to switch from Ndongo to alliance with the Portuguese. With their help, a Ndongo force was defeated at Massangano in 1582. A full-scale attack on Ndongo's core region was mounted in 1590 but the Portuguese force was totally defeated near the River Lukala, leading to the collapse of the Portuguese alliance system. A peace negotiated in 1599 left the Portuguese largely confined to the coast. The Portuguese role in the fighting in part rested on firearms, but their skill as swordsmen was probably more significant and in battle they formed a heavy infantry core with local archers deployed on the flanks.[12]

On the Zambezi, the Portuguese settlements were destroyed by the Zimba, a nomadic warrior tribe, in 1585 and 1592; but in 1596 the Portuguese were able to help a protégé to the throne of Mwene Mutapa in modern Zimbabwe.

Philippines

The use of local troops was frequently a factor in Western expansion, and as a key part of a local co-operation that helps to focus attention on political circumstances. Thus, in the Philippines, where the Spaniards expanded control from 1565, the vulnerability of the islands to maritime attack and the limited and weak nature of local fortifications were important factors, but this was a conquest that involved relatively little warfare for there was no strong political entity in the Philippines able to mobilise resistance. The *barangay*, a comparatively small kinship group, was the sole significant political unit, and this limited the organisation of resistance. Furthermore, cultural assimilation was aided by the nature of Philippine religion – animist and without an organised ecclesiastical structure – and by the willingness of Spain to encourage effective Catholic missionary activity.

In contrast, it is significant that the Spaniards encountered most serious resistance in the Philippines from those areas where Islam had made an impact: the southern islands of Mindinao and Sulu. The first major Spanish attack on Sulu, begun in 1578, failed, as did a 1596 expedition to Mindinao. Fortunately for the Spaniards, the Philippines were at the edge of the Islamic world, distant from centres that might have provided support for co-religionists. Moreover, there was not a force-projection capability matching that of Spain, which, indeed, had planted its first settlement in the Philippines not from Spain but across the Pacific from Mexico. The Philippines was at the intersection of a number of worlds. Thus, the value of the walled settlement built by the Spaniards when they conquered Manila was demonstrated in 1574 when an attack by Lin Feng, a Chinese pirate with 62 ships and about 1000 men, was driven off. Having been defeated, Lin Feng founded a settlement at Pangasinan in Lingayen Bay. The following year, the Spaniards launched a surprise attack that destroyed most of the pirate ships before laying siege to the fortress. This siege, which ended with the flight of Lin Feng, indicated another strength of the Spanish system as Filipino auxiliaries were deployed alongside Spanish troops.

Indian Ocean

The complex role of local politics was amply displayed in Ceylon (Sri Lanka), where the Portuguese had first landed in 1505, signing a trade treaty with the kingdom of Kotte on the south-west coast, a treaty that reflected Portugal's greater political, military and, initially, commercial interest in the western part of the Indian Ocean compared to the eastern part. Whereas China had successfully intervened on the island in 1410–11, King Dharmapalla of Kotte became a vassal of the Portuguese crown in 1551 and willed the kingdom to Portugal in 1580. The Portuguese reunited Kotte, which had been divided into three principalities, and the kingdom lapsed to Portugal in 1597, but, by then, the inland kingdom of Udarata had claimed rule over the entire island in 1592 and was fighting to expel the Portuguese.[13]

The situation in Ceylon showed both that alliance with local rulers could be unstable and that it could be a valuable asset. The same was to be true of Portuguese co-operation with Iran. Initially, the Safavids accepted the Portuguese position in Hormuz, which was far from their centres of power and concern; while the Portuguese provided cannon to the Safavids, as did Ivan IV. By 1600, the Safavids had about 500 cannon. Co-operation based on strength also helped the Portuguese in East Africa, with the rulers of Malindi helping in attacking those of Mombasa. In 1589, they co-operated in capturing Mombasa, the ruler of Malindi becoming sheikh there while the Portuguese built a powerful fortress.

Naval power provided the Portuguese with a key advantage. Portuguese fortresses could be attacked by local rulers, as were Goa and Chaul in 1571, but, without naval strength, it was not possible to cut the bases off from relief by sea, which proved crucial in these cases.

Competition between Westerners

The Dutch did not land in Ceylon until 1602, and, thereafter, the Portuguese faced serious opposition which, in the end, led to them being driven from the island.[14] However, prior to that, the Portuguese benefited from not confronting Western rivals in Sri Lanka. The first Dutch fleet reached Bantam in West Java in 1596, and the English also developed a presence in the Indian Ocean that was hostile to Portugal; but, compared to the seventeenth century, it is the relative limit of rivalry between Western powers in the greater Indian Ocean that is striking. The situation was different in the Americas, where the French sought to establish bases in areas claimed by Portugal and Spain, namely Brazil and Florida, while, from 1585, war with England meant a series of challenges to the Spanish position in the Caribbean. Nevertheless, as also in South and East Asia and West Africa, there was no comparison with the degree of competition seen in the seventeenth century, a competition that became acute with the Dutch challenge to the Hispanic world, notably in the 1620s–1640s, and with conflict between the Dutch, English and French from the 1650s.

The lesser degree of competition encouraged bold plans for expansion, for example Spanish schemes for the invasion of China that Philip II rejected, and, more practically in South-East Asia, where Spanish-backed adventurers led by a Portuguese mercenary, Diego Veloso, attempted to take over Cambodia in the 1590s. Their candidate was proclaimed king in 1597, but, in 1599, the greatly-outnumbered Spaniards were killed in a successful rebellion. Limited competition with other European powers certainly helped Portugal as it developed its empire. Unlike other European states, Portugal, with its narrow demographic base, chose to devote its military resources to extra-European activity, both in Morocco or further afield. It had not been directly involved in the Italian Wars, the Franco-Habsburg struggle for predominance, nor the Wars of Religion within Christendom. Portugal thus achieved a military situation that prefigured the position of Victorian Britain, as an expansionist maritime power on the edge of Europe relatively disengaged from that continent's struggles.

When, however, in 1580, Portugal became part of the Spanish system, it was targeted by attacks on that system, and, indeed, became a tempting victim due to the wealth and apparent vulnerability of the Portuguese empire. Whereas English incursions on Portuguese interests prior to 1580 had been small-scale, thereafter these interests, bases, shipping, local alliances and commercial relationships, were directly affected by the upsurge in English attacks on the Hispanic maritime world. Portuguese East Indiamen, large carracks carrying enormous wealth, were attacked by English fleets as they staged through the Azores en route to Portugal. In 1591, the *Madre de Dios* was captured and the *Santa Clara* destroyed by a fleet of English privateers off the Azores. A third carrack, the *San Bernardo*, evaded another English force and arrived safely in Lisbon. After this, Portuguese ships avoided the Azores on their return journeys from the East. The first English ships in the Indian Ocean arrived in 1591, seizing three Portuguese vessels in 1592, and in 1595 an English privateering fleet captured the major Portuguese base of Pernambuco in Brazil. The contrast with earlier in the century was readily apparent.

Siberia

Open frontiers and the wealth of Asia attracted expansion in another direction from the early 1580s, as the Russians exploited the conquest of

Kazan and Astrakhan to advance to the Ural mountains and then across the accessible southern Urals; although the effort devoted was far less than that expended in bitter rivalry with Poland and Sweden. Firearms played a major role in the conquest of the Tatar khanate of Sibir from 1582 to 1598 as the Tatars, despite their advantage in numbers and mobility, lacked firearms. The Russians anchored their presence with the construction of forts, including at Tobolsk on the River Ob, near the site of Sibir, in 1587 and at Samara, Ufa and Tyumen in 1596.[15] The forts maximised the defensive potential of firearms. The role of adventurers and entrepreneurs, predominantly Cossacks, in this eastward expansion was crucial to its success. In some respects, this expansion matched the process of Spanish conquest in the New World, with initial successes often followed by a more difficult process in which the enforcement of a new order owed much to the disruptive impact of divisions among the local people and the devastating consequences of European disease.

The Americas

Initial contact between Europe and the Americas in the early modern period came first from the arrival of Christopher Columbus in the West Indies in 1492. His voyages were part of a pattern of Iberian expansion, with, as an important element, non-Iberian navigators and economic interests taking advantage of the support of the expansionist crowns of Portugal and Castile. These rulers, in turn, sought to supplement their own resources with those they could recruit to their service. This expansionism was territorial and religious as well as economic. Drawing on their long-standing ideological crusading role in driving the Moors and Islam from Iberia, a task apparently achieved with the fall of the last Moorish kingdom, Granada, in 1492, the crowns of Portugal and Castile had already taken the fight into North Africa. They also seized the islands of the eastern Atlantic, the Canaries, Madeira, the Azores and the Cape Verde Islands, which served as important stopping-places on the route to the West Indies and South America. Portugal, moreover, established bases in West Africa, from which it obtained gold and slaves and sought allies against the Moors, while continuing to explore the route round southern Africa into the Indian Ocean.

In contrast, following Columbus, Castile made the running in the Americas, with, as a result, Portugal restricted there to Brazil which had been discovered as part of the Portuguese effort to find better winds and currents to push forward the search for a route into the Indian Ocean. Moreover, Portugal did not seek to establish a territorial presence in North America to the north of the Castilian zone; although Portuguese interests were to play a role there, notably in fishing, and more recent Portuguese influence is readily found in maritime New England. In the Papal division of the New World in 1493 followed by the Treaty of Tordesillas in 1494, North America was allocated to Castile, or Spain as it can be termed after the union of the inheritances of Castile and Aragon. North America's relative lack of appeal to contemporaries was shown by the absence of Portuguese attempts to circumvent this restriction, although, in addition, Portugal was not well placed to defy neighbouring Spain in this, while from 1580 to 1640, after a successful invasion, the kings of Spain were also kings of Portugal.

The Spanish conquest of the Caribbean was incomplete, with only some of the larger islands, principally Hispaniola, Cuba and Puerto Rico, seeming attractive for seizure and settlement. This left later opportunities on different islands for other European powers, notably France, England and the Dutch, and ensured that the natives remained dominant in certain islands, such as St Vincent. However, the Spaniards brought European diseases, notably smallpox, and the inroads of disease helped ensure that the demographic balance in the West Indies rapidly changed, and also greatly demoralised the native population. Once seized, these islands, especially Cuba, where a harbour was developed at Havana from 1511, became important bases for Spanish activity, fulfilling a role that was lacking as far as the Atlantic seaboard of North America was concerned. Offshore islands, such as Newfoundland and Bermuda, played only a minor part as far as English settlement in the seventeenth century was concerned. In contrast, Cuba provided Spain with a springboard for the invasion of Mesoamerica.

In 1519, Hernán Cortés landed at Veracruz with about 450 soldiers, 14 small cannon and 16 horses. His overthrow of the Aztec empire, based in Mesoamerica in what is now central Mexico, was rapidly achieved. Montezuma, the Aztec leader, was fascinated by Cortés, worried that he might be an envoy from a powerful potentate, and unwilling to act decisively against him; although the account that Montezuma saw him as a god has been questioned. Cortés reached Tenochtitlán, the Aztec capital, without having to fight his way there. In 1520, the situation deteriorated from the Spanish point of view. A massacre of the Aztec nobles in the courtyard of the Great Temple helped lead to an Aztec rising, and Cortés had to flee Tenochtitlán, having had Montezuma killed. Against formidable resistance, Cortés fought his way back into the city in 1521.

In some respects, this conquest was a remarkable step, but it was also part of a wider pattern of territorial change in 1515–30 with the overthrow of the Mamluk empire, the Lodi sultanate, and the kingdom of Hungary. Each, in its way, was a striking achievement, and, together, they serve as a reminder of the possibility of change and, in particular, of the extent to which states which lacked any real grounding comparable to the engaged and mobilised mass publics of the nineteenth and twentieth centuries could readily fall when their rulers and élites were overthrown. This process was eased, and, in part, achieved, by recruiting part of the existing élite and reconciling it to the new rulers. Thus, many of the Rajputs were swiftly recruited by the Mughals, while the Ottomans rapidly used Mamluk troops and administrators, the former playing an impressive part in the capture of Rhodes in 1522.[16]

The Spanish conquest of much of Central and South America in the early and mid-sixteenth century fits into this pattern. The Spaniards exploited existing divisions within Central Mexico, notably forming an alliance with the Tlaxcaltecs, a people surrounded by Aztec territory, subordinated to the Aztecs, and resentful. They and other allies provided significant numbers to help in the conquest of Tenochtitlán in 1521. Native support was essential in order to match the massive numerical superiority of the Aztecs, who also learned to alter their tactics to counter Western arms, especially firepower.[17] In Mesoamerica, the battle superiority of the Spaniards, which owed much to steel helmets and swords, promised those who allied with them a good chance of victory, but the availability and willingness of many of the Mesoamericans to co-operate against the Aztecs reflected the nature of the Aztec empire, in particular the absence of a practice and theory of assimilation.

Subsequent Spanish expansion from the Aztec territories owed much again to local support, including frequently in distant lands and against those who were not traditional enemies. In 1524–6, resuming earlier (pre-Spanish) patterns of attempted expansion from Central Mexico, Pedro de Alvarado invaded Guatemala with Nahua allies, overrunning the area only to undermine his success (and that of his allies) by excessive violence and harsh demands for tribute and labour. As a result of continuing opposition, his brother Jorge recruited between 5000 and 10,000 native warriors for his invasion of Guatemala in 1527, but he only succeeded in 1529 after large-scale butchery of the population. The importance of native support, which provided fighting power, intelligence, and the logistics of porterage as well as obtaining and preparing supplies, was probably greater than that of other factors in Spanish success: the impact of new diseases, of Spanish military technology, and of divisions among the local population.[18]

Subsequently, Viceroy Antonio de Mendoza used 10,000 local allies in the Mixton War of 1540–2. Moreover, indigenous local soldiers were employed as a defence force, so that in Nueva Galicia by the 1590s local *flecheros* (bowmen) were guarding roads and silver mines, receiving fiscal and legal advantages in return.[19]

In South Africa, although Pizarro rapidly conquered the Inca world, capturing the ruler, Atahualpa, in November 1532, and occupying the capital, Cuzco in 1533, he faced serious opposition, not least in 1536 when Manco Inca brought a degree of cohesion to the resistance. At that point, the Spaniards were not only successful because their fighting quality brought success in battle. In addition, sufficient local people supported the invaders and their puppet emperor to provide Spain with major battlefield and political advantages. Memory of Inca oppression played a role.[20] Leadership was also important, with the assassination of Manco Inca being important to Spanish success. Nevertheless, the conquest took over seven years.

In part, this length of time reflected the extent to which the Spaniards sought conquest, not raiding. Military action was followed by the symbolic ownership shown by naming the new landscape.[21] This process was complemented by the arrival of colonists and their crops and livestock, by Christian proselytisation and the destruction of rival religious rituals, and by the introduction of administrative and tenurial structures, for example the town-based patterns of control based on Classical Rome.[22] In addition, the degree of Spanish acceptance of local élites and local material cultures, as well as of local adaptation to the Spaniards, were important factors. Urbanisation was also important to the grounding of Ottoman power and governance, with cities such as Sarajevo, Mostar and Plovdiv created or greatly expanded in the Balkans.

It is possible, alongside the slaughter, to paint a more benign account of the Spanish conquest and, in particular, to discuss the Christianity of Spanish America as syncretic: drawing on local roots and practices[23] as well as being European in its origins. This account of a melded sacred space can then serve as a key indicator of a more general pattern of co-operation, as consensus was elicited, and this pattern can then be seen as the basis for the politics of Spanish America. In particular, a causal line can be drawn from syncretism and consensus to stability. This stability can be seen as a central characteristic of Spanish America, as well as a possible reason why its society proved less dynamic, both then and subsequently, than that of British America.

Yet, such an account ignores both much of the process by which the Spaniards established their presence and also the comparative dimension. In the Americas, there was a typecasting of native societies as harsh, primitive and uncivilised, and this typecasting encouraged not only total war and cruelty on the part of the conquerors, as in Mexico, but also a determination to extirpate the distinctive features of their society.[24] There was a destruction of native religious sites and an extirpation of practices deemed unacceptable, these practices being discussed by Spanish commentators to demonstrate the superiority of Spanish rule. While Christian worship in Spanish America might contain elements of compromise, there was no compromise about Christianity. The Inquisition became important to the campaign to end native religion, as with the burning of idols.[25]

The situation was different to the position across much of Eurasia where there were important confessional tensions, but without conquest by the Ottomans, Mughals and Manchus leading to the ending of other religious practices. Yet, the Spaniards and their descendants never outnumbered the indigenous or mixed population, so, although the Spaniards could make unremitting war on the pagan deities, as well as use control over native labour to lessen the position of the indigenous nobility, they left large tracts of land in the hands of co-operative natives, particularly those who had readily allied themselves with the conquest.[26]

Spanish practice was to be followed by other Europeans. Proselytism was regarded as a product of superiority, a justification for conquest, and as a way to secure control. The net outcome was an assault on native culture far greater than that seen for example by conquerors, non-Western and Western, in India, and, as a consequence, a disruption of native society that contributed, alongside disease, to its breakdown. The result, established from the outset in the New World, was a pattern of conquest that was more total than that generally seen elsewhere. It was a pattern that looked in particular to the Iberian *Reconquista* and can be seen as arising from a belief in Christian manifest destiny. Yet, the harshness of Spanish rule was strengthened by key aspects of Western history and public culture in the sixteenth century. The assault by a revived Islam in the shape of the Ottoman empire, an assault that also involved the enslavement of Christians, was particularly relevant to Spanish attitudes. The marked increase in religious violence within Christendom due to the Reformation was also pertinent, particularly the general practice of post-Reformation treatment of the heterodox, not least their dehumanisation by presentation as animals.

Extreme violence extended to the response to other Westerners in the New World, despite, and, in part due to, the extent to which Westerners were outnumbered. Thus, in 1565, a Spanish force slaughtered Huguenots (French Protestants) who had established a presence in Florida. The difficulty of controlling and caring for captives was a factor in prisoner massacres, but the central drive was that of a religious intolerance and self-righteousness, and the deliberate destruction of those held to be threats. This practice was not tempered in the case of fellow Christians with the large-scale enslavement seen between Christians and Muslims in the Mediterranean.

The treatment of the defeated raises a question about the structural use of geopolitical ideas, or, rather, suggests that these ideas have to be understood in a flexible fashion, for the very varied conduct of conquerors on the world scale in the fifteenth and sixteenth centuries introduces a powerful element of agency in the shape of the choices made by contemporaries. Moreover, countering any simplistic usage of a form of geopolitics 'plus' to explain policy, in this case geopolitics plus demographics, demographic imbalance was not the sole factor in the case of Spanish policy in the Americas, as later also initially with that of the British in North America. Instead, as already indicated, similar imbalances can be seen elsewhere, notably with Muslim invaders of Hindustan, but without comparable results in terms of the treatment of local religions; although Muslim rulers of India were ready to enslave non-Muslim captives.

With the Aztecs and Incas, the Spaniards faced the consequences of over-throwing empires, but, elsewhere in North and South America, the context was different as they were opposed by tribes. That remark, however, should not be taken to imply that circumstances were similar in all cases. Instead, there was considerable variety in environment, economic development, social patterns and political organisation. Some tribes were sophisticated, for example the emerald-mining Musica of the highland interior of Colombia, who were conquered in a rapacious Spanish expedition of 1536.[27] Yet, combined with difficult terrain, native opposition could pose formidable difficulties as for the Portuguese in the Brazilian forests. Operating in Venezuela, Panama and Colombia from the 1580s, Vargas Machuca recorded both the dangers posed by traditional native weapons and tactics, such as poison arrows, rocks rolled down from on high, ambushes and pits, as well as native ability to respond to Spanish capability and limitations, such as profiting from the damaging impact of rain on gunpowder.[28]

To a considerable extent, the scope and nature of the Portuguese and Spanish empires reflected the strength of local resistance. Where local support was absent, for example in central Chile, Western forces faced grave difficulties in the Americas. In Chile, the Spaniards were pushed back from the Southern Central Valley in 1598–1604: thereafter, the River Bió Bió was a frontier beyond which the Araucanians enjoyed independence.

In northern Mexico, the Spaniards encountered opposition from the nomadic warriors of the Gran Chichimeca, who used their archery to deadly effect in terrain that was often difficult for the Spanish cavalry. The Spaniards, in turn, raised allied native forces, so that the conflict became another version of the long-standing struggle between nomadic and sedentary peoples. The Spaniards found their opponents difficult to fix, and the conflict took too much of the profit produced by the silver mines of the region, while there was also the challenge posed by the natives capturing and using Spanish horses in order to win greater mobility.

In the event, an abandonment by the Spaniards of their aggressive policies, including slave-raiding, and a switch to a more peaceful process of bribing opponents with gifts, combined with Christian missionary activity, helped lessen tension.

Indeed, cultural dominance and the destruction of independent indigenous activity was not the only situation in the Americas, not least because of the significance of the frontier, a 'middle ground' of great depth. This 'middle ground' was not so much a zone or region as, for long, a description of part of the area and practice of European activity in North America. Thus, the practice of European activity was not fixed. In northern Mexico, the alteration in Spanish policy provided an opportunity to increase settlements and establish forts, and thus to change the landscape of settlement.[29]

Rumours of bullion encouraged Spanish expeditions north from Mexico into the American interior, such as that of Francisco Vásquez de Coronado into what is now New Mexico, and thence into the Great Plains in 1540. The rumours proved erroneous, just as English explorers, such as Martin Frobisher in the 1570s, did not find the bullion they sought in North American waters, in his case the Canadian Arctic.[30] There were certainly no benefits to match those found in Mexico. Similarly, there was no follow-up to the expedition of Hernando De Soto who, between 1539 and 1542, brutally pillaged the Lower Mississippi and nearby lands. In 1541, he won a battle with the Choctaw at Mobile (Selma, Alabama), in which his cavalry was able to dominate the open ground without competition. After De Soto's death, de Moscoso pressed on in 1542–3 into what is now eastern Texas. The diseases brought by this expedition proved devastating for local people.

The lack of benefit is not the sole reason why European interest in America north of Mexico was limited, but it was important. In 1598, the Spaniards were able to press north to establish a position in what they called New Mexico. Nevertheless, the settlement of Santa Fé was very much to be an outlier, not least because it did not have the Pacific access that had been anticipated. Further south, helped by the malaria the Spaniards unwittingly introduced, much of the Yucatán, the centre of Mayan civilisation, was conquered in 1527–41, but the Itzás of the central Petén were not defeated until 1697.[31]

Unlike Central America, Florida proved a sphere of European competition. With coasts on the Atlantic and the Gulf of Mexico, it was readily accessible, and, in many respects, an equivalent to the major islands of the West Indies. Thus, Florida was part of the Caribbean, which helped explain Spanish interest, although it was far less than that in Mexico and Venezuela. Spain established bases in Florida, but the first fort at St Augustine, built in 1565, was burned down by the Timucua the following spring. Spain also made a major effort at proselytism among the native population. Settlements that were Spanish–native were founded.

In the event, Huguenots (French Protestants) established a base in Florida in 1564, in part in order to threaten the route back to Europe taken by the Spanish treasure ships from Veracruz, and in part as a consequence of the French Wars of Religion. Philip II of Spain was a key supporter of the Guise faction, the main opponent of the Huguenots in France. Florida also represented French attempts to benefit from the Atlantic, at least in the shape of the entrepreneurial energy of Atlantic and Channel ports such as Dieppe and La Rochelle, the latter the key Huguenot strongholds.

Just, however, as the French in the 1550s failed to challenge the Portuguese in Brazil successfully, so French Florida rapidly fell victim to Spanish counter-attack, and, in particular, to the greater ability of Spain to deploy power from nearby Cuba, a key capability as Spain was under considerable pressure in Europe in the 1560s, notably from the Ottomans in the Mediterranean. Deployment from Cuba was an impressive display of Spanish effectiveness and resilience, and one that set a pattern that was seen up to the Spanish ability to reconquer West Florida from Britain in 1779–81, and to the initially successful attempts in the 1810s to resist the Latin American Wars of Independence.

The Spaniards re-established their position in Florida in 1565, but it was less extensive than prior to the French arrival. Indeed, after the 1560s, Florida was very much a marginal colony and, as such, not an effective base for Spanish power projection further north, nor a source of profit or lobbying that provided an encouragement for such action. There was some Spanish activity further north, including missionaries in the Chesapeake Bay area, but it was not sustained.

This situation set an effective limit to Spanish America, and thus provided the English with a margin of opportunity when they attempted (unsuccessfully) to establish a colony at Roanoke on the North Carolina Banks in the 1580s, and (successfully) in Virginia from 1607. Moreover, as Carolina was only established in the 1660s and Georgia in the 1730s, the lack of Spanish interest in northward expansion was also significant in creating what was, from the European perspective, a vacuum into which the British could expand. This view was mistaken, in that there were many Native Americans in the region, but correct in so far as the future was to lie with the European powers.

The failure of French Florida was also instructive because it indicated the extent to which colonial enterprise that might otherwise have succeeded could be cut short by European action. This was a lesson that was to be underlined in the mid-seventeenth century by the failure of the Swedes in the Delaware Valley at the hands of the Dutch, and by that of the Dutch in Brazil and the Hudson Valley at the hands of Portugal and England, respectively.

French interest in North America was also to be seen in the valley of the St Lawrence, a region free from any Spanish presence, but one that was to prove difficult for settlement due to the impact of the harsh climate on agriculture. Contact began in 1534 when Jacques Cartier did not find the route to the Orient he pursued. As with much European activity else-where, a quest for precious metals became important. Cartier sought them from his second voyage in 1535 and he returned from his 1541 expedition with what he thought was gold and diamonds, only for it to be worthless pyrites and quartz, an experience later shaped by the English explorer Martin Frobisher.

English interest in North America in the sixteenth century proved episodic, especially in the first half. John Cabot's voyages were not followed up, and, whereas Henry VII (r. 1485–1509) had taken a role in European diplomacy while avoiding serious conflict, and supported Cabot, Henry VIII (r. 1509–47) was far more concerned about continental power politics and eager to spend much of his wealth, and as much of that of his subjects as he could grab, on war. Entrepreneurial English merchants in mid-century were more interested in the opportunities offered by the slave trade from West Africa to the West Indies, and then, as relations deteriorated with Spain from the 1560s, in the loot to be gained from the Spanish empire, than they were in North America. Lands beyond the Spanish empire could be claimed, with Francis Drake claiming California as New Albion in 1579 during his circumnavigation of the world, and colonists landed on Roanoke Island in what is now North Carolina in 1585 and 1588 only to fall victim to disease, starvation or Native Americans.[32] However, despite growing inter-est in the idea of an English Protestant Atlantic empire,[33] English overseas settlement focused on Ireland, while commercial expansion looked to the East Indies, the Mediterranean and Russia.

The situation was to change in the early seventeenth century, and it is easy to trace a line from sixteenth-century ideas and initiatives to later settlements. There is much basis for this analysis, not least with the growth in geographical knowledge of, and speculation about, the North Atlantic. However, the striking point by 1600 was the contrast between England or France, and Spain, the king of which, from 1580 to 1640, was also ruler of Portugal. As yet, the English Atlantic was very limited as a territorial reality: seafarers sailed in numbers to the rich fishing grounds off Newfoundland and established temporary settlements on the island that were closely linked to the fisheries. While economically significant, this presence, however, did not measure up in terms of power politics. The role of the English state in trans-oceanic activity was greatly restricted, and this was even more the case of that of Scotland. The French Atlantic was also very limited.

Other features of European North America also lay mostly in the future, including large-scale African slavery. This point requires underlining as an important aspect of imperial geopolitics was that of power over people, and a crucial dimension of this power was to be provided by enslavement and the movement of slaves. Initially, the labour force for the European colonies appeared provided by the native population of North America, and this element remained the key element in Mexico and Peru. However, the inroads of disease hit this native population hard, particularly smallpox, which broke out in Mexico in 1520, the year after Cortés arrived. Smallpox appears to have killed at least half the Aztecs, including Montezuma's brother and successor, the energetic leader Cuitlahuac, and to have greatly hit the morale of the survivors. Disease weakened potential resistance to European control in the Americas, and acted like enslavement in disrupting social structures and household and communal economics, leading to famine. From the European perspective, however, disease also had a savage effect on the potential labour force.

More generally, Spanish colonial policies and practices, including the end of native religious rituals, affected local society and limited the possibility of post-epidemic population recovery. The resulting problem was compounded by the commercial opportunities created by plantation agriculture and by mining, each of which required large workforces. The obvious solution was to obtain slaves from the native population outside the span of European territorial control. The Spaniards carried out large-scale slaving in the sixteenth century among natives in Honduras and Nicaragua[34] and the Portuguese in Brazil; this slaving proving an aspect of warfare. The benefits gained from the sale of slaves helped to destabilise native society by encouraging conflict between tribes in order to seize people for slavery, which was a process also seen in West Africa. People were commodified as a result, which proved a central aspect of the way in which the slave trade affected relations between Europeans and Native Americans.

Despite the benefits gained from the slave trade within the Americas, there were also problems for the colonists including the availability and cost of slaves, with native resistance and flight proving key factors. Moreover, control over native labour within the area of Spanish control was affected by royal legislation, which sought to address clerical pressure to treat the natives as subjects ready for Christianisation, rather than as slaves. Indeed, native slavery was formally abolished in the *Leyes Nuevas* of 1542. However, aside from the rebellion this legislation helped cause among the Spaniards in Peru, the implementation of edicts took time and was frequently ignored by local officials and landowners. Furthermore, systems of tied labour, especially the *encomienda* (land and native families allocated to colonists), and forced migration, notably the *repartimiento*, under which a part of the male population had to work away from home, represented *de facto* slavery.[35] Native slaves remained important in frontier regions distant from the points of arrival of African slaves, such as northern Mexico. Nevertheless, the equations of opportunity and cost were to favour the purchase of slaves in West Africa and their shipment across the Atlantic. Initially, Africans were shipped into Spanish America via Spain, but, from 1518, *asientos* or licences were granted for their direct movement. As it was initially more expensive to supply Spanish America with African slaves than with native slaves, the Africans were often used as house slaves, a form of high-value slavery that indicated their cost. By the mid-sixteenth century, the situation had changed and, rather than providing a marginal part of the labour force, Africa was becoming steadily more important as a source of slaves, not least because it was believed that Africans were physically stronger than natives. African slaves remained more expensive than native labour which could be controlled in various ways, including by making service an element of debt repayment, but the number of African slaves transported across the Atlantic increased greatly over the following century.

Western Expansion and the Military Revolution

Western expansion was no mere footnote to developments within Christendom. Indeed, at the world scale, the early modern period can be dovetailed into a modernising and teleological view of these developments[36] if emphasis is placed upon this expansion, and/or if the situation elsewhere is treated as a series of parallels. The latter approach suggests that Western success was a product of better following the same course that the other major powers were on. In turn, the reasons for this apparent contrast are employed to establish a global hierarchy of military proficiency, which encourages a neglect of the non-Western powers, or a treatment of them as failures and/or victims.

These approaches, however, are problematic, not least if a technologically driven Military Revolution is presented as the key causative factor behind a Western rise to dominance. Although the Western Europeans indeed created the first global empires, this achievement was only partly due to military developments and, moreover, did not amount to dominance. In addition, it is unclear that it is appropriate to read across from one success or group of successes in order to suggest a shift in global military capability. Advocates of a Military Revolution tend to work with the big picture and overall trends, employing individual cases as illustrations more than evidence. However, this method invites questions about the applicability and contextualisation of the illustrations cited, and thus directs attention to the issue of how overall trends are to be judged. Is the Portuguese failure in Morocco to receive more or less attention than Spanish success against the Incas, and, if so, which criteria are at play? In addition, if Western capability is discussed in terms of particular successes, and these successes then 'explained' accordingly, then the value of this explanatory model is lessened because it fails to account for expansion such as those of the Ottomans, Safavids, Mughals and others. For example, the great event in sixteenth-century India was the creation of the Mughal empire, not the establishment of Portuguese power in parts of the Indian littoral. Although creating significant new trade links, Portugal was even more marginal in the histories of Japan, China and Iran.

The situation was very different for the Philippines, South-East Asia and the East Indies, although, in each case, the emphasis should rather be on parts of the region in question. Thus, the major Portuguese impact in Malacca, north-west Sumatra, west Java and the Moluccas, was scarcely matched in Dai Viet, Thailand or Borneo, while the Spanish presence in central Luzon was not seen in most of the rest of that island, let alone across all parts of the Philippine archipelago. There is no simple case of successful littoral power-projection by the Western powers into divided polities, as that was not true of Japan. Moreover, Siam was vulnerable to attack from Burma, and not to Western powers, and Aden was captured by the Ottomans, not the Portuguese. More generally, there was an interactive quality to Portuguese expansion.[37]

The impression of relatively limited Western military impact may become more pertinent in military history if scholarship in the twenty-first century focuses more attention on East and South Asia than was the case in general histories of war written in the twentieth century. The particular impact as far as the story of Western expansion is concerned, may well be to make the overrunning of key areas of Central and South America in the sixteenth century appear less significant than in twentieth-century accounts. Looked at differently, the 'Gunpowder Revolution' may have been important for the early Spanish conquests in the New World, which were achieved with very few Spaniards, but the role of gunpowder weaponry was limited in these conquests which were not in principle very different from other cases, both earlier and contemporaneous, of warriors conquering agricultural societies with much larger populations. Gunpowder weapons were employed in only some of these conquests and were not a precondition for them. Gunpowder neither set the goal, nor was the agent that explains all.

On the other hand, it is possible to emphasise the Western achievement not only by focusing on the naval dimension but also by drawing a distinction between a Western military revolution, in which new ways of war were invented around the opportunity presented by firearms, and, on the other hand, non-Western use of firearms, as it can be suggested that it was only in the West that there was a sustained transformation of the culture of war. In contrast, in the Ottoman empire and Morocco, firearms were adopted as useful force-multipliers, as more, or differently used, weapons, but the underlying culture of warfare remained the same, and this was even more the case in Iran, India and China. However, this assessment needs to take note of the extent to which there was still change in these areas, let alone the Ottoman empire and Morocco. In the case of China, the response to Portuguese weaponry, first encountered in the 1520s, was one of emulation, with the Jiajing emperor ordering both the manufacture of similar cannon and training in their use. Chinese firepower was to be important, on land and sea, in the war with Japan in the 1590s, while Japanese handgunners outperformed the impressive Korean archers in the initial invasion of 1592. Furthermore, the extent of the transformation of the culture of war in the West by 1600 was less apparent than was to be the case by 1700.

Conclusions

Alongside technology it is appropriate to emphasise political and economic practices. Thus, Douglas Peers, while criticising the 'epistemology of opposition in which the two sides are delimited in terms of essential differences from each other', added: 'The types of command economy that began to emerge in early modern Europe allowed its rulers to maximise the resources at hand so as to keep their armies up to strength and their armories properly outfitted', but also pointed out that this type of economy was not a Western monopoly.[38]

Linked to this point, the effectiveness of any Western transformation of the culture of war on land is unclear, and should not be exaggerated, in so far as the West's ability to expand at the expense of other powers was concerned. Indeed, the pace of the Muslim assault on European Christendom by land and sea greatly slackened in the last two decades of the century, in part because of the strength of the response, but also due to the Ottoman focus on war with the Safavids and, to a lesser extent, because of Moroccan expansion across the Sahara. A consideration of the Muslim assault, which was to resume with the eventually successful invasion of

Venetian-ruled Crete in 1645, and to be followed by offensives against Austria and in Ukraine, provides a questioning context for the habitual stress on Western expansion.

Moreover, it is necessary not to primitivise other systems. In particular, it is clear that the Ottomans created a highly effective military system, and the Ottoman army, and even more navy, of 1600 were very different to those of 1450, such that there was a sustained transformation in Ottoman warmaking. Numerous Western observers commented on the discipline and organisation of the Ottoman army on the march. Its effectiveness included the use and organisation of firearms. Thus, although it was not until the mid-sixteenth century that the majority of the *janissaries* carried firearms, the Ottomans made stronger and more reliable musket barrels than their Western counterparts, which were constructed with longitudinal seams, whereas the Ottomans used flat sheets of steel coiled into a spiral which produced great strength in the barrel. As was noted during the siege of Malta in 1565, their musket fire was more accurate than that of their Christian opponents. As far as organisation was concerned, the Ottomans had a separate corps of gunners, and another of gun-carriage drivers, leading to a cohesion and continuity in the artillery that was largely absent as far as most Western armies were concerned. Benefiting, moreover, from their self-sufficiency in workmen and raw materials, the Ottomans proved a crucial source of firearms technology in the Islamic world.[39] This provision was linked to the impressive and planned effort that enabled the Ottomans to mount naval efforts in the Indian Ocean. These efforts have been presented as part of a 'globally informed political response' to Portuguese power, although the extent of this commitment has been queried.[40]

At every point, it is necessary to look at the situation in the sixteenth century in its own terms, and not to define and analyse it in the light of later developments: some of these emerged clearly from the context of the sixteenth century, but the latter cannot be understood correctly in this teleological manner. Both the extent of transformation in the West and the contrast between Western and non-Western militaries were more limited than is often realised.

8 Warfare, Social Contexts, and State Development

War interacted with the full range of human activities, political, social, economic and cultural. This interaction varied greatly in character, in part as a consequence of environmental constraints and in part due to the nature of socio-political development. Thus, the former helped ensure that, across much of the world, there was a low density of population, with consequences for the nature of warfare including the number of troops that could be deployed. In these areas, the tendency was for all fit adult males to be warriors, and for conflict to be local in extent and in some respects similar to hunting. However, the range of causes of conflict included the pressure for revenge, the drive to seize hostages, the extension of political influence and the linked quest for prestige, and overlapping cultural factors such as religious pressures and witchcraft claims.[1]

Without suggesting that such situations and pressures were static, there was a fundamental continuity in the social context of warfare in these areas, many of which were stateless. Personal ownership of weaponry was a feature of these societies and was indeed crucial to their military character. This ownership and the limited control wielded by tribal authorities made the borrowing of outside techniques by such societies highly unlikely. Partly as a consequence, the West defined barbarians as militarised, but individualistic; while the civilised, in contrast, were members of states created by war and in which battlefield arms were centrally organised.

In practice, conditions in both types of society varied greatly. Thus, the Oromo warriors of East Africa might seem primitive to outsiders, but, far from being static, their fighting techniques developed, as in the 1580s when they adopted the use of body-length shields made of stiff ox-hide, which protected them from archers. The practice of warriors shaving most of their head to show that they had killed someone was different in form to that seen elsewhere, but matched a widespread pattern of displaying prowess at the individual and collective levels.[2]

The standard emphasis on the proficiency of gunpowder forces deployed by developed, bureaucratic states fails to give sufficient weight to the strength and vitality of other militaries. Thus, southern Iraq was dominated by tribal confederacies that were able to challenge Ottoman rule. Fortified positions could hold them off, so that the Jawazir tribe besieged Basra unsuccessfully in 1549, 1566 and 1596, but, in turn, Ottoman campaigns against the tribe failed. Such campaigning was generally an interlude in the tributary dimension of relations. Conflict, certainly in the Asian context, was mostly avoided by tributary arrangements that, as long as they were paid, usually sufficed to keep the (nomadic) fringe in check. This was true for the Ottomans with the Arabs and Kurds, with the Safavids for the Arabs, Kurds, Lezghis, Baluchis, Türkmen and Uzbeks, for the Russians in the Caucasus, and for the Chinese.

These outsiders could pose a formidable threat. The Chinese might regard the Mongols and Manchus as barbarians, but they were capable of considerable sophistication, scale and success. Indeed, in 1592, the Chinese reported the Manchu leader Nurhaci as able to deploy 30,000–40,000 cavalry and 40,000–50,000 infantry.[3] Just over half a century later, the Manchu were to capture Beijing. Aside from great diversity among those regarded as barbarians, the situation in more defined states also varied considerably, with, for example, the provision of men, horses and arms frequently provided by methods that did not match the more bureaucratic centralisation seen for example in China, and, to a lesser extent, the Ottoman empire.

Reform and Recruitment

In contrast to areas of low density of population and tribal societies, regions with a highly competitive and combative international system could lead to pressures for governmental change, although there was relatively little on display in Central Asia, where there was such competition. Despite such exceptions, there was a widespread interaction between international ambitions, enhanced military capability, especially the development of permanent forces, and administrative reform. Burgundy under Charles the Bold (r. 1467–77), Mughal India under Akbar (r. 1556–1605), Burma under Bayinnaung (r. 1551–81) and Iran under Abbas I (r. 1587–1629), provided examples of this process.[4]

However, such reform should not necessarily be seen in terms of modern concepts. Instead, reform often centred on the search for a new consensus with the socially powerful, rather than on bureaucratic centralisation, not that the latter process was without its ideological tensions, legal difficulties, serious administrative limitations and grave political problems. The pursuit of a new consensus was centralising – in that it focused the attention of regional élites on the centre – but not centralised. Indeed, military strength was not largely a matter of bureaucratic sophistication and development, although that was an element and was, indeed, particularly significant in China and, to an important but lesser extent, the Ottoman empire. Instead, the co-operation of key social groups with rulers was necessary in order to produce recruits and resources, with this co-operation being seen in both naval and land capability. The emphasis on the role of these groups, and specifically, of private entrepreneurs, in mobilising resources for war on land and at sea helps explain the degree to which the inherent strength and adaptability of economies, societies and states may have been more important than the particular characteristics of their military systems.[5]

Competitive military systems that put a premium on the size of armed forces and the sophistication of their weaponry enhanced the position of centralising rulers able to deploy the necessary resources, while those international and military systems that were not dominated by such armies and navies did not lend themselves to control by such rulers. In turn, rulers could help alter the situation, as with the Ottoman empire under Mehmed II who brought a measure of control over the autonomous tendencies represented by the frontier *beys*, who controlled the cavalry in their regions. Mehmed's successes helped ensure that *beys* served in the army.[6]

Consensus was less necessary if rulers employed foreign mercenaries such as the Swiss troops hired under the French alliance of 1521[7] or slave forces, the latter being particularly common with Islamic states, notably the Ottoman empire, Morocco and Achin. The Mamluks of Egypt, one-time slaves, used black slave soldiers from sub-Saharan Africa. In contrast, the Ottomans' 'slaves of the Sublime Porte' were maintained by a system of *devsirme* (collection), a slave system of considerable sophistication, with boys conscripted in the empire. Their training was described in *The Laws of the Janissaries*, which was written in the early seventeenth century. Boys were regarded as easier to train and subdue than men. The best-looking were allocated to the palace to receive an education in the palace schools and serve the person of the Sultan, while the physically strong were chosen to work in the palace gardens, but most were destined for the élite *janissary* corps. First, however, they were assigned to Turkish farmers in Anatolia in order to accustom the boys to hardship and physical labour, and to teach them some basics of Islam and, more significantly, Turkish, which was the language of the corps and the imperial élite. Recalled after about seven or eight years, and based in the barracks of the novices near the palace entrance, the novices were used for palace and imperial tasks, such as transporting firewood to the palace or manning troop ferries, or working as palace laundrymen and apprentices in the naval dockyards, and on construction projects. The circumcision of the boys when they arrived for the first time at Constantinople was designed to assert their Muslim future and was a clear instance of symbolic power over the slave soldiers-to-be.[8] Slaves were also used in the Ottoman galleys, as in those of other powers. Thus, when Mehmed II captured Trebizond in 1461, he took 1500 youths to serve as galley slaves.

The role of slave soldiers indicated the highly differing patterns of recruitment and command across the world, as the degree of professionalism and control resulting from this method were very different to those produced by tribal structures, tenurial dependents or contracted soldiers hired through semi-independent foreign or domestic agents. Yet, despite the value of firm governmental control, seen notably with both Ottoman forces and the Chinese, who did not use slave soldiers, there was no clear developmental pattern in military organisation. The tendency in Western literature is to place a progressive interpretation on the rise of the state and its attempt to monopolise force and to develop a professionalised state-run military. This approach, however, fails to give sufficient weight to the vitality of other military systems and developments, such as the adaptability and professionalism of mercenaries, a type of military service seen not only in the West,[9] but also in other areas with developed military labour markets, such as north and south India. In the expeditions against Suwār of Dhu'l-Kadr in the late 1460s and early 1470s, the Mamluk sultan Qaytbay found it difficult to get his Egyptian cavalry fief holders to serve, instead, and hired infantry, including archers, in Syria, closer to the sphere of hostilities.[10]

Although paid soldiers were the key element in Western Europe, obligatory levies played a major role in many parts of the world. Such levies, however, did not necessarily provide effective forces for the field forces of rulers. Instead, these levies were more important in local defence than in expeditionary warfare, and obligation could be as much owed to the local community as to the distant ruler. The value of citizens' militia could also be shown in operations against the ruler, as with the successful defence of the Dutch town of Leiden against Spanish siege in 1574. The military activity of local forces overlapped with the maintenance of law and order. Thus, in the Ottoman empire, peasant village militias were significant in providing defence against robbers and brigands.[11]

Alongside those who hired out their military services, a hiring in which patronage and image played a role alongside payment in ensuring service, there were free military communities such as those that flourished thanks to the disturbed nature of the frontier between Christendom and Islam.[12] The most important were the Barbary corsairs of North Africa, the Cossacks, and the Knights of Malta. In the Adriatic, the comparable group was the Uskoks of Senj, an Adriatic port under the nominal control of the Austrian Military Frontier in Croatia. Senj came to play a major role in the incessant conflict in Dalmatia (the coastal region of modern Croatia), a conflict that does not attract attention because it was not one of large-scale campaigns. The Uskoks, who lived entirely on raiding the Ottomans and, to a lesser extent, the (Christian) Venetians, originated in nearby Austrian territories threatened by the Ottomans, but later they came from all the Croatian–Ottoman and Venetian–Ottoman border areas, their grievances channelled into warfare fuelled by ideals of holy honour and vengeance.[13] Alongside coexistence, such ideals also played a role on other religious frontiers, for example between Muslims and Hindus in India.

In contrast to free military communities, soldier colonies were generally an aspect of central control. Thus, much of the Chinese army was based in military colonies, mostly near the frontiers, where soldier-farmers, provided by the government with seeds, animals and tools, produced food while also manning the fortified strongholds that the colonies contained, strongholds that, in turn, protected the storehouses and granaries. However, in the fifteenth century, this system deteriorated, in part because of the impact of Mongol attack, but largely because the officers tended to take over the colonies, using the soldiers as a labour force. Thus, the military came to approximate to the landed system found in many other states, for example much of the Ottoman empire, not least because Chinese officers were largely a hereditary group. For example, the rebellion of the garrison in the important frontier city of Ningxia in 1592 involved Pübei, a Mongol in Chinese military service who had recently retired with the rank of regional military commissioner, a rank inherited by his son who used a Chinese name, Pu Cheng'en, and who also rebelled. Moreover, the family had over a thousand 'household men', veterans who took personal orders from the commander.[14] The rebels rapidly seized a number of border fortresses, only to fail after several attempts, to take the town of Pinglu by assault. This failure robbed the rebels of the appearance of success and thus helped the government as it rallied its forces. Ningxia was besieged, eventually falling as a result of the combination of the siege with divisions among the defenders. The change in the Chinese colonies affected military effectiveness as the colonists became more farmers than soldiers. Much of the army was raised from a hereditary soldiery, although mercenaries became more important in China during the sixteenth century, in part in response to the deterioration of the hereditary element, including large-scale desertion.

Co-operation and bureaucracy

In contrast to state-driven and directed systems, consensus played an important role in the development of Western European maritime capability as, in order to sustain the sophisticated administrative systems required to maintain fleets, it was necessary to obtain the support of mercantile groups. The disadvantage of not having such support was amply shown in Poland in the late sixteenth century, when Gdansk (Danzig), the major port, refused both to provide the Crown with ships to assist operations in Livonia and to support efforts to create a royal fleet. In 1570, the king pushed through a charter giving the crown greater authority in the maritime sphere, but, after coming to the throne in 1575, Stephan Bartory, having failed to coerce Gdansk and under pressure from the expansionism of Ivan IV, 'the Terrible', of Russia, annulled the charter and made further concessions in return for a payment.

The willingness and ability of Western European societies to organise their resources for maritime enterprise were combined with a degree of curiosity about the unknown world, a wish to question, rather than to accept, received knowledge. This independence of mind and action was especially manifest in the explorers: they sought governmental support, but were not constrained by it. Yet, the global links that individuals established could only become a sustainable military reality with resources and institutional support. The willingness of Western European governments to decide that such a goal was important reflected views on spatial possibilities and on the acceptance of new developments that were not shared by all states.

Governments not only set goals; they also sought to realise them, within the context of differing political circumstances, by altering political parameters and allocating resources.[15] To these ends, some states developed what were, by earlier, although scarcely by nineteenth-century, standards, impressive bureaucracies that sustained far-reaching patterns of activity and action. In Europe, the thesis of transformative military change has been linked to the development of the modern state:

> In 1400 A.D. no prince could prevail against any substantive portion of his feudal barons unless he enjoyed the active support of a similar number of the barons. In 1600 A.D. most princes could be confident that their standing army would suppress all but the most widespread rebellions.[16]

However, the argument looks less clear if focus is devoted to the French Wars of Religion, the Dutch Revolt, or the rebellions against Spanish rule in the 1640s. Nevertheless, the economics of war certainly favoured the development of large states, as professional disciplined infantry, cannon and fortifications, were all best provided by large states able to raise taxation from societies that had relatively effective economies. However, it is unclear how far centralisation was a product of force as opposed to a range of political, cultural and social functions.[17]

As a separate point, the cost of supporting the military burden of war and peacetime expenditure in turn threatened political stability, both creating new tasks for the military and making it harder for them to fulfil these tasks. Such strains could be seen not only in Christian Europe, as when the city of Ghent opposed exceptional war levies by Charles V in 1539, but also more generally. Thus, repeated campaigns put a serious strain on Ottoman resources as well as affecting the popularity of the regime. This strain led to Mehmed II's expropriation of some properties belonging to charitable trusts and private individuals which caused further discontent. Yet again, however, it is misleading to isolate only one factor as this cost was more supportable if the economy was growing and population numbers rising, and less so in other circumstances. The general expansion of the world population in the sixteenth century, as well as widespread economic growth, were important in enabling states to sustain conflict.

War, especially, but not only, civil war, could trigger a reversion to more primitive military arrangements. Whatever the formal situation, the general practice was for private entrepreneurs to organise and for local populations to pay. In the early seventeenth century, the structures for the financing, supply and control of Western European armies proved inadequate to the burdens that the sustained warfare of the Thirty Years War (1618–48) was to create, and there had earlier been comparable problems in the late sixteenth century. Nevertheless, a bleak picture would be inappropriate as, by global standards, Western military administration, if less impressive than that of China and the Ottomans, and in many respects much less so, was well developed, and had been so for centuries. In addition, accounts of deficiencies in army administration are not too helpful as a guide to the situation at sea, where the introduction of numbers of specialist warships led to a development of admiralties. Indeed, Western European warriordom, its ethos and practices, depended heavily on clerks, although the Ottomans proved more successful in achieving a concentration of resources, and in deploying them with less need to consult local élites. This success was crucially important to the logistical sophistication that underpinned Ottoman operations.

The extension of state control for both the Ottomans and their Christian rivals was easier at sea, because navies required substantial fixed, and recurrent, expenditure, and operated from a limited number of ports.

Furthermore, much of Europe's coastline, especially the Atlantic coastline, was under the control of a small number of powers that did not wish to encourage naval forces that were not under control. The situation in the Mediterranean was different, but, even so, there also the net result was a concentration of naval power. Much of the piracy was from outside areas under the authority of the major states, notably from the Barbary States, the Knights of St John at Malta, and the Uskoks of Senj. However, in France, England and Scotland, there was extensive piracy, especially in areas distant from central control, such as Devon and Cornwall in England and the port of La Rochelle in France.

Despite such activity, and often in co-operation with it, the major states played a key part in naval power, and the role of government in developing and sustaining their naval strength was central. Thus, alongside the Ottomans and the Venetians, Spanish bureaucracy showed remarkable agility, dedication and inventiveness in keeping the fleets supplied. In a pattern seen more generally in Western Europe, private contractors and public officials worked fruitfully together. Forest legislation sought to conserve timber stocks, efforts were made to provide sailors and soldiers with nutritious food and good medical care, and severe discipline was enforced on erring fleet commanders and bureaucrats alike.[18] In contrast, although the Portuguese challenge led to a greater focus from 1505, the Mamluks earlier lacked a sustained naval commitment, and had no continuity in shipbuilding or naval preparedness.[19]

More generally, the compromises between rulers, élites and local communities that were important to order within states could also become the base for a degree of centralisation into major organisations. The latter were to be important in sixteenth- and, even more, late seventeenth-century Europe, although they became much more significant in the nineteenth and twentieth centuries. In agricultural societies, such as Europe in the period 1450–1600, organisations could directly involve only a small minority of the population, although some armed forces employed several per cent of the male population and military organisations could be important as part of a process of transformation.

Government also set norms for the military. The enforcement and acceptance of discipline was a crucial aspect of state control of war and was central to the transformation of martial élite culture as knights became officers. This process helped to ensure the continuation of ancestral political and social privilege, but their technically different battlefield roles required a more predictable and disciplined response, and this response helped improve the effectiveness of Western forces. Training became more significant, as it was only thanks to training and discipline that different types of troops could combine effectively in battle tactics. Advances in technology themselves were often of limited use without such combination, as was shown by the need for vulnerable handgunners to combine with pikemen.

Officership

Precisely because an expansion of governmental military strength was a matter largely of co-opting élites through patronage, rather than coercing them, it proved difficult to limit unofficial military activity. Military entrepreneurship could be redirected through more regular military channels, especially thanks to a system of the aristocratic proprietorship of regiments, but it proved far harder to suppress feuds, brigandage and duels enjoying élite support. Nevertheless, aristocratic proprietorship of regiments and the raising of troops from friends and tenants[20] was a key instance of the patronage mechanisms that proved a central element linking politics and war. For example, the relationship between rulers and the aristocracy was important to France's eastward advance, with the extension of patronage networks serving to consolidate control,[21] although this process could also have an authoritarian dimension as well as dividing the local élite with some being exploited, particularly in order to pay the burden of war.[22]

If war was a forcing house of change, it was also designed to prevent it, both in terms of changes in territorial power and the prevailing political, social and ideological practices and norms. Armies suppressed rebellions, such as that in Lower Austria in 1597,[23] and maintained or strengthened social and spatial patterns of control. At the same time, the extent to which the social élite was willing to co-operate with military change, including the organisation of armies around a state-directed structure, varied. Thus, in Christian Europe, the service basis for landownership that, from the late fifteenth century, provided Russia with cavalry, and that was given a new iteration by the granting of *pomestie* land by Ivan IV, was not matched in Western Europe, although, in 1497, John I, king of Poland, confiscated the estates of landowners who had refused to take part in the campaign against Wallachia that year. This service basis also provided the Ottomans with cavalry, whereas in Egypt the Ottomans rewarded their cavalry with wages, not land. When they gave support by providing land, the Ottomans controlled the process so that, in 1582, those who refused to serve against the Safavids were deprived of their *timars* (fiefs), while the *timars* of others killed fighting the Venetians in Cyprus in 1570–1 were given to colleagues who had shown bravery.[24] Timar holders were not only expected to serve in person but also to provide troops for the army.

Across the world, the hierarchy and collective discipline of officership could work and be made most effective if it rested on a definition of noble honour and aristocratic function in terms of military service. Moreover, nobles were seen as particularly suited to this service because of their nobility. Despite different cultural manifestations, these assumptions were seen around the world. In Japan, commanders were favoured by chronicles extolling their prowess, and that of their lineage, chronicles that focused on honour. Thus, those discussing the invasions of Korea in the 1590s presented the Japanese as greatly outnumbered by the Chinese, while, in turn, Chinese historians played up the successes of the Wanli emperor in order to eulogise ruler, dynasty and state. Although he never took the field, the emperor was an active supreme commander.[25]

More generally, romantic images of war were disseminated, and if military memoirs in the West offered a reality that was far from chivalric, that did not make conflict appear an undesirable pursuit.[26] Indeed, the revival of chivalry in the late fifteenth century[27] in the West has implications for those who have sought to analyse changing military patterns largely through technological progress or the putative steady march of an emerging professionalism. Poland provides an instance of the combination of institutional change and the identification of honour with military service. As king from 1575 to 1586, Stephan Bathory was a successful war-leader who both created a permanent force of hussars as both royal bodyguard and cadre for the wartime army, and made such service fashionable for the nobles.

A definition of aristocratic honour with reference to military service was encouraged by the emphasis on honour, service and glory by as well as for rulers. Their peacetime courts and wartime campaigns provided opportunities for dramatising patronage through displays of prowess and munificence, as with the central role of hunting in court life and also the use of tournaments and other forms of mock combat.[28] Henry II of France was fatally injured in a joust in 1559. As a child, the future king Sebastian of Portugal, like many royal heirs, was encouraged to show a penchant for war games. Troops reviews proved part of the same process, in both peace and war. Thus, in 1580, Philip II reviewed the Spanish army near Badajoz before it invaded Portugal. Some operations took on the characteristics of an aristocratic review, such as Charles V's campaign against Tunis in 1535 which was accompanied by large numbers of Spanish and Italian nobles. Yet, campaigning was also dangerous for aristocrats. Alba's father died in 1510 on the Djerba expedition, Louis XII's nephew, Count Gaston of Foix, commander of the French army in Italy, was killed leading a cavalry charge at the battle of Ravenna in 1512, while, in 1544, René Prince of Orange, stadholder (governor) of Holland, was killed by a cannonball while besieging a position in France.

Many rulers fought as part of the process of command. In 1501, Babur fired a crossbow while defending Samarqand from Uzbek assault, and he subsequently fired a more conventional Central Asian bow.[29] In contrast, his grandson Akbar fired a musket, as at the siege of Chitor. Shah Tahmasp I of Iran (r. 1524–76) was helped in asserting his authority in the face of conflict over control of the regime until 1533 by victories, notably at Jam over the Uzbeks in 1528. In 1537, he gained prestige when he recovered Herat and captured Kandahar. Princes were also expected to show prowess, and such displays were particularly important in monarchical systems that lacked primogeniture, as merit was displayed by these means. At Başkent in 1473, both the Aqquyunlu and the Ottoman flanks were commanded by the sons of the rulers.

In turn, the image and results of battles were displayed in order to secure glory for participants and, in doing so, sustained the way in which such glory was gained. This was true of rulers and of other commanders. Bravery in the field was seen as an important attribute of command. Thus, in 1496, the Spanish commander Gonzalo de Córdoba gained great renown by being one of the first into the breach in the walls of French-held Ostia. The ceremonial entries of French monarchs celebrated royal valour and success,[30] while Francesco II Gonzaga, Marquess of Mantua presented his performance at the battle of Fornovo in 1495, where he had fought bravely and captured many prisoners, albeit failing to block the French march north, as a victory; and Andrea Mantegna's painting the *Madonna della Vittoria* was produced accordingly. Similarly, Francesco's additions to his ancestral seat at Gonzaga were decorated with scenes from family military history while the palace of San Sebastiano he built provided an opportunity for the display of what he saw as an apt comparison, Mantegna's series the *Triumphs of Caesar*, painted from 1482 to 1492.[31] Francis I fought at Marignano and Pavia being captured at the latter, while Titian painted a splendid equestrian portrait of Charles V to celebrate his victory at Muhlberg in 1547. More generally, horsemanship brought and reflected status, which gave cavalry service a social value.[32]

Bravery was rewarded not only with honour, but also with more tangible rewards. These included both land at home for officers and also booty.[33] Thus, in the Morea in 1460, Sultan Mehmed II, after his troops were repulsed in their first attack on Kastrion, addressed his troops: 'he promised splendid rewards to those who should fight well, and stated that the fortress would be pillaged. Then he gave the order to attack.' The women and children of the captured town were enslaved. In 1462, one-third of the population of captured Mitylene (Mitilini) was enslaved and distributed to the soldiers; although, as a reminder of a different form of violence, all the captured Italian mercenaries were killed. Tursun Beg, a government surveyor, wrote of operations in the Morea in 1459, 'After these conquests ... every tent had the appearance of a slave market with pretty young girls and boys thronging the entrances.'[34] Nicosia was savagely sacked by the Ottomans in 1570.

Resources and Information

Honour and glory might act as lubricants for obedience while defeat caused a loss of support by nobles, as Babur discovered in 1501, but this factor does not explain why success was obtained at the expense of different cultures. Resources and environments were significant factors here. Thus, Western Europe was able to utilise a wide-ranging resource base, one that was enhanced by trans-oceanic expansion. There was heavy forest cover and abundant mineral resources in Western Europe, both of which were essential for naval construction and metallurgy. There was also access to larger quantities of cheaper metal than was available elsewhere, and some of this metal, in the form of nails, was used to hold Western European ships together. In contrast, the planks of Indian Ocean ships were sewn together with rope, and therefore vulnerable to the recoil of heavy guns and to storms at sea.

Given the limited nature of the data, it is difficult to compare Western European and Chinese economic development but, at the very least, Western Europe, with its water mills, windmills, heavy forge work and mechanical clocks, had one of the most advanced industrial systems of the time. Along with a relative openness to new ideas, this economic strength helped Western Europeans in their adaptation and improvement of technology developed elsewhere, such as gunpowder or ship design. Knowledge provided a significant advantage to the Western navies. Thus, the English, who arrived in the Indian Ocean to challenge the Portuguese, were able, thanks to the use of the telescope and the compass, which were rarely employed on Indian vessels, as well as to better maps and cartographic techniques, like measurement by degrees, to probe and follow new routes that were generally ignored by Indian vessels.[35] Western expansion benefited from the willingness to acquire, incorporate and apply knowledge of the (to them) new worlds, while, crucially, there was a willingness to use new knowledge to challenge inherited frameworks of knowledge, not least the prestige of the Classical tradition.[36] In contrast, Chinese writers displayed scant sympathetic interest in the Indian Ocean expeditions of Zheng Ho, which were seen as a foolish extravagance.[37]

Furthermore, Western European powers were well advanced in the field of international finance and funding debts, enabling states, notably Spain,[38] in part to finance their activities, not least their expensive fleets, through an international credit system and through far-reaching sources of wealth. Thus, Spain could realise the potential wealth of Central and South American silver mines by turning to German and Italian bankers. Although agriculture and mining were major sources of wealth, finance and credit were linked to trade and the latter were particularly important to rulers seeking cash with which to pay their soldiers and contractors.

The urban-based nature of trade underlined the value of controlling or overawing towns, and this control played a key role in campaigns in many parts of the world. Thus, in Central Asia, campaigning revolved around the major cities, notably Merv, Herat, Samarqand, Kandahar, Kabul and Meshed. After his victory over Babur at Sir-e-pul in 1501, the Uzbek leader, Muhammad Shaybni, attacked Samarqand, finally starving the city so as to force Babur to abandon it. Delhi and Agra were key points of contention in northern India.

In part, the control of towns was a military and governmental process within states, seen most clearly when town walls were breached and when town militia were subordinated to royal garrisons, the latter frequently based in a separate citadel within the urban fortifications.[39] Rebellious Rotterdam was starved into surrender by Habsburg forces in 1489, and rebellion by Ghent was overcome in 1492 and 1540. The city of Groningen acted as a centre of regional opposition, resisting Habsburg attempts to bring it under control in 1505–6 and 1514. In turn, in 1536, the city successfully resisted an attempt by Duke Karel of Gelderland to take control. A popular revolt in the city of Utrecht in 1525 had won support from the Duke of Gelderland and France. After the revolt was suppressed in 1528, in large part because of troops and money provided by the province of Holland, work began on a large citadel, the Vredenburg, within the city walls. It was designed to intimidate the city guilds. This fortress was to be demolished in 1577 as part of the rejection of Habsburg control. The suppression of rebellion in Ghent in 1540 was followed by the construction of a citadel. The citadel being built by the Spaniards in Siena helped lead the latter to rebel against Spanish rule in 1552.

Yet, the relationship between town and ruler was one in which such force was generally secondary to more complex patterns of interaction. The same was true of rural areas, although hostility to peasant assertiveness helped encourage a violent response when aristocratic controls were challenged, as in Hungary in 1514, Germany in 1525 and Transylvania in 1596.

Whereas land and agriculture provided a key basis of power when soldiers were rewarded for service with land, any switch to cash rewards increased the significance of trade. Protracted warfare encouraged this process, especially if accompanied by scorched earth policies, by devastating agricultural zones. Rivalry and confrontation with the Ottomans from the 1470s put pressure on the Mamluks, who needed to spend more on the army and also increasingly paid them with money rather than lands granted as fiefs. This expenditure helps explain Mamluk concern over trade routes,[40] a concern that subsequently contributed to Portuguese–Ottoman rivalry in the Indian Ocean for dominance in the trade between South Asia and Western Europe.

Compared to most non-Western states, although not for example Japan, the Western states proved better able to monetarise their economies and thus to raise taxation and support military activity from governmental funds. This ability reflected the benefits of conquering the New World, where the great silver-producing centre of Potosí in modern Bolivia was established by the Spaniards in 1545. Yet, more than conquest was at issue for there were also significant pre-existing long-term developments in the West, including a prominent role for trade, notably the international trade that provided a source of customs revenue. This revenue was both a product of the division of the West into a number of states and a cause of the determination to define borders, control particular sites and routes, and defend trade and fisheries.[41] Conflict in the Baltic in the late sixteenth century owed much to a wish to dominate trade routes, with the port of Riga proving the main prize in Livonia, while Ivan IV sought to develop Russian trade through the River Narva.

Political pluralism in the West was accentuated by religious developments, in the shape both of the Protestant Reformation and of the failure of the attempt to defeat it, for the end result was a variety of competing governmental centres. This competition encouraged not only conflict but also a search for best practice in war. The role of debate and choice in military organisation and force structure, are also reminders of a dynamic aspect of Western culture, its relative freedom of discussion. Commentators could debate the value of mercenaries or militia, pikemen or swordsmen, musketeers or heavy cavalry.

This situation was a world away from that in nomadic and semi-nomadic societies where there was less military specialisation, notably in fortification and siegecraft. While the agricultural surplus and taxation base of settled agrarian societies permitted the development of logistical mechanisms to support permanent specialised military units, nomadic peoples generally lacked such units and had a far less organised logistical system.

In war, they often relied on raiding, but that did not mean a lack of ability for their battlefield techniques, such as feints, entailed considerable skill. Babur wrote of his defeat at Sir-e-pul in 1501:

> The enemy's right having routed my left, now attacked me in the rear ... . The enemy now began to charge us both in front and rear, pouring in showers of arrows ... . In battle, the great reliance of the Uzbeks is on the *tulughmeh* (or turning the enemy's flank). They never engage without using the *tulughmeh*. Another of their practices is to advance and charge in front and rear, discharging their arrows at full gallop, pell-mell ... and, if repulsed, they in like manner retire full gallop.[42]

The excellent training of the Mongols and other Inner Asian warriors have been traced to hunting;[43] but there was no theoretical literature in these cultures to aid in any debate over methods.

Bellicosity

Different state systems did not necessarily mean contrasting values, and vice versa. The bellicose values of Central Asian warriors were matched in Western Europe, notably among younger sons.[44] In contrast, China was closer in governmental values to the states of Western Europe than it was to tribal societies, but the general passivity of the Chinese élite was similar to neither. The military establishment scarcely enjoyed a central place in Ming society, not least because the military was nominally hereditary, whereas the norms of civilian society were merit-orientated. Moreover, the civil service bureaucrats who were powerful under the Ming had scant commitment to the goals of the military, and, as a result, the prestige of military service was limited. This situation led to a lack of interest in war, let alone in expansionism, and to only limited commitment to the state of the military,[45] although there is room for a reinterpretation stressing the extent to which emperors had an important military role.[46] The attitude of the next, Manchu, dynasty, however, was to be more bellicose, and this bellicosity was linked to an abandonment of the Ming willingness to coexist, however reluctantly, with the Mongols.[47]

The Ming attitude was certainly not shared by those who set the ideological norm in the Christian and Muslim worlds, as war in both was in part vindicated by the continued strength of the idea of conflict with the infidel. The Church played an important role in keeping the idea of holy war alive, and it remained particularly important in Mediterranean culture. Current hostility was inscribed into the past. Thus Francs Francken I's *Triptych of the Calvary* (1585) showed Christ escorted by Romans with an Ottoman flag. The ferocity of fighting, as on Malta in 1565, testified to the strength of religious antagonism between Christian and Muslims. At the same time, the Papacy was prepared to support violence against fellow-Christians before the Reformation led to the additional practice of seeing many Christians as heretics. Thus, as temporal rulers in Italy, the Popes, for example Julius II (r. 1503–13), played a major role in the Italian Wars (1494–1559).

There was no comparable political role for senior Islamic clerics, but they did not bring their spiritual influence to bear in encouraging peace with fellow-Muslims. Instead, differences within Islam fed into political tensions between and within states. The establishment of the Shi'a Safavid empire proved extremely disruptive and a cause of conflict with Muslim powers to both west and east. Sects also played a role in civil warfare within China and Japan, as with the 1587 rebellion in Shandong in China backed by the White Lotus–Maitreya sect.

The differing ideological context for warfare between Christendom/ Islam and Ming China was not simply one of a contrast between monotheism and polytheism, but, in part, reflected differing tendencies and emphases in the religious sphere. The role of such tendencies served to underline the extent to which cultural factors, such as bellicosity and the emphasis on honour and glory, were not a constant element across the world. At the same time, causal patterns varied. For example, monotheism might be important in encouraging bellicosity, but other factors also played a role. Evaluating them, however, is difficult and there is a danger that misleading stereotypes are adopted. For example, conventionally, there is an emphasis for the Mamluks and the Japanese on individual prowess and élite warriors. These were indeed a significant part of the culture and mythos of Mamluk and Japanese warfare, but a smaller part of the reality of conflict. Moreover, in Japan, individual prowess and élite warriors were not a particularly important phenomenon as the emphasis had long-since shifted to generalship, large-scale troop movements, and the manipulation of logistics. In addition, the mystique of bladed weapons and hand-to-hand fighting on medieval battlefields was an invention of the late nineteenth century, when Japanese military planners were considering how to defeat Western technology.

Any emphasis on the individual warrior underlined and risked undermining the often complex pattern of order in military systems, as concepts of subordination meant relatively little when the stress was on individual prowess. Yet, this stress was not necessarily incompatible with organised systems of warfare. For example, galley fighting in part served to display the merit of the prominent warriors who commanded the galleys and who led boarding parties. The same was true with fortifications in that those who led storming parties into breaches, or who resisted attack in these breaches, acquired great renown.

This renown both served as a reminder of the extent to which forms of warfare, whether old or new, served to display valour and other traditional knightly skills, and also recognised the extent to which such skills were still pertinent for the leadership required from officers in military units. However much the emphasis for the latter might be on the discipline and predictability required to get the most out of combined arms forces, for example the archers and shield-bearers of Jolof formations in West Africa, there was also a need for leadership in conflict, whether battle, skirmishes, advances or retreats. Moreover, as patterns of order buckled or broke down under the unpredictable strains of fighting or the multiple problems of operations, so it was necessary to put an emphasis on leadership. Gunpowder and discipline were not incompatible with such traditional military skills, but these skills required adaptation for new environments.

Military Challenges

This adaptation was a matter not only of the use of new weaponry and related changes in the balance between arms, but also of the different physical environments that troops and commanders had to confront. For the Ottomans, but even more for the Portuguese and Spaniards as their empires spread, the contrast between the environments faced in 1450 and those confronted between 1570 and 1600 was astonishing. Between 1500 and 1600, the change was also striking for the Mughals. Alongside physical environments, there were also contrasting political, social and religious contexts. For example, Alfonso d'Avalos, Marquis of Vasto (1502–46), an Italian-born Spaniard, not only served in Italy against the French, including at the battles of Pavia (1525) and Ceresole (1544), but also campaigned against the Ottomans in Hungary in 1532 and served on the successful expedition against Tunis in 1535.

Moreover, alongside international challenges, there was the need to consider domestic opposition. For example, large-scale bandit operations south of Beijing from 1509 led to operations by troops that were only successful in 1512. The use of troops in this policing function was seen in states across the world, and reflected the lack of alternative police forces able to maintain order. Banditry was a common feature in many rural regions, for example, in Europe, in Albania, Apulia, Calabria, Jülich and Sicily. The violence involved in some policing, and the size of possible problems, encouraged the use of troops. Frontier zones provided particular cover for often large-scale brigandage. The financial and judicial authority of rulers was rejected and their agents ignored, intimidated or challenged.

Banditry and feuding were not easy to suppress.[48] In Italy, for example in Lombardy and the Veneto, there was a rise in violence and a revival of feuds at the close of the sixteenth century. Brigandage, frequently associated with the social élite, remained a marked feature of Sicilian society, while, in the kingdom of Aragon in Spain, there were serous feuds, including that in the 1570s and 1580s, between the Count of Chinchón, a leading minister, and the Duke of Villahermosa, the most prominent noble. This struggle encompassed rivalry at court and fighting in the localities. Alongside feuds there was violent factionalism which could be linked to ethnic, regional and religious tensions. In 1474, *conversos* (converted Jews) and 'Old Christians' fought in the streets of Córdoba in Spain, a conflict that was related to those between urban and aristocratic factions.

Such fighting was a more pronounced instance of a violent lawlessness and a practice of pursuing ideas of justice and order through violence. These tendencies challenged long-standing governmental attempts to monopolise warfare as an aspect of sovereignty and a function of rule. Theoretically asserted for long,[49] these powers were pushed by assertive rulers.

Conversely, there were attempts to challenge the claims of rulers. Thus, the death of Duke Charles 'the Bold' of Burgundy in battle in 1477 left his daughter Mary (r. 1477–82) both vulnerable in the face of rebellions and short of money and troops. Rebellion in Flanders led Mary to concede the *Grand Privilège* of 1477, under which the ruler was obliged to seek the consent of the provincial estates in order to raise taxes and troops. A renewed rebellion in Flanders in 1488, in which Philip of Cleves (see p. 47) was prominent, was suppressed in 1492 and, the following year, the privileges granted in 1477 were declared void by the States General. In the early 1590s, the Transylvanian Diet sought to bring the army under the control of the Estates and in 1594 refused to endorse the declaration of war against the Ottomans, only for the prince to use the army to arrest the leaders of the opposition who were then killed.[50]

Rivalries in imperial and royal courts and among ruling élites also led to the use of the military. In China in 1457, imperial bodyguards were employed to replace Jingdi as emperor by his predecessor and half-brother, Yingzong. Four years later, there was an attempted coup in the capital mounted by disaffected generals controlling the garrison, but it was suppressed by loyal troops. Élite risings were not only staged in the capital. Thus, in the Chinese province of Shaanxi in 1510, Prince Anhua staged an uprising against what he presented as bad administration, only to be quickly captured in a ruse. Nine years later, the Prince of Ning, who was after the imperial throne, staged a rebellion, only to be swiftly defeated, not least because fireboats destroyed his fleet on a lake.

The distinction between rebellion and war was rarely clear in frontier areas. For example, opposition to Safavid rule in Khurasan was of interest to the hostile Uzbeks. Conversely, the suppression of rebellion there, as in 1581 when the shah of Iran, Muhammad Khudabanda, overcame the rebellious governor of Herat, lessened Uzbek options. The equation of rebellion with war was complicated by the extent to which states had numerous inner frontiers. Their character varied, but such frontiers often marked the division between sedentary agrarian societies that were largely under control and regions, often forested, arid or mountainous, where the agriculture was less intensive and the control far less.[51]

These inner frontiers were particularly seen in China in the case of areas occupied by non-Han peoples, notably in south-west China. In the 1590s, tensions over Han intrusions and governmental authority interacted with internal rivalries in the Yang clan, which had hereditary overlordship over Bozhou, the mountainous region bordering the three provinces of Sichuan, Guizhou and Huguang, resulting in conflict with the government, a conflict in which the Miao people eventually supported Yang Yinglong, who was able to deploy about 100,000 men. The course of the conflict reflected the contrast between an empire that needed to balance differing commitments over a wide area and, on the other hand, a local force that lacked such problems but, in this case, was unable to benefit from external support.

Ming efforts were limited while conflict with Japan in Korea took precedence, but in 1599 Wanli approved a counter-offensive. The initial force was destroyed in 1599, as a result of an effective feint by Yang, but in 1600 over 200,000 troops were deployed. Most were provincial and tribal forces but, crucially, there were also experienced units from the war in Korea which led each advancing column. Captured Japanese units of handgunners also fought for the Ming. In the face of converging columns, the mountains and ravines provided no refuge, Yang committed suicide, and the hereditary overlordship was ended. Alongside such conflicts and overlapping with them sometimes, there were intermittent border wars with Burma, with Chinese attacks in 1582–4, while the Burmese, in turn, attacked in the 1590s.

Conclusions

Inner frontiers were more transitional zones than clear divisions of sovereignty, and this factor accentuated the extent to which control frequently rested, at lest in part, on the appearance of power and the offering in return of a degree of deference, rather than obedience. At the same time, the means of coercion and defence were present, as clearly with fortification systems, which offered both defence and bases for attack.[52] Fortifications provided some of the most impressive surviving works of the century, notably parts of the Great Wall of China and also fortresses in Europe, such as the town walls of Berwick in England.

In most cases, these fortifications were constructed by states, which is one among many reasons for the dominance of the military narrative and analysis by their activities. However, the target of governmental power were not only the challenges posed by other states, but also those raised by a range of foreign and domestic forces that, while different, could also be deadly.

9 Conclusions

Assessing Military Change

The period covered by this book is conventionally considered in terms of a gunpowder revolution; but, while a fruitful thesis, this approach also faces a number of problems. First, it is unclear why, if the earlier introduction of gunpowder in China did not lead to revolutionary changes, the situation should have been different, or be regarded as different, in the West. Gunpowder provided the basis for different forms of handheld projectile weaponry and artillery on land and sea, but the technique of massed projectile weaponry was not new. More specifically, it is possible to regard gunpowder weaponry as an agent, not a cause, of changes in warfare. Thus, far from concentrating simply on technology, Michael Roberts and Geoffrey Parker argued that weapons (technology) were important as they were marshalled by doctrine and cultural habit of use (technique).[1] More recently, in addition to dismissing the idea of a military revolution centred on guns, Peter Lorge has suggested that the large, disciplined, trained infantry armies created in China were the necessary basis for subsequent developments in weapons use, developments that were to be emulated in Europe.[2]

There is also, as this book has indicated, the need to consider how best to incorporate into any description of military change armies that do not correspond to the metanarrative, the overall approach. The armies in question, for example those of the Safavids and Uzbeks, were frequently not infantry-based, but those warriors fighting on foot in North America and Australasia can also be considered. Any discussion of such forces invites a re-evaluation of comparative global military advantage and capacity, of the extent to which it is appropriate to consider military progress in terms of the use of gunpowder, especially siege artillery, and, subsequently, its use by infantry employing volley fire. Such progress also came with heavy costs, literally so. Thus, major fortresses could still be taken in the West, as was Antwerp by the (Spanish) Army of Flanders in 1585 and Amiens by Henry IV of France in 1597, but the resources and time required to mount successful sieges, four months in the case of Maastricht by the Spaniards in 1579, and even assaults, placed a heavy burden on states.

It is also necessary to reopen the question of how best to measure success, specifically the extent to which, as is usually done, the territorial nature of power and, therefore, conquest are the crucial criteria, so that control over land is seen as the basis for assessment. Instead, for example, it is possible also to place weight on successful raiding, which was another way to derive benefit from land and trade, and indeed to exercise a degree of control over both. The issue of how best to measure success relates to that of military effectiveness, through the question of how far capability should be considered in terms of the fitness of particular forces for the purpose of distinctive goals.

For example, the emphasis in land operations on regular forces at the cutting edge of sophistication is taken even further when considering navies, but the extent to which alternative means of naval organisation and operation should be regarded as of lesser value is unclear. In particular, the assumption rests on the idea that the monopolisation of commerce protection and violence by state forces was inherently more progressive than the use of privately organised armed forces, including armed merchantmen and privateers. The success of the English and Korean fleets against the Spaniards and Japanese, respectively, does, however, suggest that this assumption is well-grounded as far as major battles at sea were concerned.

Moreover, there is the issue of how far, and how best, to distinguish between changes in weaponry and their wider context, specifically the training, systematisation, and large-scale deployment of such weaponry on land and sea. The rate of change is also at issue.[3] If we see the major technological innovations in Europe relating to gunpowder as occurring prior to 1500 and argue, instead, that in the sixteenth century there was essentially incremental change, frequently at a sluggish rate but, nevertheless, an increase in the number of gunpowder weapons, then we have to decide how to rank the relative importance of these two processes. Irrespective of their value against both similar and different forces, many of the changes used to define the Military Revolution, or associated with it, such as larger armies, greater military expenditure, new tactics, and the *trace italienne*, all had medieval precedents. This approach can be amplified by considering the evolutionary theories of many historians of technology, with the resulting emphases on users, not designers, and on stability, not breakthroughs.

International Comparisons

Sixteenth-century developments in the West made gunpowder weaponry normative, which is to say that drill, tactics and assumptions were all increasingly focused in a particular way, while remaining far from identical.

Yet, elsewhere in the world, the focus was different and the standardisation less pronounced. To treat this contrast as failure may be pertinent from the perspective of the late nineteenth century, but is far less helpful if judging sixteenth-century forces on their own merit. Indeed, tactical flexibility in some contexts meant a mix of weaponry very different from that of leading Western armies.

At the same time, the foreign threat to Christendom, that of the Ottomans, did involve a military that was far more similar than what appeared to be the exotic forces encountered by Westerners in the Americas and sub-Saharan Africa. This similarity was also seen in the depiction of war. The Ottomans might be presented as unchristian, barbarous and cruel, but their military could also seem familiar as with the artillery shown by Johann Haselberg in his 1530 pictorial map of the recent Ottoman advance. Printed in Nuremberg, the map was accompanied by a booklet that called for a crusade in response.[4]

It can be argued that Western forces acquired a tactical and organisational superiority that enabled them to use gunpowder weaponry tactics more effectively than their opponents, but this argument, while valuable, also suffers from Eurocentricity in its application. The thesis focuses on the ability to keep cohesion and control in battle, and to make effective use of units, and this disciplined unitisation of armies is generally discussed in terms of the Renaissance and related intellectual developments. Printing was important in strengthening the consciousness of a specific military tradition, not least as printed manuals on gunnery, tactics, drill, siegecraft and fortification spread techniques far more rapidly than word of mouth or manuscript. Manuals also permitted a degree of standardisation that, at least in the long term, both helped to increase military effectiveness and was important for cohesion and the utilisation of military resources. Maps permitted the sharing of information. More generally, printing and literacy fostered discussion of military organisation and methods, and encouraged a sense of system, affecting and reflecting cultural assumptions.[5] Wartime propaganda also deployed notions of the common good that helped develop a sense of patriotism.

Printing certainly transformed the writing about war in Christian Europe, but not in China, where printing was invented. On the world scale, printing powerfully accentuated the contrast between the military memory in the Western world, where printing developed most rapidly and comprehensively, and most of the rest of the world; although the oldest extant fully-fledged drill manual for firearms was Japanese, *Inatomi teppô densho*, appearing in 1595. Moreover, there was a military manual publishing boom in late Ming China that encompassed the compilation of technical manuals, training works, encyclopedias and campaign histories.

However, if applauding Western methods of discourse, specifically the ready reproduction of ideas and instructions through a culture of print, it is necessary to allow for the difficulty of assessing the impact of this print culture for the conduct of war, at least in the sixteenth century. The extent to which the greater availability of printed material indicates that it had a major impact on operations is unclear, not least because the selection of commanders put more of an emphasis on birth than education. Military education was largely on the job, and there were few military academies.

Moreover, there is a tendency towards the primitivisation of the conceptual methods and organisational effectiveness of other forces that partly rests on prejudice and ignorance and that underplays the availability of information on the ability of non-Western cultures to develop new military solutions. Such primitivisation is particularly dubious if the emphasis in Western forces is on unit cohesion, a meritocratic military culture, and the role of expertise and training. These characteristics are applied to such a core force as the Spanish Army of Flanders,[6] but are also characteristics that were not dependent on technology or state development and that can be readily seen elsewhere. Rather than presenting non-Western forces as hordes, it is instructive to note their flexibility in battle conditions, as with Babur's description of the beginning of the battle of Sir-e-pul in 1501: 'When the lines of the two opposite armies approached each other, the extremity of their right wing turned my left flank, and wheeled upon my rear. I changed my position to meet them.'[7]

A Military Revolution?

The continued appeal of the theory of the Military Revolution reflects not only the high quality of the work of its leading current proponent, Geoffrey Parker, but also the extent to which the idea fulfils a need for selecting the apparently key developments in military history,[8] amid the often bewildering mass of conflicts, and for explaining the general impact of war on state development and international power in this period and over a longer time scale.[9] There is also a close relationship between the idea of a military revolution and discussion of the modern military situation.[10]

Yet, the thesis of a military revolution in this period also faces problems. As far as Christian Europe is concerned, the thesis's emphasis on firepower and *trace italienne* fortifications fails to capture, first, the extent to which the key theme was adaptation, rather than revolutionary change, and, secondly, the diversity of developments in the region, including the continued importance of cavalry, notably in France, where the cavalry made full use of the new wheel-lock pistol, and Poland.[11] Moreover, the French Wars of Religion saw a decline in the strength of the French artillery[12] that contributed to a shift towards a more mobile style of war prefiguring that which was to be seen in the latter stages of the Thirty Years' War.

In addition, the thesis of a military revolution has only limited traction outside Christian Europe for a number of reasons. In particular, the diffusion of Western methods was limited, while the extent to which the expansion of Western power can be attributed to the Military Revolution is questionable. Other factors played a major role, notably the disunity of opponents and the ability to win local support, as in Mexico.

Lastly, there were other dynamic powers in the world whose success is not necessarily explicable in terms of a Western-style military revolution or, indeed, of developments that paralleled those in the West. It is of course possible to understand those Koreans who, underplaying the important role of resources and organisational support, explained Chinese superiority over the Japanese in the 1590s in terms of technology: 'Military affairs are simple. Big cannons defeat small cannons and many cannon defeat few cannon.'[13] However, this factor was not central in the case of the Uzbeks or the Safavids. Complexity thus emerges as the central conclusion, a complexity that is enhanced by the avoidance of the often misleading clarity offered by single-source accounts of key episodes.[14]

Postscript

The historian sinks himself in his writing on the whole in the British academic tradition. The intellectual, pedagogic and cultural preference in academic life is for concealing the role of the author and, in particular, for letting the material apparently dictate the treatment. I would like to depart from that convention here because, while thinking about and writing this book, I asked myself repeatedly how far my approach was affected by changes in the world since I first wrote a book on the subject, my short *A Military Revolution? Military Change and European Society 1550–1800* (1991). In particular, I have wondered about the influence of declining American hegemony and rising Chinese power, and was struck by the need to address some of the themes offered in my *Rethinking Military History* (2004).

Re-reading my books on the subject in chronological order, I feel it clear that my concerns about technological emphases, still more determinism, and my unhappiness with Western-centred accounts, were there from the outset and preceded the problems that were to be encountered by Western power in Iraq and Afghanistan after the conquest of the first in 2003 and the overthrow of the Taliban government in the second in 2001. So, possibly, I should turn the question round and ask whether readers will be more receptive to my approach because of recent and current events. I certainly feel that a military history for the new millennium needs to devote due weight to Asia, the continent not only with the most people but also, in the twenty-first century, as in 1450–1600, with much military power. Parallels, of course, cannot be taken far, for the world is very different; but they serve to suggest the need to rethink the chronology and geography of world history and the accompanying patterns of analysis and causation.

Notes

1: Introduction

1. For an important recent discussion of this example which is of wider relevance, J.C. Scott, *The Art of Not Being Governed: An Anarchist History of Upland Southeast Asia* (New Haven, Connecticut, 2009) and review article by V. Lieberman, 'A zone of refuge in Southeast Asia? Reconceptualising interior spaces', *Journal of Global History*, 5 (2010), pp. 333–46.

2. D. Harrison, *Social Militarisation and the Power of History: A Study of Scholarly Perspectives* (Oslo, 1999), p. 194.

3. L.E. Grinter, 'Cultural and Historical Influences on Conflict in Sinic Asia: China, Japan and Vietnam', in S.J. Blank et al (eds), *Conflict and Culture in History* (Washington, 1993), pp. 117–92.

4. J. Lynn, *Women, Armies, and Warfare in Early Modern Europe* (Cambridge, 2008).

5. P. Withington, *Society in Early Modern England* (Cambridge, 2010).

6. T.T. Allsen, *Culture and Conquest in Mongol Eurasia* (Cambridge, 2001).

7. J. Thornton, 'Warfare, slave trading and European influence: Atlantic Africa 1450–1800', in J. Black (ed.), *War in the Early Modern World* (London, 1999), p. 133.

8. T. May, *The Mongol Art of War: Chinggis Khan and the Mongol Military System* (Yardley, Pennsylvania, 2007).

9. I.A. Khan, 'Coming of gunpowder to the Islamic world and North India: Spotlight on the role of the Mongols', *Journal of Asian History*, 30 (1996), pp. 27–45.

10. B.F. Manz, *The Rise and Rule of Tamerlane* (Cambridge, 1989).

11. J. Muldoon and F. Fernández-Armesto (eds), *The Expansion of Latin Europe, 1000–1500: The Medieval Frontiers of Latin Christendom* (Aldershot, 2008).

12. A.S. Atiya, *The Crusade of Nicopolis* (London, 1934).

13. J.M. Bak, 'Hungary and Crusading in the Fifteenth Century', in N. Housley (ed.), *Crusading in the Fifteenth Century: Message and Impact* (Basingstoke, 2004), pp. 116–27.

14. B.S. Hall, 'The Corning of Gunpowder and the Development of Firearms in the Renaissance', in B.J. Buchanan (ed.), *Gunpowder* (Bath, 1996), pp. 93–4.
15. K. Chase, *Firearms: A Global History to 1700* (Cambridge, 2003), p. 51.
16. E.L. Dreyer, *Zheng He: China and the Oceans in the Early Ming Dynasty, 1405–1433* (New York, 2007).

2: Conflict, 1450–1500

1. G. Raudzens, 'In Search of Better Quantification for War History: Numerical Superiority and Casualty Rates in Early Modern Europe', *War and Society*, 15 (1997), pp. 1–30.
2. F. Mote, 'The Tu-Mu Incident of 1449', in F. Kierman and J. K. Fairbank (eds), *Chinese Ways in Warfare* (Cambridge, Massachusetts, 1974), pp. 243–72.
3. A.I. Johnston, *Cultural Realism: Strategic Culture and Grand Strategy in Chinese History* (Princeton, New Jersey, 1995), pp. 236–42.
4. M. Rossabi, 'The tea and horse trade with Inner Asia during the Ming', *Journal of Asian History*, 4 (1970), pp. 136–68.
5. M. Elvin, *The Pattern of the Chinese Past* (London, 1973), pp. 95–7.
6. P.C. Perdue, *China Marches West: The Qing Conquest of Central Eurasia* (Cambridge, Massachusetts, 2005).
7. J.E. Herman, *Amid the Clouds and Mist: China's Colonization of Guizhou, 1200–1700* (Cambridge, Massachusetts, 2007).
8. K. Kazuo and K.A. Grossberg, 'Shogun and Shugo: The Provincial Aspects of Muromachi Politics', in J.W. Hall and T. Takeshi (eds), *Japan in the Muromachi Age* (Berkeley, California, 1977), pp. 65–87.
9. T. Conlan, 'Largesses and the Limits of Loyalty in the Fourteenth Century', in J.P. Mass (ed.), *The Origins of Japan's Medieval World: Courtiers, Clerics, Warriors, and Peasants in the Fourteenth Century* (Stanford, California, 1997), pp. 39–64.
10. J. Gommans, 'Warhorse and gunpowder in India c. 1000–1850', in J. Black (ed.), *War in the Early Modern World* (London, 1999), p. 113.
11. I benefited from discussing this topic with Simon Digby.
12. L. Kaba, *Sonni Ali-Ber Ali* (Paris, 1977); I.B. Kale and G. Comte, *Askia Mohamed* (Paris, 1976).
13. R. Irwin, 'Gunpowder and Firearms in the Mamluk Sultanate Reconsidered', in M. Winter and A. Levanoni (eds), *The Mamluks in Egyptian and Syrian Politics and Society* (Leiden, 2004), pp. 117–39; A. Fuess, 'Les Janissaires, les Mamlouks et les armes à feu. Une comparison des systèmes militaires Ottoman et Mamlouk à partir de la moitié du quinzième siècle', *Turcica*, 41 (2009), pp. 209–27; C. Petry, *Protectors or Praetorians? The last Mamlūk Sultans and Egypt's Waning as a Great Power*

(Albany, New York, 1994), p. 46. I have benefited from the advice of Albrecht Fuess.

14. S. Har-El, *Struggle for Domination in the Middle East: The Ottoman–Mamluk War 1485–91* (Leiden, 1995).

15. J.R. Melville-Jones (ed.), *The Siege of Constantinople 1453* (Amsterdam, 1972); K. DeVries, 'Gunpowder Weaponry at the siege of Constantinople, 1453', in Y. Lev (ed.) *War, Army and Society in the Eastern Mediterranean, 7th–16th Centuries* (Leiden, 1996); R. Crowley, *Constantinople: The Last Great Siege, 1453* (London, 2005); M. Philippides and W.K. Hanak, *The Siege and the Fall of Constantinople in 1453* (Farnham, 2011).

16. P. Wittek, *The Rise of the Ottoman Empire* (London, 1938), pp. 50–1.

17. G. Ágoston, 'Behind the Turkish War Machine: Gunpowder Technology and War Industry in the Ottoman Empire, 1450–1700', in B.D. Steele and T. Dorland (eds), *The Heirs of Archimedes. Science and the Art of War through the Age of Enlightenment* (Cambridge, Massachusetts, 2005), p. 106.

18. K. DeVries, 'The Lack of a Western European Military Response to the Ottoman Invasions of Eastern Europe from Nicopolis to Mohács', *Journal of Military History*, 63 (1999), pp. 555–7.

19. C. Heywood, 'Bosnia Under Ottoman Rule, 1463–1800', in M. Pinson (ed.) *The Muslims of Bosnia-Herzegovina: Their Historic Development from the Middle Ages to the Dissolution of Yugoslavia* (Cambridge, Massachusetts, 1994), pp. 23–4.

20. C. Heywood, *Writing Ottoman History* (Aldershot, 2002), no continuous pagination, section 16, pp. 5, 12.

21. A. Williams, '*Sacra Militia*, the Order of St John: Crusade, Corsairing and Trade in Rhodes and Malta, 1460–1631', in M. Fusaro et al. (ed.), *Trade and Cultural Exchange in the Early Modern Mediterranean* (London, 2010), p. 146.

22. D. Kolodziejczyk, 'Inner Lake or Frontier? The Ottoman Black Sea in the Sixteenth and Seventeenth Centuries', in F. Bilici et al. (eds), *Enjeux politiques, économiques et militaires en Mer Noire* (Braila, 2007), pp. 125–39.

23. Kritovoulos, *History of Mehmed the Conqueror* trans. C.T. Riggs (Princeton, New Jersey, 1954), p. 171.

24. Irwin, 'Gunpowder and Firearms', p. 124.

25. Ibid., p. 136.

26. H. Inalcik and R. Murphey (eds), *The History of Mehmed the Conqueror by Tursun Beg* (Minneapolis, Minnesota, 1978), p. 62.

27. J.E. Woods, *The Aqquyunlu: Clan, Confederation, Empire: A Study in 15th/9th Century Turko-Iranian Politics* (Minneapolis, Minnesota, 1976), pp. 132–44; T. Stavrides, *The Sultan of Vezirs: The Life and Times of the Ottoman Grand Vezir Mahmud Pasha Angelović 1453–1474* (Leiden, 2001), pp. 176–8.

28. A.H. Burne, 'The Battle of Castillon, 1453', *History Today*, 3 (1953), pp. 249–56; M. de Lombarès, 'Castillon (17 juillet 1453), dernière bataille de la guerre de Cent Ans, première victoire de l'artillerie', *Revue historique des armées* (1976), pp. 7–31.

29. C. Heywood, *Writing Ottoman History* (Aldershot, 2002), no continuous pagination, section 16, p. 19; R.D. Smith and K. DeVries, *The Artillery of the Dukes of Burgundy, 1363–1477* (Woodbridge, 2005).

30. S. Morillo, 'The "Age of Cavalry" Revisited', in D.J. Kagay and L.J.A. Villalon (eds) *The Circle of War in the Middle Ages* (Woodbridge, 1999), pp. 57–8.

31. S. Pepper, 'The Siege of Siena in its International Context', in M. Ascheri, G. Mazzoni and F. Nevola (eds), *L'Ultimo Secolo della Repubblica di Siena* Siena, 2008), pp. 451–66, esp. pp. 453–60.

32. W. Cook, 'The Cannon Conquest of Násrid Spain and the End of the Reconquista', *Journal of Military History*, 57 (1993), pp. 43–70.

33. G. Phillips, *The Anglo-Scots War 1513–1550. A Military History* (Woodbridge, 1999).

34. R. Vaughan, *Charles the Bold* (London, 1973); D. Reichel (ed.), *Grandson, 1476* (Lausanne, 1970).

35. M.E. Mallett and J.R. Hale, *The Military Organisation of a Renaissance State: Venice, c. 1400–1617* (Cambridge, 1984).

36. P. Krenn, P. Kalaus and B.S. Hall, 'Material Culture and Military History: Test-Firing Early Modern Small Arms', *Material History Review*, 42 (1995), pp. 101-9; T. Richardson, 'Ballistic Testing of Historical Weapons', *Royal Armouries Yearbook*, 3 (1998), pp. 50–2.

37. L.J.D. Collins, 'The military organisation and tactics of the Crimean Tatars during the sixteenth and seventeenth centuries', in V.J. Parry and M.E. Yapp (eds), *War, Technology and Society in the Middle East* (Oxford, 1975), pp. 257–76; D. Morgan, 'The Mongol Empire in World History', in L. Komaroff (ed.), *Beyond the Legacy of Genghis Khan* (Leiden, 2006), p. 435.

38. P. Purton, *A History of the Late Medieval Siege, 1200–1500* (Woodbridge, 2010), p. 394.

39. *Ibid.*, p. 405.

40. A.R. Bell, *War and the Soldier in the Fourteenth Century* (Woodbridge, 2004).

41. R. Higham, 'Public and Private Defence in the Medieval South West: Town, Castle and Fort', in Higham (ed.), *Security and Defence in South-West England before 1800* (Exeter, 1987), pp. 40–2.

42. S. Pepper, 'The Face of the Siege: Fortification, Tactics and Strategy in the Early Italian Wars', in C. Shaw (ed.), *Italy and the European Powers. The Impact of War, 1500–1530* (Leiden, 2006), pp. 33–40.

43. D. Abulafia (ed.), *The French Descent into Renaissance Italy, 1494–95: Antecedents and Effects* (Aldershot, 1995); D.C. Nicolle, *Fornovo, 1495* (London, 1999).
44. D. Bornstein, 'Military Manuals in Fifteenth-Century England', *Mediaeval Studies*, 37 (1975), pp. 469–77.
45. L.H.J. Sicking, 'Philip of Cleves' *Instruction de toutes manières de guerroyer* and the fitting out of warships in the Netherlands during the Habsburg-Valois wars', in J. Haemers et al. (eds), *Entre la ville, la noblesse et l'état: Philippe de Clèves* (Turnhout, 2007), p. 120.
46. N. Vatin, *Sultan Djem: un prince ottoman dans l'Europe du XV siècle d'après deux oeuvres contemporaines* (Ankara, 1997); J. Freely, *Jem Sultan: The Adventures of a Captive Turkish Prince in Renaissance Europe* (London, 2004).

3: Conflict, 1500–1535

1. S. Chandra, *Medieval India From Sultanat to the Mughals* (Delhi, 2000), pp. 28–9.
2. L. King (ed.), *Memoirs of … Babur* (2 vols, Oxford, 1921), II, 186–7.
3. *Ibid.*, 288–308.
4. P. Jackson and L. Lockhart (eds), *The Cambridge History of Iran*, VI (Cambridge, 1986), p. 183.
5. *Memoirs of … Babur*, II, 67–8.
6. *Ibid.*, 74–5.
7. M. Bruinessen and H. Boeschoten, *Evliya Çelebi in Diyarbekir* (Leiden, 1988), pp. 13–15.
8. M. Mazzaoui, 'Global Policies of Sultan Selim, 1512–1520', in D.P. Little (ed.), *Essays on Islamic Civilization* (Leiden, 1976), pp. 224–43.
9. R. Irwin, 'Gunpowder and Firearms in the Mamluk Sultanate Reconsidered', in M. Winter and A. Levanoni (eds), *The Mamluks in Egyptian and Syrian Politics and Society* (Leiden, 2004), pp. 136–8.
10. J. Waterson, *The Knights of Islam: The Wars of the Mamluks* (St Paul, Minnesota, 2007).
11. G. Casale, *The Ottoman Age of Exploration* (Oxford, 2010), pp. 31, 212.
12. I. Beldiceaunu-Steinherr, 'Le règne de Selim Ier: tournant dans la vie politique et réligieuse de l'empire ottoman' *Turcica*, 6 (1975), pp. 35–48.
13. F. Szakály, 'Nándorfehérvár [Belgrade], 1521: the Beginning of the End of the Medieval Hungarian Kingdom', in G. Dávid and P. Fodor (eds), *Hungarian–Ottoman Military and Diplomatic Relations in the Age of Süleyman the Magnificent* (Budapest, 1994), pp. 47–76.
14. R.D. Smith and K. DeVries, *Rhodes Besieged: A Story of Stone, Cannon and Men, 1480–1522* (forthcoming).

15. M.A. Bakhit, *The Ottoman Province of Damascus in the Sixteenth Century* (Beirut, 1982), p. 33.
16. M. Rady, 'Jagaello Hungary', in F. Döry, *The Laws of the Medieval Kingdom of Hungary IV, 1490–1526*, ed. P. Banyó and M. Rady (Budapest, 2010), pp. xxviii.
17. G. Perjés, *The Fall of the Medieval Kingdom of Hungary: Mohacs 1526–Buda 1541* (Boulder, Colorado, 1989), pp. 251–7.
18. I. Zombori (ed.), *Fight against the Turk in Central-Europe in the First Half of the Sixteenth Century* (Budapest, 2004).
19. H. Kamen, *The Duke of Alba* (New Haven, Connecticut, 2004), p. 13.
20. G. Dávid and P. Fodor (eds), *Hungarian–Ottoman Military and Diplomatic Relations in the Age of Süleyman the Magnificent* (Budapest, 1994) and *Ottomans, Hungarians and Habsburgs in Central Europe: The Military Confines in the Era of Ottoman Conquest* (Leiden, 2000).
21. J.D. Tracy, *Emperor Charles V's Crusades against Tunis and Algiers: Appearance and Reality* (Minneapolis, Minnesota, 2001).
22. M. Carr, *Blood and Faith: The Purging of Muslim Spain, 1492–1614* (London, 2009), pp. 74–7.
23. F. Soyer, *The Persecution of the Jews and Muslims of Portugal: King Manuel I and the End of Religious Tolerance, 1496–7* (Leiden, 2007).
24. T. Tamrat, *Church and State in Ethiopia, 1270–1527* (Oxford, 1972), pp. 294–300.
25. R. Pankhurst, *The Ethiopian Borderlands* (Lawrenceville, New Jersey, 1997), pp. 222–3.
26. P.M. Holt and M.W. Daly, *A History of the Sudan* (4th edn, London, 1988), pp. 28–30.
27. R. Law, *The Horse in West African History* (Oxford, 1980).
28. R. Law, 'Horses, Firearms, and Political Power in Pre-Colonial West Africa', *Past and Present*, 72 (1976), p. 120.
29. D.K. Abbass, 'Horses and Heroes: the Myth of the Importance of the Horse to the Conquest of the Indies', *Terrae Incognitae*, 18 (1986), pp. 21–41, esp. 40–1.
30. A.P. Vayda, *Maori Warfare* (Wellington, 1960); N.B. Dukas, *A Military History of Sovereign Hawai'i* (Honolulu, Hawai'i, 2004), pp. 2–26.
31. I. Goldman, *Ancient Polynesian Society* (Chicago, Illinois, 1970), pp. 556–7.
32. G. Parker, *The Grand Strategy of Philip II* (New Haven, Connecticut, 1998).
33. Though see G. Agostón, 'Information, ideology and limits of imperial policy: Ottoman grand strategy in the context of Ottoman-Habsburg rivalry', in V. Aksan and D. Goffman (eds), *The Early Modern Ottomans: Remapping the Empire* (Cambridge, 2007), pp. 75–103.
34. S.J. Gunn, 'The French Wars of Henry VIII', in J. Black (ed.), *The Origins of War in Early Modern Europe* (Edinburgh, 1987), pp. 28–51.

35. L. Silver, *Marketing Maximilian: The Visual Ideology of a Holy Roman Emperor* (Princeton, New Jersey, 2008).
36. J. Tracy, *Emperor Charles V, Impresario of War: Campaign Strategy, International Finance, and Domestic Politics* (Cambridge, 2002), p. 38.
37. F. Baumgartner, *Louis XII* (Stroud, 1994).
38. G. De Gaury, *The Grand Captain, Gonzalo de Cordoba* (London, 1955).
39. S. Pepper, 'The Face of the Siege: Fortification, Tactics and Strategy in the Early Italian Wars', in C. Shaw (ed.), *Italy and the European Powers: The Impact of War, 1500–1530* (Leiden, 2006), pp. 33–56.
40. B. Hall, *Weapons and Warfare in Renaissance Europe* (Baltimore, Maryland, 1997).
41. G. Phillips, *The Anglo-Scots Wars 1513–1550. A Military History* (Woodbridge, 1999).
42. Phillips, *Anglo-Scots Wars 1513–1550*, p. 41.
43. M. Arfaioli, *The Black Bands of Giovanni: Infantry and Diplomacy during the Italian Wars, 1526–1528* (Pisa, 2005).
44. R. Finlay, *Venice Besieged: Politics and Diplomacy in the Italian Wars, 1494–1534* (Aldershot, 2008).
45. M. Tanner, *The Last Descendant of Aeneas: The Habsburgs and the Mythic Image of the Emperor* (New Haven, Connecticut, 1993); H. Kleinschmidt, *Ruling the Waves: Emperor Maximilian I, the Search for Islands and the Transformation of the European World Picture* (Utrecht, 2008).

4: Conflict, 1535–1575

1. K. So, *Japanese Piracy in Ming China during the Sixteenth Century* (East Lansing, Michigan, 1975); T. Brook, *The Confusions of Pleasure: Commerce and Culture in Ming China* (Berkeley, California, 1998).
2. A. Waldron, *The Great Wall of China: From History to Myth* (Cambridge, 1990), pp. 125–39.
3. L.C. Goodrich and F. Chaoying, *Dictionary of Ming Biography, 1368–1644* (New York, 1976), pp. 6–9.
4. A. Chan, *The Glory and Fall of the Ming Dynasty* (Norman, Oklahoma, 1982), pp. 51–63; H. Serruys, 'Four Documents Relating to the Sino-Mongol Peace of 1570–1571', *Monumenta Serica*, 19 (1960), pp. 1–66.
5. L.Y. Andaya, 'Interactions with the Outside World and Adaptation in Southeast Asian Society, 1500–1800', in N. Tarling (ed.), *The Cambridge History of South-East Asia* (2 vols, Cambridge, 1992), I, 380–95; A. Reid, *Southeast Asia in the Age of Commerce , 1450–1680: II, Expansion and Crisis* (New Haven, 1993), pp. 219–29.
6. S. Morillo, 'Guns and Government: A Comparative Study of Europe and Japan', *Journal of World History*, 6 (1995), pp. 75–106.
7. G. Parker, *The Military Revolution* (2nd edn, Cambridge, 1996), pp. 140–1.

8. T. Conlan, *Weapons and Fighting Techniques of the Samurai Warrior, 1200–1877* (London, 2008).

9. C.R. Tsang, *War and Faith: Ikkō-Ikki in Late Muromachi Japan* (Cambridge, Massachusetts, 2007).

10. B.A.K. Matta, *Sher Shah Suri: A Fresh Perspective* (Karachi, 2005).

11. S. Digby, *War Horse and Elephant in the Delhi Sultanate* (Oxford, 1971), pp. 23–82; R.K. Phul, *Armies of the great Mughals, 1526–1707* (1978), pp. 64–6.

12. J.F. Richards, *The Mughal Empire* (Cambridge, 1993), p. 288.

13. P. Barua, *State and War in South Asia*, pp. 35–6.

14. R.J. Barendse, 'Trade and State in the Arabian Seas: A Survey from the Fifteenth to the Eighteenth Century', *Journal of World History* (2000), pp. 210–11.

15. S. Subrahmanyan, *The Political Economy of Commerce: Southern India, 1500–1650* (Cambridge, 1990), pp. 151–3.

16. J.E. Mandaville, 'The Ottoman Province of al-Hasa in the Sixteenth and Seventeenth Century', *Journal of the American Oriental Society*, 90 (1970), pp. 490–3.

17. R. Matthee, 'The Safavid–Ottoman Frontier: Iraq-i-Arab as seen by the Safavids', in K.H. Karpat and R.W. Zens (eds), *Ottoman Borderlands* (Madison, Wisconsin, 2003), pp. 157–73.

18. H. Kamen, *The Duke of Alba* (New Haven, Connecticut, 2004), p. 19.

19. G. Agoston, 'Information, Ideology, and Limits of Imperial Policy: Ottoman Grand Strategy in the Context of Ottoman–Habsburg Rivalry', in V. Aksan and D. Goffman (eds), *The Early Modern Ottomans: Remapping the Empire* (Cambridge, 2007), pp. 75–103, esp. 77. For sources of information on the outside world, S. Faroqhi, *The Ottoman Empire and the World Around* (London, 2004), pp. 179–210.

20. G. Veinstein, 'Some Views on Provisioning in the Hungarian Campaigns of Suleyman the Magnificent', in Veinstein (ed.), *Etat et Société dans l'Empire Ottoman, XVIe–XVIIIe siècles* (Aldershot, 1994), pp. 177–85.

21. D. Goffman, *The Ottoman Empire and Early Modern Europe* (Cambridge, 2002), p. 65.

22. De L. Jensen, 'The Ottoman Turks in Sixteenth-Century French Diplomacy', *Sixteenth-Century Journal*, 16 (1985), pp. 451–70.

23. M. Kunt and C. Woodhead (eds), *Süleyman the Magnificent and His Age: The Ottoman Empire in the Early Modern World* (London, 1995).

24. M. Abin, *Ethiopia and the Red Sea* (London, 1980), pp. 126–7.

25. A.N. Kurat, 'The Turkish Expedition to Astrakhan in 1569 and the Problem of the Don–Volga Canal', *Slavonic and East European Review*, 40 (1961), pp. 7–23.

26. W.E.D. Allen, *Problems of Turkish Power in the Sixteenth Century* (London, 1963), pp. 36–7.

27. A. el-Moudden, 'The *Sharif* and the Padi Shah: Some Remarks on Moroccan–Ottoman Relations in the Sixteenth Century', in S. Deringil and S. Kuneralp (eds), *Studies on Ottoman Diplomatic History, V: The Ottomans and Africa* (Istanbul, 1990), pp. 27–34.

28. R. Murphey, 'A Comparative Look at Ottoman and Habsburg Resources and Readiness for War *c* 1520 to *c* 1570', in G. Hernán and D. Maffi (eds), *Guerra y Sociedad en la Monarquía Hispánica* (2 vols, Madrid, 2006), I, 76, 102.

29. D. Behrens-Abouseif, *Egypt's Adjustment to Ottoman Rule* (Leiden, 1994), p. 42.

30. M. Carr, *Blood and Faith: The Purging of Muslim Spain 1492–1614* (London, 2009), pp. 159–84.

31. F. Gonzáles de Léon, *The Road to Rocroi: Class, Culture, and Command in the Spanish Army of Flanders, 1567–1659* (Leiden, 2009).

32. G. Parker, *The Army of Flanders and the Spanish Road, 1567–1659: The Logistics of Spanish Victory and Defeat in the Low Countries' Wars* (2nd edn, Cambridge, 2004).

33. S. Carroll, *Noble Power during the French Wars of Religion: The Guise Affinity and the Catholic Cause in Normandy* (Cambridge, 1998).

34. See also p. 206.

35. J. Meyer, *The Art of Combat: A German Martial Arts Treatise of 1570*, ed. I. Forgeng (London, 2005); D. Randall, 'Providence, Fortune, and the Experience of Combat: English Printed Battlefield Reports, circa 1570–1637', *Sixteenth-Century Journal*, 35 (2004), pp. 1053–77.

36. R. Murphey, 'The Garrison and its Hinterland in the Ottoman East, 1578–1605', in A.C.S. Peacock (ed.), *The Frontiers of the Ottoman World* (Oxford, 2009), p. 369.

37. S. Pepper, 'The Siege of Siena in its International Context', in M. Ascheri, G. Mazzoni and F. Nevola (eds), *L'Ultimo Secolo della Republica di Siena* (Siena, 2008), p. 466.

38. W.E.D. Allen, *Problems of Turkish Power in the Sixteenth Century* (London, 1963), p. 38.

39. M. Greene, 'The Ottomans in the Mediterranean', in V. Aksan and D. Goffman (eds), *The Early Modern Ottomans: Remapping the Empire* (Cambridge, 2007), p. 110.

5: Conflict, 1575–1600

1. A. Burton, *The Bukharans: A Dynastic, Diplomatic and Commercial History, 1550–1702* (New York, 1997), p. 117.

2. M.E. Berry, *Hideyoshi* (Cambridge, Massachusetts, 1982).

3. K.M. Swope, 'Turning the Tide: The Strategic and Psychological Significance of the Liberation of Pyongyang in 1593', *War and Society*, 21 (2003), pp. 1–22.

4. K.M. Swope, 'Deceit, Disguise, and Dependence: China, Japan, and the Future of the Tributary System, 1592–1596', *International History Review*, 24 (2002), pp. 757–1008.

5. S. Turnbull, *Samurai Invasion: Japan's Korean War, 1592–1598* (London, 2002), although see criticisms in K.M. Swope's 'Crouching Tigers, Secret Weapons: Military Technology Employed During the Sino-Japanese-Korean War, 1592–1598', *Journal of Military History*, 69 (2005), pp. 11–42. See also Swope, *A Dragon's Head and a Serpent's Tail: Ming China and the First Great East Asian War, 1592–1598* (Norman, Oklahoma, 2009).

6. The numbers given for both sides vary considerably.

7. E.W. Bovil, *The Battle of Alcazar* (London, 1952); W. Cook, *The Hundred Years War for Morocco: Gunpowder and the Military Revolution in the Early Modern Muslim World* (Boulder, Colorado, 1994).

8. L. Kaba, 'Archers, Musketeers and Mosquitoes: The Moroccan Invasion of the Sudan and the Songhay Resistance, 1591–1612', *Journal of African History*, 22 (1981), pp. 457–75.

9. M. Abir, *Ethiopia and the Red Sea* (London, 1980), p. 136.

10. T. Tamrat, *Church and State in Ethiopia, 1270–1527* (Oxford, 1972), p. 301.

11. G. Ágoston, 'Habsburgs and Ottomans: Military Changes and Shifts in Power', *Ottoman Studies Association Bulletin*, 22 (1998), pp. 126–41.

12. C. Keyvanian, 'Maps and Wars: Charting the Mediterranean in the Sixteenth Century', in B. Kolluoğlu and M. Toksöz (eds), *Cities of the Mediterranean: From the Ottomans to the Present Day* (London, 2010), p. 60.

13. G. Ágoston, 'Gunpowder for the Sultan's Army', *Turcica*, 25 (1993), pp. 75–96, 'Ottoman Artillery and European Military Technology in the Fifteenth and Sixteenth Centuries', *Acta Orientalia Academiae Scientarum Hungaricae*, 47 (1994), pp. 32–47 and 'Disjointed Historiography and Islamic Military Technology: The European Military Revolution and the Ottomans', in M. Kaçan and Z. Durukal (eds), *Essays in Honour of Ekmeleddin Ihsanoğlu* I (Istanbul, 2006), pp. 567–82.

14. G. Pálffy, *The Kingdom of Hungary and the Habsburg Monarchy in the Sixteenth Century* (Boulder, Colorado, 2009), pp. 114–17.

15. M.C. Paul, 'the Military Revolution in Russia, 1550–1682', *Journal of Military History*, 68 (2004), pp. 36–7.

16. D. Potter, *Renaissance France at War: Armies, Culture and Society, c. 1480–1560* (Woodbridge, 2008).

17. M.P. Holt, *The French Wars of Religion, 1562–1629* (Cambridge, 1995).

18. G. Oestreich, *Neostoicism and the Early Modern State* (Cambridge, 1982).

19. G. Parker, 'The "Military Revolution", 1955–2005', *Journal of Military History*, 69 (2005), p. 208.
20. G. Parker, 'The Limits to Revolutions in Military Affairs; Maurice of Nassau, the Battle of Nieuwpoort, and the Legacy', *Journal of Military History*, 71 (2007), pp. 331–72.
21. C. Brady, *The Chief Governors: The Rise and Fall of Reform Government in Tudor Ireland, 1537–1588* (Cambridge, 1994); N. Canny, *Making Ireland British, 1580–1650* (Oxford, 2001).

6: Naval Capability and Warfare

1. For an account of capability, D. McNab, B.W. Hodgins and D.S. Standen, '"Black with Canoes": Aboriginal Resistance and the Canoe: Diplomacy, Trade and Warfare in the Meeting Grounds of Northeastern North America, 1600–1821', in G. Raudzens (ed.), *Technology, Disease and Colonial Conquests, Sixteenth to Eighteenth Centuries* (Leiden, 2001), pp. 237–92.
2. D.J.B. Trim and M.C. Fissel (eds), *Amphibious Warfare, 1000–1700: Commerce, State Formation, and European Expansion* (Leiden, 2006).
3. H. Inalcik and R. Murphey (eds), *The History of Mehmed the Conqueror by Tursun Beg* (Minneapolis, Minnesota, 1978), p. 62.
4. G. Agoston, 'Muslim–Christian Acculturation: Ottomans and Hungarians from the Fifteenth to the Seventeenth Centuries', in B. Bennassar and R. Sauzet (eds), *Chrétiens et Musulmans à la Renaissance* (Paris, 1994), p. 296.
5. S. Subrahmanyam, *The Career and the Legend of Vasco da Gama* (Cambridge, 1997).
6. A. Naohiro, 'The Sixteenth-Century Unification', in J.W. Hall (ed.), *The Cambridge History of Japan, IV: Early Modern Japan* (Cambridge, 1991), p. 54.
7. M. Newitt, 'Portuguese Amphibious Warfare in the East in the Sixteenth Century, 1500–1520', in Trim and Fissel (eds), *Amphibious Warfare*, pp. 103–21; F. Bethencourt and D. Ramada Curto (eds), *Portuguese Oceanic Expansion, 1400–1800* (Cambridge, 2007).
8. J. Hathaway, 'A Forgotten Province: A Prelude to the Ottoman Era in Yemen', in D. Wasserstein and A. Ayalon (eds), *Mamluks and Ottomans* (Abingdon, 2006), p. 201.
9. S. Özbaran, *The Ottoman Response to European Expansion: Studies on Ottoman–Portuguese Relations in the Indian Ocean and Ottoman Administration in the Arab Lands During the Sixteenth Century* (Istanbul, 1994); P. Brummett, 'The Ottomans as a World Power: What We Don't Know about Ottoman Sea-power', *Oriente Moderno*, 81 (2001), pp. 1–21.

10. A. Reid, 'Sixteenth-century Turkish Influence in Western Indonesia', *Journal of Southeast Asian History*, 1 (1969), pp. 395–414.

11. S. Özbaran, 'Ottoman Naval Policy in the South', in M. Kunt and C. Woodhead (eds), *Süleyman the Magnificent and his Age* (London, 1995), pp. 58–64; G. Casale, *The Ottoman Age of Exploration* (Oxford, 2010), pp. 163–78.

12. W. Floor, *The Persian Gulf: A Political and Economic History of Five Port Cities, 1500–1730* (Washington, DC, 2006).

13. Kritovoulos, *History of Mehmed the Conqueror*, trans. C.T. Riggs (Princeton, New Jersey, 1954), p. 185.

14. A.C. Hess, 'The Evolution of the Ottoman Seaborne Empire in the Age of Oceanic Discoveries, 1453–1525', *American Historical Review*, 75 (1969–70), p. 1906.

15. L.J. Libby, 'Venetian Views of the Ottoman Empire from the Peace of 1503 to the War of Cyprus', *Sixteenth-Century Journal*, 9 (1978), pp. 103–26.

16. J.F. Guilmartin, 'The Earliest Shipboard Gunpowder Ordnance: An Analysis of Its Technical Parameters and Tactical Capabilities', *Journal of Military History*, 71 (2007), pp. 667–8.

17. U. Alertsz, 'The Naval Architecture and Oar Systems of Medieval and Later Galleys', in R. Gardiner and J. Morrison (eds), *The Age of the Galley: Mediterranean Oared Vessels since Pre-Classical Times* (London, 2004), pp. 142–62.

18. P. Brummett, 'The Overrated Adversary: Rhodes and Ottoman Naval Power', *Historical Journal*, 36 (1993), p. 541.

19. M. Balard, 'Genoese Naval Forces in the Mediterranean during the Fifteenth and Sixteenth Centuries', in J.B. Hattendorf and R.W. Unger (eds), *War at Sea in the Middle Ages and the Renaissance* (Woodbridge, 2003), pp. 137–49; T.A. Kirk, *Genoa and the Sea: Policy and Power in an Early Modern Maritime Republic, 1559–1684* (Baltimore, Maryland, 2005).

20. D. Brewer, *Greece, The Hidden Centuries* (London, 2010), pp. 58–64.

21. J.F. Guilmartin, *Gunpowder and Galleys: Changing Technology and Mediterranean Warfare at Sea in the Sixteenth Century* (2nd edn, Annapolis, Maryland, 2003), pp. 42–56.

22. Y.N. Harari, 'Martial Illusions: War and Disillusionment in Twentieth-Century and Renaissance Military Memoirs', *Journal of Military History*, 69 (2005), p. 61.

23. E. Bradford, *The Great Siege* (London, 1961); Guilmartin, 'The Siege of Malta and the Habsburg–Ottoman Struggle for Domination of the Mediterranean', in Trim and Fissel (eds), *Amphibious Warfare*, pp. 149–80.

24. Guilmartin, *Gunpowder*, pp. 221–52 and 'The Tactics of the Battle of Lepanto Clarified: The Impact of Social, Economic, and Political Factors on Sixteenth-century Galley Warfare', in C.L. Symonds (ed.), *New Aspects of Naval History* (Annapolis, 1981), pp. 41–65; N. Capponi, *Victory of the*

West: The Story of the Battle of Lepanto (London, 2006). For recent Turkish work, see I. Bostan, 'Inebahti Deniz Savasi', in *Türkiye Dinayet Vakfi Islam Ansiklopedisi* vol. 22 (Istanbul, 2000), pp. 287–9. I owe this reference to Gabor Ágoston.

25. C. Imber, 'The Reconstruction of the Ottoman Fleet after the Battle of Lepanto', in Imber, *Studies in Ottoman History and Law* (Istanbul, 1996), pp. 85–101.

26. Guilmartin, *Gunpowder*, pp. 253–73.

27. T. Nelson, 'Slavery in Medieval Japan', *Monumenta Nipponica*, 59 (2004), pp. 465–6.

28. R.A. Stradling, *The Armada of Flanders: Spanish Maritime Policy and European War, 1568–1668* (Cambridge, 1992).

29. C. Martin and G. Parker, *The Spanish Armada* (London, 1988).

30. E. Tenace, 'A Strategy of Reaction: The Armadas of 1596 and 1597 and the Spanish Struggle for European Hegemony', *English Historical Review*, 118 (2003), pp. 855–82.

31. D. Goodman, *Spanish Naval Power, 1589–1665: Reconstruction and Defeat* (Cambridge, 1996).

32. S. Souchek, 'Islamic Charting in the Mediterranean', in J.B. Harley and D. Woodward (eds), *The History of Cartography: Cartography in the Traditional Islamic and South Asian Societies* (Chicago, Illinois, 1992), pp. 263–92.

33. A. Barrera-Osorio, *Experiencing Nature: The Spanish American Empire and the Early Scientific Revolution* (Austin, Texas, 2006), p. 131.

7: The Expansion of the West, 1450–1600

1. G. Casale, *The Ottoman Age of Exploration* (Oxford, 2010).

2. T. Nelson, *Japanese Overseas Settlements to 1650* (Abingdon, 2010); R.J. Antony (ed.), *Elusive Pirates, Pervasive Smugglers: Violence and Clandestine Trade in the Greater China Seas* (Hong Kong, 2010).

3. D. Ostrowski, *Muscovy and the Mongols: Cross-Cultural Influences on the Steppe Frontier, 1304–1589* (Cambridge, 1998), pp. 187–8.

4. J. Pelenki, *Russia and Kazan: Conquest and Imperial Ideology, 1438–1560s* (The Hague, 1974).

5. T. Armstrong (ed.), *Yermak's Campaign in Siberia: A Selection of Documents Translated from the Russian Chronicles* (London, 1975).

6. J. Vogt, 'Saint Barbara's Legions: Portuguese Artillery in the Struggle for Morocco', *Military Affairs*, 41 (Dec. 1977), pp. 176–82; M.M. Elbl, 'Portuguese Urban Fortifications in Morocco: Borrowing, Adaptation, and Innovation along a Military Frontier', in J.D. Tracey (ed.), *City Walls: The Urban Enceinte in Global Perspective* (Cambridge, 2000), pp. 349–85.

7. D. Goffman, *The Ottoman Empire and Early Modern Europe* (Cambridge, 2002), p. 232.
8. N. Capponi, *Victory of the West*, pp. 142–4.
9. M.A. Bakhit, *The Ottoman Province of Damascus in the Sixteenth Century* (Beirut, 1980), pp. 94, 98, 225.
10. M. Newitt (ed.), *The Portuguese in West Africa, 1415–1670: A Documentary History* (Cambridge, 2010), pp. 163–4.
11. R. Gray, 'Portuguese Musketeers on the Zambezi', *Journal of African History*, 12 (1971), p. 531.
12. J. Thornton, 'The Art of War in Angola, 1575–1680', *Comparative Studies in Society and History*, 30 (1988), pp. 362–78 and 'Firearms, Diplomacy, and Conquest in Angola: Cooperation and Alliance in West Central Africa, 1491–1671', in W.E. Lee (ed.), *Empires and Indigenes: Intercultural Alliance, Imperial Expansion, and Warfare in the Early Modern World* (New York, 2011).
13. C.R. de Silva, *Portuguese Encounters with Sri Lanka and the Maldives* (Farnham, 2009).
14. T. Abeyasinghe, *Portuguese Rule in Ceylon, 1594–1612* (Colombo, 1966).
15. V.A. Kivelson, '"Exalted and Glorified to the Ends of the Earth": Imperial Maps and Christian Spaces in Seventeenth- and Early Eighteenth-century Russian Siberia', in J.R. Akerman (ed.), *The Imperial Map: Cartography and the Mastery of Empire* (Chicago, Illinois, 2009), p. 72.
16. M. Winter, 'The Re-emergence of the Mamluks following the Ottoman Conquest', in T. Philipp and U. Haarmann (eds), *The Mamluks in Egyptian Politics and Society* (Cambridge, 1988), pp. 87–106, esp. 91–2, 105.
17. R. Hassig, *Mexico and the Spanish Conquest* (London, 1994); M. Restall, *Seven Myths of the Spanish Conquest* (Oxford, 2003).
18. M. Restall and F. Asselbergs, *Invading Guatemala: Spanish, Nuala, and Maya Accounts of the Conquest War* (University Park, Pennsylvania, 2007); D.A. Daniel, 'Tactical Factors in the Spanish Conquest of the Aztecs', *Anthropology Quarterly*, 65 (1992), pp. 187–94.
19. L.E. Matthew and M.R. Oudijk (eds), *Indian Conquistadors: Indigenous Allies in the Conquest of Mesoamerica* (Norman, Oklahoma, 2007).
20. A.F. Galindo, *In Search of an Inca: Identity and Utopia in the Andes* (Cambridge, 2010), p. 26.
21. C. Jacob, *The Sovereign Map: Theoretical Approaches in Cartography throughout History* (Chicago, Illinois, 2006), p. 205.
22. R. Kagan, *Urban Images of the Hispanic World, 1493–1793* (New Haven, Connecticut, 2000); S. MacCormack, *On the Wings of Time: Rome, the Incas, Spain, and Peru* (Princeton, New Jersey, 2007).
23. E. Wake, *Framing the Sacred: The Indian Churches of Early Colonial Mexico* (Norman, Oklahoma, 2010).

24. I. Clendinnen, '"Fierce and Unnatural Cruelty": Cortés and the Conquest of Mexico', in S. Greenbalt (ed.), *New World Encounters* (Berkeley, California, 1993), pp. 12–47.

25. P.L. Don, *Bonfires of Culture: Franciscans, Indigenous Leaders, and the Inquisition in Early Mexico, 1524–1540* (Norman, Oklahoma, 2010); M.A. Nesvig, *Ideology and Inquisition: The World of the Censors in Early Mexico* (New Haven, Connecticut, 2009).

26. C. Gibson, *The Aztecs under Spanish Rule: A History of the Indians of the Valley of Mexico, 1519–1810* (Stanford, California, 1964); J. Lockhart, *The Nahuas After the Conquest: A Social and Cultural History of the Indians of Central Mexico* (Stanford, 1992).

27. J.M. Francis, *Invading Colombia: Spanish Accounts of the Gonzalo Jiménez de Quesada Expedition of Conquest* (University Park, Pennsylvania, 2007).

28. B. de Vargas Machucha, *The Indian Militia and Description of the Indies*, ed. K. Lane (Durham, North Carolina, 2008).

29. P. Powell, *Soldiers, Indians and Silver: The Northward Advance of New Spain, 1550–1600* (Berkeley, California, 1952).

30. T.H.B. Symons, *Meta Incognita: A Discourse of Discovery. Martin Frobisher's Arctic Expeditions, 1576–1578* (Hull, 1999).

31. G.D. Jones, 'The Last Maya Frontiers of Colonial Yucatán', in M.J. MacLeod and R. Wassertrom (eds), *Spaniards and Indians in Southeastern Mesoamerica: Essays on the History of Ethnic Relations* (Lincoln, Nebraska, 1983), pp. 64–91.

32. K.O. Kupperman, *Roanoke: The Abandoned Colony* (Savage, Maryland, 1984).

33. P.C. Mancall, *Hakluyt's Promise: An Elizabethan's Obsession for an English America* (New Haven, Connecticut, 2007).

34. A. Galley, *The Indian Slave Trade* (New Haven, 2002); B. Rushforth, '"A little flesh we offer you": The Origins of Indian Slavery in New France', *William and Mary Quarterly*, 60 (2003), pp. 777–808.

35. L.B. Simpson, *The Encomienda in New Spain: The Beginning of Spanish Mexico* (3rd edn, Berkeley, California, 1966); W.L. Sherman, *Forced Native Labour in Sixteenth-Century Central America* (Lincoln, Nebraska, 1979); O.N. Bolland, 'Colonization and Slavery in Central America', in P.E. Lovejoy and N. Rogers (eds), *Unfree Labour in the Development of the Atlantic World* (Ilford, 1994), pp. 11–25.

36. For example, the editorial introduction to F. Tallett and D.J.B. Trim (eds), *European Warfare 1350–1750* (Cambridge, 2010), p. 7.

37. J.E. Wills, 'Maritime Asia, 1500–1800: The Interactive Emergence of European Domination', *American Historical Review*, 98 (1993), pp. 83–105.

38. D. Peers (ed.), *Warfare and Empires: Contact and Conflict between European and Non-European Military and Maritime Forces and Cultures* (Aldershot, 1997), pp. xvii–xxix.
39. G. Ágoston, *Guns for the Sultan: Military Power and the Weapons Industry in the Ottoman Empire* (Cambridge, 2005).
40. G. Casale, *The Ottoman Age of Expansion* (Oxford, 2010), p. 202; see critical review by S. Soucek in *Archivum Ottomanicum*.

8: Warfare, Social Contexts, and State Development

1. R.J. Chacon and R.G. Mendoza (eds), *North American Indigenous Warfare and Ritual Violence* (Tucson, Arizona, 2007).
2. R. Pankhurst, *The Ethiopian Borderlands* (Lawrenceville, New Jersey, 1997), pp. 287, 281.
3. F.W. Mote and D. Twichett, *The Cambridge History of China. VII: The Ming Dynasty, Part 1* (Cambridge, 1988), p. 576.
4. V. Lieberman, *Strange Parallels: Southeast Asia in Global Context c. 800–1830* (2 vols, Cambridge, 2003, 2009).
5. J. Glete, *War and the State in Early Modern Europe: Spain, the Dutch Revolt and Sweden as Fiscal-Military States, 1500–1660* (London, 2002), esp. p. 215.
6. T. Stavrides, *The Sultan of Vezirs: The Life and Times of the Ottoman Grand Vezir Mahmud Pasha Angelović* (Leiden, 2001), pp. 191–2.
7. J. McCormack, *One Million Mercenaries: Swiss Soldiers in the Armies of the World* (London, 1993).
8. C. Imber, *The Ottoman Empire* (2nd edn, Basingstoke, 2009), pp. 123–7.
9. M. Mallett, *Mercenaries and Their Masters: Warfare in Renaissance Italy* (London, 1974); J. France (ed.), *Mercenaries and Paid Men: The Mercenary Identity in the Middle Ages* (Leiden, 2008).
10. C.F. Petry, *Twilight of Majesty: The Reigns of the Mamluk Sultans al-Ashrāf Qaytbay and Qansuh al-Ghawbri in Egypt* (Seattle, Washington, 1993), p. 62–3.
11. G. Ágoston, 'A Flexible Empire: Authority and its Limits on the Ottoman Frontiers', in K.H. Karpat and R.W. Zens (eds), *Ottoman Borderlands* (Madison, Wisconsin, 2003), pp. 26–7.
12. J.E. Thomson, *Mercenaries, Pirates, and Sovereigns: State-Building and Extra-territorial Violence in Early Modern Europe* (Princeton, New Jersey, 1994).
13. C.W. Bracewell, *The Uskoks of Senj: Piracy, Banditry, and Holy War in the 16th-Century Adriatic* (Ithaca, New York, 1992).
14. K.M. Swope, 'All Men are Not Brothers: Ethnic Identity and Dynastic Loyalty in the Ningxia Mutiny of 1592', *Late Imperial China*, 24 (2003), pp. 79–129.

15. S. Gunn, D. Grummitt and H. Cools, *War, State, and Society in England and the Netherlands, 1477–1559* (Oxford, 2007).
16. R. Bean, 'War and the Birth of the Nation State', *Journal of Economic History*, 33 (1973), p. 203.
17. J.R. Hale, *War and Society in Renaissance Europe, 1450–1620* (London, 1985), pp. 248–51.
18. C.R. Phillips, *Six Galleons for the King of Spain: Imperial Defense in the Early Seventeenth Century* (Baltimore, Maryland, 1992).
19. A Fuess, 'Rotting Ships and Razed Harbors: The Naval Policy of the Mamluks', *Mamlūk Studies Review*, 5 (2001), pp. 45–71, esp. p. 60.
20. S. Adams, 'The English Military Clientele, 1542–1618', in C. Giry-Deloison and R. Mettam (eds), *Patronages et Clientélismes 1550–1750* (Lille, 1990).
21. D. Potter, *War and Government in the French Provinces: Picardy, 1470–1560* (Cambridge 1993).
22. D. Dee, *Expansion and Crisis in Louis XIV's France: Franche-Comté and Absolute Monarchy, 1674–1715* (Rochester, New York, 2009), esp. pp. 177–9.
23. J. Berenger, 'La révolte paysanne de Basse-Autriche de 1597', *Revue d'Histoire Economique et Sociale*, 53 (1975), p. 479.
24. M.A. Bakhit, *The Ottoman Province of Damascus in the Sixteenth Century* (Beirut, 1980), pp. 101, 103.
25. K.M. Swope, 'Bestowing the Double-edged Sword: Wanli as Supreme Military Commander', in D. Robinson (ed.), *Culture, Courtiers, and Competition: The Ming Court* (Cambridge, Massachusetts, 2008), pp. 61–115.
26. Y.N. Harari, *Renaissance Military Memoirs: War, History, and Identity, 1450–1600* (Woodbridge, 2004).
27. M. Vale, *War and Chivalry: Warfare and Aristocratic Culture in England, France and Burgundy at the End of the Middle Ages* (London, 1981); K. Stevenson, *Chivalry and Knighthood in Scotland 1424–1513* (Woodbridge, 2006).
28. T.T. Allsen, *The Royal Hunt in Eurasian History* (Philadelphia, Pennsylvania, 2006); R.J. Knecht, *The French Renaissance Court* (New Haven, Connecticut, 2008).
29. *Babur... Memoirs*, I, 152, 186.
30. N. Russell and H. Visentin (eds), *French Ceremonial Entries in the Sixteenth Century: Event, Image, Text* (Toronto, 2007); R.J. Knecht, *Renaissance Warrior and Patron: The Reign of Francis I* (Cambridge 1994).
31. M. Bourne, *Francesco II Gonzaga: The Sober Prince as Patron* (Rome, 2008).
32. K. Raber and T.J. Tucker (eds), *The Culture of the Horse: Status, Discipline and Identity in the Early Modern World* (Basingstoke, 2005).
33. F. Redlich, *De Praede Militare: Looting and Booty, 1500–1815* (Wiesbaden, 1956).

34. Kritovoulus, *History of Mehmed the Conqueror*, trans. C.T. Riggs (Princeton, New Jersey, 1954), pp. 154–5, 182; H. Inalcik and R. Murphey (eds), *The History of Mehmed the Conqueror by Tursan Beg* (Minneapolis, Minnesota, 1978), p. 44.

35. R.J. Barendse, *The Arabian Sea: The Indian Ocean World of the Seventeenth Century* (Armonk, New York, 202), p. 454.

36. A. Barrera-Osorio, *Experiencing Nature:The Spanish American Empire and the Early Scientific Revolution* (Austin, Texas, 2006), pp. 128–30.

37. W. Franke, 'Historical Writing during the Ming', in F.W. Mote and D. Twitchett (eds), *Cambridge History of China: VII, Part 1* (Cambridge, 1988), p. 773.

38. I.A.A. Thompson, '"Money, money and yet more money!" Finance, the Fiscal-State, and the Military Revolution: Spain 1500–1650', in C.J. Rogers (ed.), *The Military Revolution Debate* (Boulder, Colorado, 1995), pp. 273–98.

39. N. Rubinstein, 'Fortified Enclosures in Italian Cities', in D.S. Chambers, C.H. Clough and M.E. Mallett (eds), *War, Culture and Society in Renaissance Venice* (London, 1993), pp. 1–8; M. Wolfe, *Walled Towns and the Shaping of France: From the Medieval to the Early Modern Era* (Basingstoke, 2009).

40. F.J. Appélaniz Ruis de Galarreta, *Pouvoir et finance en Méditerranée prémoderne: le deuxième État mamelouk et le commerce des épices, 1382–1517* (Barcelona, 2009).

41. L. Sicking, *Neptune and the Netherlands: State, Economy and War at Sea in the Renaissance* (Leiden, 2004).

42. *Babur ... Memoirs*, I, 148–9.

43. T. May, 'The Training of an Inner Asian Nomad Army in the Pre-Modern Period', *Journal of Military History*, 70 (2006), pp. 617–36.

44. R. Rapple, *Martial Power and Elizabethan Political Culture: Military Men in England and Ireland, 1559–1594* (Cambridge, 2009).

45. Mote and Twitchett, *Cambridge History of China: VII, Part 1* (Cambridge, 1988), p. 376.

46. D. Robinson, *Bandits, Eunuchs, and the Son of Heaven: Rebellion and the Economy of Violence in Mid-Ming China* (Honolulu, Hawai'i, 2001); K.M. Swope, 'Bestowing the Double-edged Sword: Wanli as Supreme Military Commander', pp. 63–7.

47. P.C. Perdue, 'Culture, History, and Imperial Chinese Strategy: Legacies of the Qing Conquests', in H. Van de Ven (ed.), *Warfare in Chinese History* (Leiden, 2000), p. 27.

48. E. Muir, *Mad Blood Stirring: Vendetta and Factions in Friuli during the Renaissance* (Baltimore, Maryland, 1998); J.B. Netterstrom and B. Poulsen (eds), *Feud in Medieval and Early Modern Europe* (Aarhus, 2007).

49. J. Firnhaber-Baker, 'Seigneurial War and Royal Power in Later Medieval Southern France', *Past and Present*, 208 (Aug. 2010), p. 75.
50. G. Barta et al., *History of Transylvania* (Budapest, 1994), p. 294.
51. For India, J. Heesterman, 'Warrior, Peasant and Brahmin', *Modern Asian Studies*, 29 (1995), pp. 637–54.
52. K.M. Swope, 'Clearing the Fields and Strengthening the Walls: Defending Small Cities in Late Ming China', in K.R. Hall (ed.), *Secondary Cities and Urban Networking in the Indian Ocean Realm* (Boulder, Colorado, 2008), pp. 123–54.

9: Conclusions

1. M. Roberts, *The Military Revolution, 1560–1660* (Belfast, 1956); W.H. McNeill, *The Age of Gunpowder Empires, 1450–1800* (Washington, 1989); G. Parker, *The Military Revolution: Military Innovation and the Rise of the West, 1500–1800* (2nd edn, Cambridge, 1996).
2. P. Lorge, *The Asian Military Revolution* (Cambridge, 2008) and unpublished paper 'The World History of Guns and Gunpowder'. I would like to thank Peter Lorge for letting me read this piece. S. Laichen, 'Ming–Southeast Asian Overland Interactions, c. 1368–1644' (Ph.D. thesis, Michigan, 2000).
3. C.J. Rogers (ed.), *The Military Revolution Debate: Readings on the Military Transformation of Early Modern Europe* (Boulder, Colorado, 1995).
4. P.H. Meurer and G. Schilder, 'Die Wandkarte des Türkenzuges 1529 von Johann Haselberg und Christoph Zell', *Cartographica Helvetica*, 39 (2009), pp. 27–42; P. Barber and T. Harper, *Magnificent Maps. Power, Propaganda and Art* (London, 2010), pp. 32–3.
5. J.R. Hale, 'Printing and Military Culture of Renaissance Venice', *Medievalia et Humanistica*, 8 (1977), pp. 21–62; C. Wilkinson, 'Renaissance Treatises on Military Architecture and the Science of Mechanics', in J. Guillaume (ed.), *Les Traités d'architecture de la Renaissance* (Paris, 1988), pp. 467–76; H. Kleinschmidt, *Tyrocinium Militare: Militärische Körperhaltungen und bewegungen im Wandel zwischen dem. 14 und dem. 18. Jahrhundert* (Stuttgart, 1989); H.J. Webb, *Elizabethan Military Science* (Madison, Wisconsin, 1965).
6. F. González de Léon, *The Road to Rocroi: Class, Culture, and Command in the Spanish Army of Flanders, 1567–1659* (Leiden, 2009).
7. *Babur … Memoirs*, I, 148.
8. B.S. and D.S. Bachrach, 'Saxon Military Revolution, 912–973? Myth and Reality', *Early Medieval History*, 15 (2007), pp. 186–222.
9. B. Downing, *The Military Revolution and Political Change: Origins of Democracy and Autocracy in Early Modern Europe* (Princeton, New

Jersey, 1990); D.R. Headrick, *Power over Peoples: Technology, Environments, and Western Imperialism, 1400 to the Present* (Princeton, New Jersey, 2010), pp. 151–4.

10. C.J. Rogers, '"Military Revolutions" and "Revolutions in Military Affairs": A Historian's Perspective', in T. Gongora and H. von Riekhof (eds), *Towards a Revolution in Military Affairs? Defense and Security at the Dawn of the Twenty-First Century* (Westport, Connecticut, 2000), pp. 21–35.

11. R.S. Love, '"All the King's Horsemen": The Equestrian Army of Henri IV, 1585–1598', *Sixteenth-Century Journal*, 22 (1991), pp. 511–33.

12. J.B. Wood, *The King's Army: Warfare, Soldiers and Society during the Wars of Religion in France, 1562–1576* (Cambridge, 1996), p. 182.

13. K.M. Swope, 'Crouching Tigers, Secret Weapons: Military Technology Employed During the Sino-Japanese-Korean War, 1592–1598', *Journal of Military History*, 69 (2005), p. 37.

14. R. Irwin, 'Gunpowder and Firearms in the Mamluk Sultanate Reconsidered', in M. Winter and A. Levanoni (eds), *The Mamluks in Egyptian and Syrian Politics and Society* (Leiden, 2004), pp. 138–9.

Selected Further Reading

The footnotes to this book and to the books listed here provide details of other relevant works.

General

Black, J. *Rethinking Military History* (2004)

Braudel, F. *The Mediterranean and the Mediterranean World in the Age of Philip II* (1973)

Chase, K. *Firearms: A Global History to 1700* (2003)

Cipolla, C.M. *Guns and Sails in the Early Phase of European Expansion 1400–1700* (1965)

Parker, G. *The Military Revolution: Military Innovation and the Rise of the West, 1500–1800* (2nd edn, 1996)

Steele, B. and Dorland, T. (eds) *The Heirs of Archimedes: Science and the Art of War through the Age of Enlightenment* (2005)

Thompson, J.E. *Mercenaries, Pirates and Sovereigns: State-building and Extraterritorial Violence in Early Modern Europe* (1994)

East and South Asia

Barfield, T.J. *The Perilous Frontier: Nomadic Empires and China* (1989)

Berry, M.E. *Hideyoshi* (1982)

Berry, M.E. *The Culture of Civil War in Kyoto* (1992)

Gommans, J. *Mughal Warfare* (2002)

Kiernan, F. and Fairbank, J. (eds), *Chinese Ways in Warfare* (1974)

Kolff, D. *Naukar, Rajput and Sepoy: The Ethnohistory of the Military Labor Market in Hindustan, 1450–1850* (1990)

Lorge, P. *War, Politics, and Society in Early Modern China, 900–1795* (2005)

Lorge, P. *The Asian Military Revolution* (2008)

Needham, J. *Military Technology: The Gunpowder Epic* (1987)

Sansom, G.B. *A History of Japan, 1334–1615* (1961)

Streusand D.E. *The Formation of the Mughal Empire* (1989)

Turnbull, S. *Samurai Warfare* (1996)

Turnbull, S.R. *Samurai Invasion: Japan's Korean War, 1592–98* (2002)

The Islamic World

Agoston, G. *Guns for the Sultan: Military Power and the Weapons Industry in the Ottoman Empire* (2005)

Ayalon, D. *Gunpowder and Firearms in the Mamluk Kingdom: A Challenge to a Medieval Society* (1956)

Cook, W. *The Hundred Years War for Morocco: Gunpowder and the Military Revolution in the Early Modern Muslim World* (1994)

Correggio, F.B. *The Siege of Malta 1565* (2005)

Digby, S. *War-horse and Elephant in the Delhi Sultanate* (1971)

Finkel, C. *The Administration of Warfare: Ottoman Campaigns in Hungary, 1593–1606* (1988)

Hess, A.C. *The Forgotten Frontier: A History of the Sixteenth Century Ibero-African Frontier* (1986)

Hodgson, M.G.S. *The Venture of Islam. III: The Gunpowder Empires and Modern Times* (1974)

Imber, C. *The Ottoman Empire, 1300–1650* (2002)

Murphey, R. *Ottoman Warfare* (2000)

Parry, V.J. and Yapp, M.E. (eds) *War, Technology and Society in the Middle East* (1975)

Woods, J.E. *The Aqquyunlu, Clan, Confederation, Empire: A Study in 15th/9th Century Turko-Iranian Politics* (1976)

Sub-Saharan Africa

Law, R. *The Horse in West African History* (1980)

Thornton, J. *Africa and Africans in the Making of the Atlantic World, 1400–1800* (2nd edn, 1998)

Thornton, J. *Warfare in Atlantic Africa, 1500–1800* (1999)

The Americas

Hassig, R. *Aztec Warfare: Imperial Expansion and Political Control* (1988)

Hemming, J. *Red Gold: The Conquest of the Brazilian Indians, 1500–1760* (2nd edn, 1995)

Christian Europe

Bak, J.M. and B.K. Király (eds) *From Hunyadi to Rákóczi: War and Society in Late Medieval and Early Modern Hungary* (1982)

Contamine, P. (ed.) *War and Competition between States* (2000)

Davies, B.L. *Warfare, State and Society on the Black Sea Steppe, 1500–1700* (2007)

Duffy, C. *Siege Warfare: The Fortress in the Early Modern World, 1494–1660* (1979)

Frost, R. *The Northern Wars, 1558–1721* (2000)
Glete, J. *War and the State in Early Modern Europe* (2002)
Hall, B. *Weapons and Warfare in Renaissance Europe* (1997)
Knecht, R. *The French Civil Wars, 1562–1598* (2000)
Mallett, M. and Hale, J. *The Military Organisation of a Renaissance State: Venice, c. 1400–1617* (1984)
Mortimer, G. (ed.) *Early Modern Military History, 1450–1815* (2004)
Parker, G. *The Grand Strategy of Philip II* (1998)
Parker, G. *The Army of Flanders and the Spanish Road, 1567–1659* (2nd edn, 2004)
Phillips, G. *The Anglo-Scots Wars, 1513–1550* (1999)
Rogers, C. (ed.) *The Military Revolution Debate: Readings on the Military Transformation of Early Modern Europe* (1995)
Tallett, F. and Trim, D.J.B. (eds) *European Warfare 1350–1750* (2010)

Western expansion

Boucher, P. *Cannibal Encounters: Europeans and Island Caribs, 1492–1763* (1993)
Diffie, B.W. and Winius, G.D. *Foundations of the Portuguese Empire, 1415–1580* (1974)
Hassig, R. *Mexico and the Spanish Conquest* (1994)
Newitt, M. *A History of Portuguese Overseas Expansion, 1400–1668* (2005)
Pelenski, J. *Russia and Kazan: Conquest and Imperial Ideology, 1438–1560* (1974)
Powell, P. *Soldiers, Indians and Silver: The Northward Advance of New Spain, 1550–1600* (1952)
Restall, M. *Seven Myths of the Spanish Conquest* (2003)

Naval

Bracewell, C.W. *The Uskoks of Senj: Piracy, Banditry and Holy War in the Sixteenth-Century Adriatic* (1992)
Brummett, P. *Ottoman Seapower and Levantine Diplomacy in the Age of Discoveries* (1994)
Glete, J. *Navies and Nations: Warships, Navies and State Building in Europe and America, 1500–1860* (1993)
Guilmartin, J.F. *Gunpowder and Galleys: Changing Technology and Mediterranean Warfare at Sea in the Sixteenth Century* (1974)
James, A. *The Ship of State: Naval Affairs in Early Modern France, 1572–1661* (2002)
Pryor, J.H. *Geography, Technology and War: Studies in the Maritime History of the Mediterranean, 649–1571* (1988)
Rodger, N. *The Safeguard of the Sea: A Naval History of Britain, 660–1649* (1997)

War and society

Canning, J. (ed.) *Power, Violence and Mass Death in Pre-Modern and Modern Times* (2004)

Cuneo, P. (ed.) *Artful Armies, Beautiful Battles: Art and Warfare in Early Modern Europe* (2002)

Cunningham, A. and Grell, O.P. *The Four Horsemen of the Apocalypse: Religion, War, Famine and Death in Reformation Europe* (2000)

Hale, J. *War and Society in Renaissance Europe, 1450–1620* (1985)

Lynn, J.A. *Women, Armies, and Warfare in Early Modern Europe* (2008)

Redlich, F. *De Praeda Militari: Looting and Booty, 1500–1800* (1956)

Ruff, J. *Violence in Early Modern Europe, 1500–1800* (2001)

Tallett, F. *War and Society in Early Modern Europe 1495–1715* (1992)

Index